UNDERSTANDING PEASANT AGRICULTURE

AN INTEGRATED LAND-USE MODEL FOR THE PUNJAB

by

Joseph H. Astroth, Jr.
University of Missouri

UNIVERSITY OF CHICAGO

GEOGRAPHY RESEARCH PAPER NO. 223

1990

Copyright 1990 by

The Committee on Geographical Studies
The University of Chicago
Chicago, Illinois

Library of Congress Cataloging-in-Publication Data

Astroth, Joseph H., 1955-
Understanding peasant agriculture.

(Research paper ; no. 223)
Bibliography: p. 161.
Includes index

1. Land use, Rural—India—Punjab—Mathematical models. 2. Agriculture—Economic aspects—India—Punjab—Mathematical models. I. Title. II. Series: Research paper (University of Chicago. Committee on Geographical Studies) ; no. 223.
HD879.P8A77   1990   333.76'13'0724   87-15099
ISBN 0–89065–127–2 (pbk.)

Geography Research Papers are available from:

The University of Chicago
Committee on Geographical Studies
5828 South University Avenue
Chicago, Illinois 60637-1583

To my parents,
JOSEPH H. ASTROTH
and
MARJORIE I. ASTROTH

CONTENTS

List of Figures	vii
List of Tables	xi
Acknowledgments	xiii
1. INTRODUCTION	1
2. AGRICULTURAL LOCATION THEORY	7
The Origins of Agricultural Location Theory	7
The Economic Approach	8
Interregional Equilibrium Models	23
The Behavioral Approach	27
Alternative Behavioral Approaches	29
Summary	31
3. MAXIMUM-LIKELIHOOD MODELING AND PEASANT AGRICULTURAL LAND USE	35
The Basic Model	35
Maximum Likelihood and Mathematical Programming Models	38
Maximum Likelihood and Agricultural Land Use	40
Some Illustrative Concepts	42
Summary	47
4. THE STUDY AREA AND RESEARCH METHODOLOGY	51
Location and Character of the Study Area	51
The Market Town of Kurali	70
The Market Town of Kharar	72
Influence of Chandigarh	77
Market Crops	86
Data Sources	88
Summary	90

5. PROCEDURE AND RESULTS OF THE TEST CASE	93
A General Maximum-Likelihood Agricultural Land-Use Model	93
Test-Case Results	102
Summary	121
6. TOWARD AN INTEGRATED APPROACH TO MODELING PEASANT AGRICULTURAL LAND USE	127
Possible Modifications and Further Testing of the Model	128
Potential Planning Applications of the Model	131
Appendix A: Marketing and Land-Use Questionnaire	133
Appendix B: Difference Matrices of Predicted and Observed Land Use	137
Bibliography	161
Index	171

FIGURES

1.	Flow Diagram of the Construction of a Mathematical Model	3
2.	The Von Thünen Three Crops–Single Market Case	12
3.	Two-Dimensional Representation of the Multiple Crops–Single Market Case	12
4.	Von Thünen Three Crops–Two Markets Case	13
5.	A Two-Dimensional Representation of the Multiple Crops–Two Markets Case	13
6.	Negative Exponential Spatial-Deterrence Functions	44
7.	Land-Use Intensity and Modal Split	44
8.	Land-Use Patterns: Von Thünen and Mixed Cropping	46
9.	Land-Use Patterns: Minimum Information and Mixed Cropping	46
10.	Land-Use Patterns: Mixed Cropping and Two Markets	48
11.	Land-Use Intensities around Two Markets	48
12.	The State of Punjab	52
13.	Location of the Study Area within Rupnagar District	53
14.	Shivalik Hills	54
15.	Market Towns and Villages of the Study Area and Surrounding Region	55
16.	Average Water Balance for Rupnagar District	58
17.	Relationship between Rainfall and Yield: Paddy	60
18.	Relationship between Rainfall and Yield: Wheat	61
19.	Percentage of Total Cropped Area Irrigated in 1982	62
20.	Villages Susceptible to Seasonal Flooding and Soil Erosion	65
21.	Dry Channel of a *Choe*	66
22.	Channelization Project for Erosion Control	66

23.	Kurali and Kharar Market Areas (*umlands*), 1982	74
24.	Major Roadways to and from Chandigarh	76
25.	Villages in Kharar Tehsil Located within the Market Area of Chandigarh	78
26.	Villages in the Study Area in which Farming Households are Involved in Commercial Dairying for the Chandigarh Market, 1982	80
27.	Villages in the Study Area in which Farming Households are Involved in Fruit and Vegetable Production for the Chandigarh Market, 1982	81
28.	Checkpoint at the Chandigarh Union Territory Boundary	84
29.	Road Network Map of Kharar Tehsil	91
30.	Villages with Residuals Greater than or Equal to 10 Percent of Total Cropped Area: Cereals and Millets	103
31.	Villages with Residuals Greater than or Less than 5 Percent of Total Cropped Area: Pulses	104
32.	Villages with Residuals Greater than or Less than 5 Percent of Total Cropped Area: Cotton	105
33.	Villages with Residuals Greater than or Less than 5 Percent of Total Cropped Area: Oilseeds	106
34.	Villages with Residuals Greater than or Less than 5 Percent of Total Cropped Area: Fruits and Vegetables	107
35.	Difference between Percentages of Predicted and Observed: Cereals and Millets	108
36.	Generalized Residual Areas: Cereals and Millets	109
37.	Difference between Percentages of Predicted and Observed: Fruits and Vegetables	111
38.	Generalized Residual Areas: Fruits and Vegetables	113
39.	Difference between Percentages of Predicted and Observed: Pulses	114
40.	Generalized Residual Areas: Pulses	117
41.	Generalized Area of Intensive Sugarcane Cultivation, 1982	118
42.	Difference between Percentages of Predicted and Observed: Oilseeds	119
43.	Generalized Residual Areas: Oilseeds	120

44. Difference between Percentages of Predicted and Observed: Cotton 122
45. Generalized Residual Areas: Cotton 123

TABLES

1.	Percentage of Net Area Irrigated to Net Area Sown, 1978-79	54
2.	Percentage of Net Area Sown More Than Once, 1978-79	56
3.	Tractors, 1977	56
4.	Chemical Fertilizer Consumption in Punjab, 1981-82	56
5.	Patterns of Rice Yields and Rainfall, 1971-72 through 1980-81	63
6.	Patterns of Wheat Yields and Rainfall, 1971-72 through 1980-81	64
7.	Percentage Distribution of Operational Holdings, 1970-71	67
8.	Percentage of Irrigated Operational Holdings in Rupnagar District by Size of Holding, 1970-71	69
9.	Mean Yields of Important Crops, 1979-80 and 1980-81	71
10.	Population of Kharar and Kurali Market Towns, 1951-81	72
11.	Total Market Demand for Khara and Kurali Markets by Crop Type, 1982	97
12.	Distance-Deterrence Parameter by Crop Type as Selected by MDIS	101

Acknowledgments

Numerous people have made intellectual and personal contributions to this research. I will not attempt to mention them all by name, for to do so would be an impossible task. I do however want to give special recognition to several critical supporters. I would like to express my appreciation to James T. Meyer, my mentor and good friend. This research project has its origins in the many hours of discussion we shared, in and out of the classroom, concerning spatial analysis and the role of modeling in geographical research. I would like to thank Norton Ginsburg for his astute guidance and criticism throughout the writing of this monograph. Colin Masica, a linguist by trade but geographer at heart, should be recognized for his unending patience as my language teacher. A.B. Mukerji and his colleagues at the Department of Geography, Panjab University, were a great help to me in completing the field portion of this study. The data collection and interview process could not have been completed without my research assistant and friend, Kranti Kumar. I would also like to extend thanks to Kit Salter, chairman of the University of Missouri Department of Geography, for his support during the critical final stages of this enterprise, and to Luther Sanders and John Beckett for their assistance in preparing many of the graphics and the initial formatting of the text. Carol Saller did the final editing and formatting of the manuscript. Her patience and endurance have been noteworthy.

Financial support for this study was provided by the following fellowship programs: National Resource Fellowship (NDEA Title VI), Fulbright-Hays Doctoral Dissertation Research Abroad, the Mellon Foundation, and the University of Chicago. I give special thanks to the United States Educational Foundation in India for their fine administrative support during my stay in India.

Finally, I would like especially to thank Kay, Justin, and Joseph for the numerous personal sacrifices they have made. Without their support and patience this manuscript would never have made it to press.

Chapter 1

INTRODUCTION

> Various reasons may be suggested for the apparent incompatibility between the economic and behavioural approaches. Their initial assumptions are in direct conflict. Economic models treat decision-making as a parameter, whereas the behavioural explanations owe their existence to the variability of this factor.[1]

Two seemingly incompatible approaches have dominated the history of agricultural location theory, a normative economic approach and a probabilistic behavioral approach. Although models of each type have offered valuable insights concerning the causes and factors underlying the general spatial patterns of agricultural land use, neither one has been successful in producing a predicted areal distribution that accurately portrays the observed spatial arrangement of a peasant rural economic landscape. These two approaches, however, are not necessarily incompatible. It follows, therefore, that the development of a more appropriate peasant agricultural land-use model requires the adoption of an "integrated approach."

Only a single attempt, however, has been made to integrate the economic and behavioral approaches to agricultural location theory.[2] Although this initial attempt shows promise as a valuable diffusion-of-innovation model, it exhibits little potential for application as an operational agricultural land-use model. The goal of this study is to introduce and empirically test the effectiveness of a new and viable integrated model of peasant agricultural land use. This new model is based on maximum-likelihood (sometimes referred to as entropy maximization) principles. A maximum-likelihood model of peasant agricultural land use results in a mixture of the

---

[1] Patrick W.E. Hart, "Problems and Potentialities of the Behavioural Approach to Agricultural Location," *Geografiska Annaler* 62B (1980): 102.

[2] Ibid., pp. 100-107.

2   UNDERSTANDING PEASANT AGRICULTURE

traditional deterministic and probability approaches. It mixes a deterministic representation of the agroeconomic environment with a probabilistic approach to the peasant farmer's agricultural land-use decision-making behavior. The result is a model grounded both upon sound economic principles and on recognition of the behavioral component in the agricultural land-use decision-making process by peasant farmers. It is this integrated model that distinguishes this monograph from previous studies concerning this topic.

The organization of this book revolves around the general approach to constructing and testing a mathematical model,[3] illustrated by the flow diagram in figure 1. The first stage in mathematical model building is the statement of a problem or hypothesis. Toward this end, chapter 2 contains a review of the problems and potentialities associated with the two traditional approaches to modeling peasant agricultural land use, the economic approach and the behavioral approach. As mentioned above, neither of these two approaches, nor an initial attempt by Hart at a "comprehensive approach," has been successful in constructing a satisfactory model.[4] Chapter 2 concludes with the proposal of two hypotheses: first, that despite the failure of a previous attempt, the most appropriate manner in which to construct an accurate model of peasant agricultural land use is through an integrated approach; second, that an integrated approach can be embodied within a maximum-likelihood methodology. This second hypothesis is developed further in chapter 3 by the use of several illustrative examples and a discussion concerning the principles that characterize a maximum-likelihood land-use model.

The second stage of reasoning involved in the formulation of a mathematical model encompasses:

1. the construction of an algebraic expression that incorporates the chief components of the system under investigation; and
2. the formulation of a set of assumptions concerning the major factors that affect the behavior of the system.

The definitions and assumptions embodied within a maximum-likelihood agricultural land-use model are described in the first half of chapter 3. They are also compared to the definitions and assumptions of other mathematical models, in particular, the von Thünen model.

The third step in model building entails the deduction of a model equation that employs mathematical reasoning and that is based upon the

---

[3]   Richard W. Thomas and Richard J. Huggett, *Modelling in Geography: A Mathematical Approach* (Totowa, N.J.: Barnes and Noble Books, 1980), pp. 5-8.

[4]   Hart, "Problems and Potentialities of the Behavioural Approach to Agricultural Location."

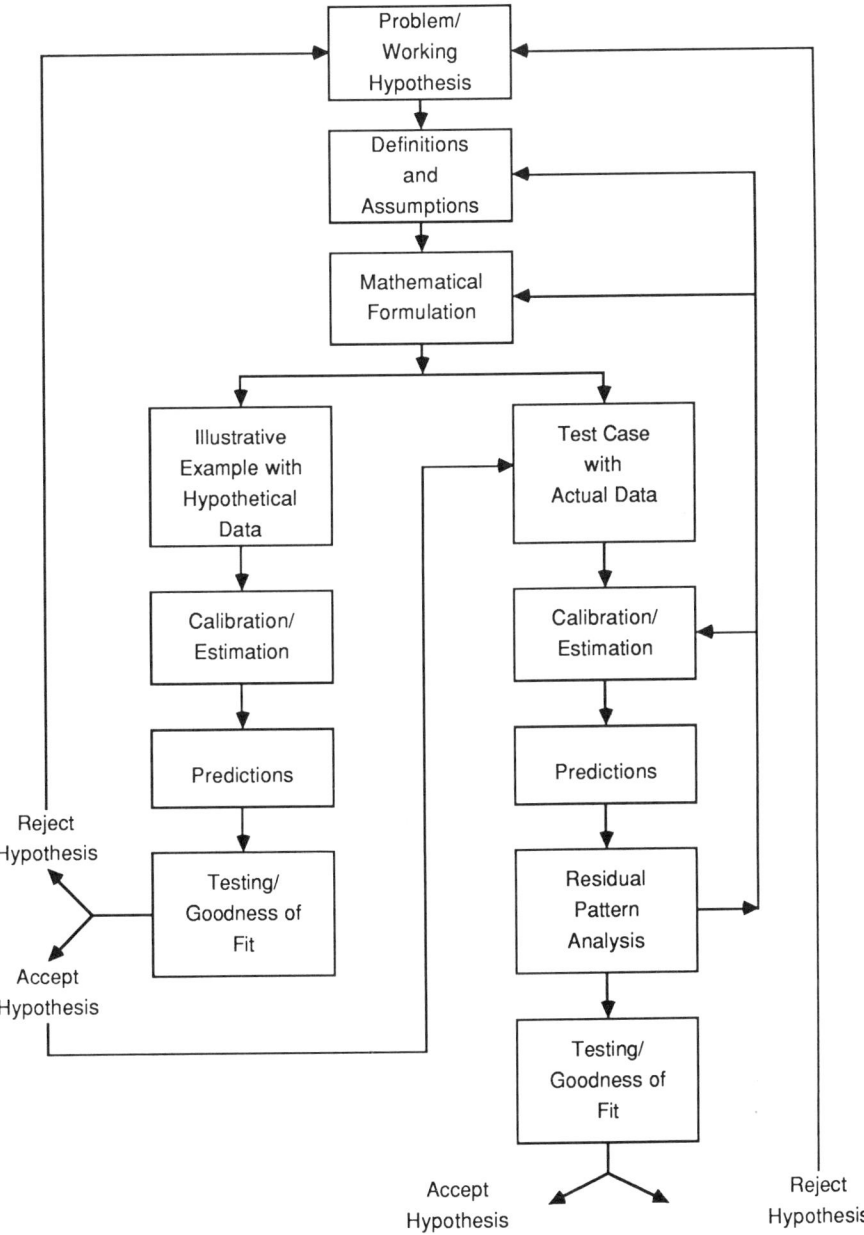

Fig. 1. Flow Diagram of the Construction of a Mathematical Model.
After Thomas and Huggett, *Modelling in Geography*, p. 7.

previously formulated set of definitions and assumptions. In this study, since a general maximum-likelihood model had already been derived by Wilson, this third step involved modifying the general equation to make it applicable to agricultural land-use modeling. These modifications are briefly discussed in chapter 3. A more detailed discussion of the mathematical formulation developed in this study may be found in chapter 5, including a test-case application of the model.

At this point in the development of a mathematical model, the goal of the scientist is to determine the suitability of the predicted values that will be obtained from the model's equation. This goal may be achieved by:

1. theoretically testing the model through the use of an illustrative example based on hypothetical data,
2. empirically testing the model by conducting a test case with data from the "real world," or
3. theoretically testing the model with contrived data and if the results are positive then carrying out an empirical test with actual land-use data.

The first option is often chosen by economists, whereas geographers, owing to the nature of their discipline, are compelled to test the model empirically in the field. In this study, the model was initially tested using hypothetical data and, on the basis of promising results, was then empirically tested using data from northern India. The procedure and methodology employed in the theoretical testing of the model are outlined in chapter 3; the test-case application is described at length in chapter 4.

The next stage in the model's development involves the estimation of the parameters in the stated mathematical equation. In the theoretical testing of the model, these parameter values were estimated from previous knowledge of peasant agricultural land-use systems. A discussion of this procedure can be found in chapter 3. In contrast, the estimation of the parameters for the test-case model involved the selection and use of a "best statistic" in the calibration process. The statistic chosen for this purpose was the minimum information discrimination statistic (MDIS). A discussion concerning the advantages and disadvantages associated with the use of MDIS, along with a complete description of the calibration procedure, is contained within chapter 5.

After the parameter estimation has been completed, the next procedural step toward formalization of the model calls for the execution of a series of test cases based on hypothetical and actual data. In both the theoretical and empirical testing of the model developed here the equation was solved using a public domain computer algorithm written by Baxter.[5] The predicted values associated with the illustrative examples are represented in graphic form in chapter 3. The modeled output from the empirical test case comprises Appendix B.

The last stage in the development of a mathematical model involves the formal testing of the model by comparing the predicted and observed values. This task is usually accomplished through the use of an appropriate goodness-of-fit statistic. If there is a satisfactory level of agreement between the predicted and observed values, then one would tentatively, pending further testing, accept the working hypothesis stated in the first stage of the model's construction. In contrast, if the fit between the modeled and actual spatial distribution is unacceptable, then one would be compelled to start over from square one with a modified working hypothesis (figure 1).

In the theoretical testing of the maximum-likelihood model constructed in this study, only the marginal elements of the data matrix were assigned values. The formal testing of the model's performance, therefore, required that a subjective judgment be made concerning whether or not the modeled results were consistent with known information regarding actual peasant agricultural landscapes. Owing to a favorable judgment concerning the performance of the model, an empirical test case was formulated and carried out based on agricultural land-use data from Kharar tehsil, Punjab, India.

As mentioned earlier, the calibration/estimation of the empirical test-case model was accomplished through the use of an appropriate goodness-of-fit statistic. This type of calibration methodology invalidates the reapplication of such a statistic in the formal testing of the model. Under these circumstances, the only true goodness-of-fit measure is to perform additional test cases in other peasant agricultural settings. In that regard, a final judgment of the model developed in this monograph remains undeclared pending the outcome of future trials in other regions of the less developed world.

Although formal testing of a model calibrated in this manner requires the completion of additional case studies, much still can be gained by examining the difference between predicted and observed values of land use in the initial trial application. Such an endeavor may reveal many valuable insights concerning both the model itself and the underlying structure of the system modeled. The results of an in-depth residual analysis could lead to redefining several of the initial assumptions, modifying the original mathematical formulation, or employing another calibration technique in future applications (figure 1). Chapter 5 contains a lengthy discussion about

---

[5] R.S. Baxter, "Entropy Maximizing Models of Spatial Interaction," *Computer Applications* 1 (1973): 57-83.

the differences between the predicted and observed agricultural land-use patterns in the test case. The spatial analysis of the residuals revealed heretofore unrecognized factors involved in the formation of agricultural land-use patterns in the study area. The incorporation of these factors, plus suggestions in regard to additional modifications of the test-case model, are discussed in chapter 6. Also included in chapter 6 is a discussion concerning possible planning applications of a peasant agricultural land-use model based on maximum-likelihood principles.

The monograph concludes with the call for further empirical testing of this integrated approach to modeling peasant agricultural land use. Based on the promising results of this initial test case, additional empirical testing not only will aid in judging the usefulness of such an approach, but also promises to shed further light on the factors that affect a peasant farmer's agricultural decision-making process.

Chapter 2

AGRICULTURAL LOCATION THEORY

The Origins of Agricultural Location Theory

A recent exchange between Chisholm and Champion in *Area* suggests that the earliest writings about agricultural location theory appeared in the middle of the eighteenth century.[1] According to Champion, the subject first appeared in Sir James Steuart's book, *An Inquiry into the Principles of Political Economy*. In this work, Steuart described a general land-use pattern that he believed existed around most urban centers.[2] According to Chisholm, Adam Smith had also shown an interest in agricultural location theory during the late 1700s.[3] In his celebrated work, *An Inquiry into the Nature and Causes of the Wealth of Nations*, Smith made several enlightening observations concerning general features of agricultural land use surrounding a "great town." He also provided a more in-depth analysis than Steuart, discussing such topics as the impact of navigable rivers, good roads, and canals on the patterns of agricultural land use, and the effect of distance from the market on the intensity of cropping.[4]

Although agricultural location theory dates to the mid-eighteenth century, the first formalized model of agricultural land use was not introduced until fifty years later. In 1817, David Ricardo proposed a normative explanation of agricultural distributions based on the principle of economic rent. He defined economic rent as the return that can be realized from a

---

[1] M. Chisholm, "Von Thünen Anticipated," *Area* 11 (1979): 37-40; A.G. Champion, "Antecedents of von Thünen," *Area* 11 (1979): 258; and Maclennan lends further support to Champion's claim in his research note: D. Maclennan, "Steuart, Smith and von Thünen," *Area* 11 (1979): 312-313.

[2] Champion, "Antecedents of von Thünen," p. 258; J. Steuart, *An Inquiry into the Principles of Political Economy* (London: 1767), p. 139.

[3] Chisholm, "Von Thünen Anticipated," pp. 37-38.

[4] Adam Smith, *An Inquiry into the Nature and Causes of the Wealth of Nations*, 6th ed., 2 vols., ed. E. Cannan (London, 1950; originally published in 1789), 1: 148, 150, 152.

given plot of land over and above that which can be obtained from an identical plot at the "margin of production." Ricardo postulated that areal variations in land rent were largely the result of soil productivity (a site factor), and land scarcity.[5] Accordingly, the margin of production is determined by environmental factors. Transport costs, the location of markets, and agricultural demand are not explicitly considered.[6]

Subsequent research on agricultural location theory may be divided into two streams of thought: an economic approach and a behavioral approach.

The Economic Approach

The von Thünen Model

Identified as the classical model of agricultural location, the von Thünen model is based on an econometric analysis of an estate in Germany that von Thünen farmed for forty years. Despite the purely descriptive nature of von Thünen's original work, ensuing scholars have transformed his observations into a normative model.[7] It is this normative model of agricultural location that I refer to throughout this monograph.

Although von Thünen had completed his treatise on agricultural location before coming in contact with Ricardo's work, it is useful to consider his ideas as following from, and building upon, those of Ricardo. In contrast to Ricardo, who attributed spatial variability in agricultural land use solely to soil fertility and rural population density, von Thünen considered the influence of transport costs, the location of markets, and the demand for each agricultural good. He replaced the factor of soil fertility with distance, while

---

[5] David Ricardo, *Principles of Political Economy and Taxation* (London: J.M. Dent & Sons, 1817). The following simple example might help to clarify Ricardian economic rent: $x is the return to a farmer from an acre of wheat on which barley is more suited; $x+y is the return to a farmer on an acre of wheat on which wheat is best suited; $y is the measure of the return per acre over and above that which is possible at the margin of production; and therefore $y is the economic rent of that acre of land.

[6] For a more detailed discussion on the basic principles of a Ricardian view of agricultural land rent see: J.B. Foust and A.R. de Souza, *The Economic Landscape: A Theoretical Introduction* (Columbus: Charles E. Merrill Pub. Co., 1978), pp. 44-47; and R.S. Thoman and P.B. Corbin, *The Geography of Economic Activity*, 3d ed. (New York: McGraw-Hill, 1974), pp. 182-183.

[7] Among the more notable are: E.M. Hoover, *Location Theory and the Shoe and Leather Industries* (Cambridge, Mass.: Harvard University Press, 1937); A. Lösch, *The Economics of Location*, translated from 2d rev. ed. by W.H. Woglon and W.F. Stolper (New Haven: Yale University Press, 1954); E.S. Dunn, *The Location of Agricultural Production* (Gainesville: University of Florida Press, 1954); and Walter Isard, *Location and Space Economy* (Cambridge, Mass.: Massachusetts Institute of Technology Press, 1956).

simultaneously allowing for a greater diversity of agricultural production. Therefore, transport costs are the cause, and rent the byproduct, of a varied agricultural landscape.

Both von Thünen and Ricardo defined economic rent in the same manner. In either framework, the crops grown on a particular plot of land will be those that yield the highest economic rent. In the von Thünen model, however, distance from the market and transport costs associated with the movement of agricultural goods to market determine the level of economic rent. Furthermore, as in the Ricardian model, economic rent is expressed as the income a farmer would realize by growing a specific crop, over that which he would receive by cultivating the same crop at the margin of production.

Unlike the production boundary in a Ricardian landscape, however, von Thünen's "agricultural frontier" is determined by a linear increase in transport cost with distance from the market. These transport costs eventually accumulate to the point where market price equals production costs plus transport cost. It is at this point that the agricultural frontier begins. Accordingly, we can calculate the economic rent for any given plot of land by solving the algebraic expression:

$$R = E(p-a) - Efk ; \qquad (1)$$

where R is the economic rent per unit area of land, k is distance from the market, and E, p, f, and a are parameters. E is the yield per unit area of land, p is the market price per unit of agricultural good, a is the production cost per unit of good, and f is the rate of transport per unit of distance for each good.[8]

The von Thünen model is subject to the following simplifying constraints:[9]

1. The landscape is an unbounded isotropic surface. Movement is unrestricted in all directions. Absolute and relative distance, therefore, are the same.

2. Transportation costs are the product of a simple linear deterrence function. Regardless of distance traveled, transport costs are the same per unit of distance.

3. The physical environment of von Thünen's "isolated state" is homogeneous, including soil fertility. Correspondingly, a given amount of labor and capital will produce exactly the same level of output on any given hectare of land.

---

[8] Dunn, *The Location of Agricultural Production*, p. 7.
[9] Foust and de Souza, *The Economic Landscape*, pp. 30-31.

10 UNDERSTANDING PEASANT AGRICULTURE

    4. A single market exists at the center of the isotropic plain.
    5. Market prices for all agricultural goods are stable and fixed. No individual or collective action by farmers is able to alter the price of crops.
    6. There is no government intervention and therefore production is solely the result of economic factors.
    7. All farmers are optimizers. They operate in a sphere of perfect information and strive to maximize profits. Given these constraints, the only variables which affect the areal distribution of agriculture are transport costs, market prices, and all possible input combinations.

The von Thünen model has been applied, with different levels of sophistication, to various situations. For comparison's sake, however, the discussion has been confined to include those applications that are useful, in this monograph, for the introduction of a maximum-likelihood approach to modeling agricultural landscapes in less developed economies.[10]

Multiple crops–single market case. The most familiar application of the von Thünen model involves a diverse agricultural landscape surrounding a single market. The land-use patterns that result are a product of the decreasing value of economic rent over distance. For example, assume that three crops, vegetables, wheat, and cotton, are demanded by a single market. Also assume a different market price per hectare (P) for each crop. The market price for vegetables (P_v) is greater than that for wheat (P_w), which is greater than that for cotton (P_c):

$$P_v > P_w > P_c.$$

The difference in market price between crops may be the result of demand (e.g., people are willing to pay a higher price for vegetables), production intensity (e.g., vegetables have a higher yield per hectare than cotton), or both. Also assume that each crop has a different transportation rate (T) such that:

$$T_v > T_w > T_c.$$

Transportation rates are a product of the perishability, bulkiness, and/or fragility of a given commodity. Vegetables are extremely perishable, frag-

---

[10] For a discussion of the wider applications of the von Thünen model see: Foust and de Souza, *The Economic Landscape*, pp. 30-47; H.F. Gregor, *Geography of Agriculture: Themes in Research* (Englewood Cliffs: Prentice-Hall, 1970), pp. 55-77; and M. Chisholm, *Rural Settlement and Land Use: An Essay in Location*, 3d ed. (London: Hutchinson University Library, 1979), pp. 13-25.

ile, and bulky crops. Cotton will keep for a long time and can be easily transported. Wheat is less perishable than vegetables, but more so than cotton.

Figure 2 depicts the multiple crops–single market scenario described above. The origin of each bid-rent curve is the market price of the agricultural good. The slope of the curve is the transportation rate. These transportation rates, in the von Thünen model, are simple linear deterrence functions: the steeper the slope, the greater the transportation rate per kilometer. As a result, vegetables are the most profitable crop from the market to distance D_v. Throughout this area, the economic rent a farmer could gain from a hectare of vegetables exceeds that of either wheat or cotton.

At D_v, however, the situation changes; from this point to D_w the economic rent per hectare of vegetables falls below that which a cultivator acquires from growing wheat. Likewise, from D_w to the margin of production (D_c), cotton yields the highest rent per hectare and therefore is the most profitable. In agreement with the restrictive behavioral assumptions of the von Thünen model, farmers at any given location have only one option. They must grow that crop, and only that crop, which yields the highest economic rent per hectare. Accordingly, farmers within this "ideal state" would produce an agricultural landscape analogous to figure 3. These belts of homogeneous land use are commonly referred to as "Thünen rings."

Multiple crops–multiple markets case. Another common application of the von Thünen model describes an agricultural landscape containing both multiple crops and multiple markets. For example, assume that the same three crops, vegetables, wheat, and cotton, are cultivated around two markets of equal demand. Furthermore, assume that both the market price and transportation rates assigned to each crop are identical to those in the previous example. Given these two assumptions, plus von Thünen's seven general constraints, the resulting agricultural land-use patterns would reflect those represented in figure 4. Note that the two bid-rent curves for cotton overlap, ultimately resulting in the development of a hexagonal market area. The cropping patterns surrounding the second market are a mirror image of those located around the first market. As in the previous example, this linear representation of the von Thünen model can be translated into a two-dimensional illustration by rotating the bid-rent curves around the net income axes, thereby creating the Thünen rings (figure 5).

Modifications of the Basic von Thünen Model

In his initial work, von Thünen presented an agricultural location theory set within a framework of ideal conditions. In subsequent works, he removed several of his limiting constraints to simulate agricultural landscapes under imperfect economic conditions. He was aware that additional

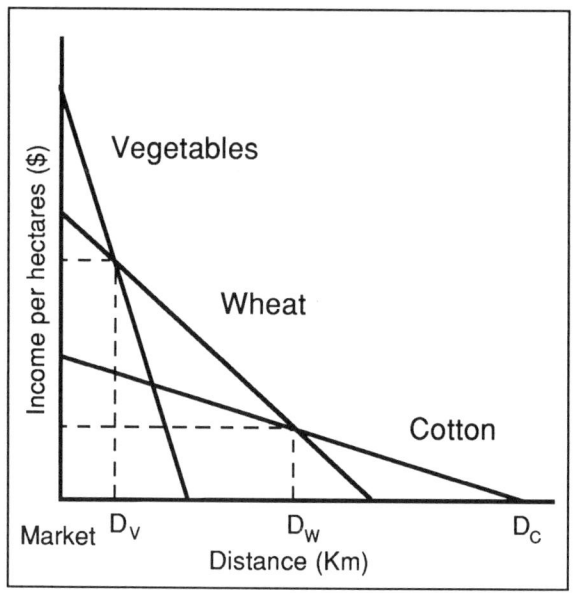

Fig. 2. The Von Thünen Three Crops–Single Market Case.

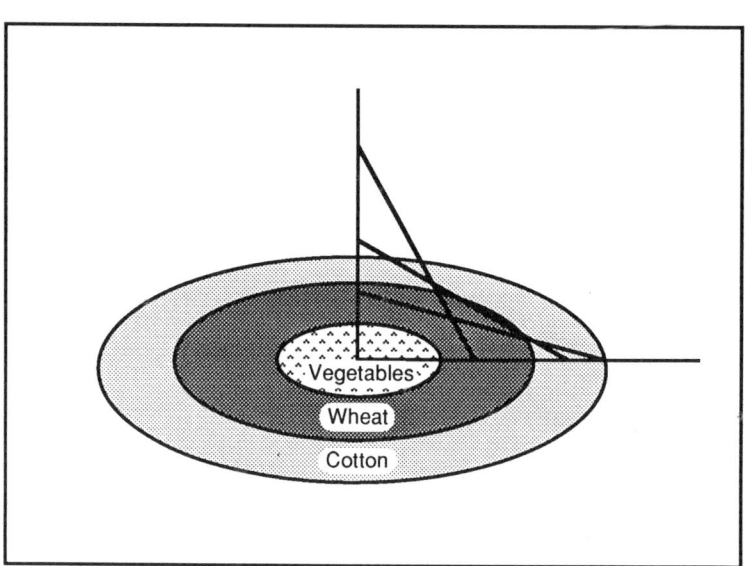

Fig. 3. Two-Dimensional Representation of the Multiple Crops–Single Market Case.

AGRICULTURAL LOCATION THEORY 13

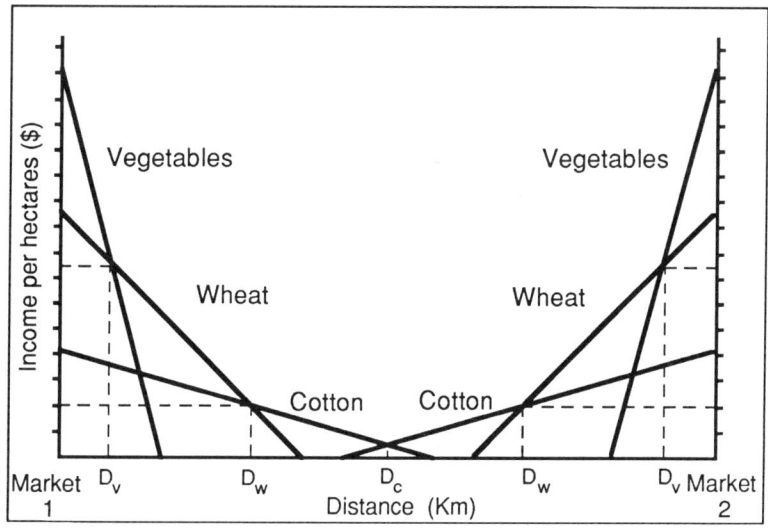

Fig. 4. Von Thünen Three Crops–Two Markets Case

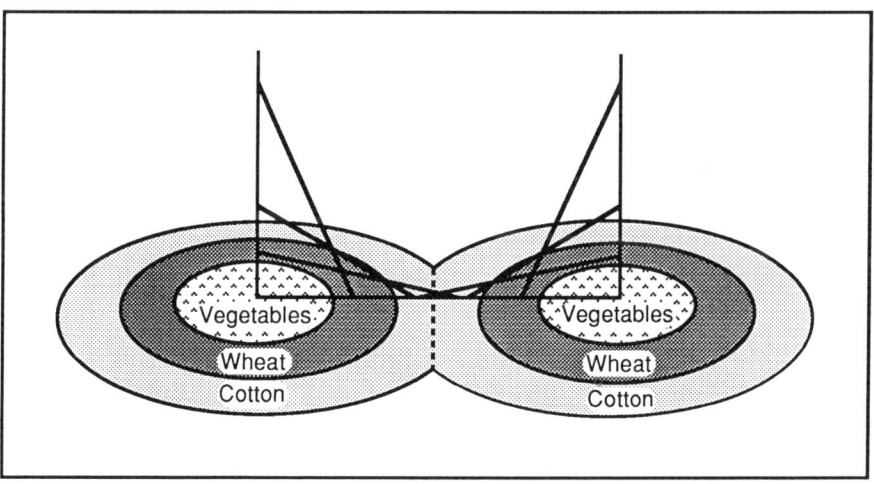

Fig. 5. A Two-Dimensional Representation of the Multiple Crops–Two Markets Case.

factors influence the location of agricultural production. "The isolated state was never meant to be something that could really exist. Once the ideal had been established, deviations from it could be analyzed."[11]

Three of the assumptions modified by von Thünen concerned the areal differentiation of production costs. Originally, he assumed that the standard of living remained constant throughout the countryside. In subsequent analyses, however, von Thünen considered the effect of variations in the standard of living. These variations were attributed to dissimilar levels of aspiration among individual farmers.[12] Von Thünen also incorporated variable prices for agricultural inputs throughout the economic landscape. Furthermore, he adjusted the ideal pattern of rural land use to reflect differences in soil fertility; consequently, production costs varied throughout the countryside.

In von Thünen's ideal model, transport costs were isotropic and strictly a linear function of distance. In later writings, however, he discussed land-use patterns that were the result of anisotropic cost surfaces. For example, he illustrated the extent a canal or navigable river distorts the ideal circular land-use pattern. Production zones are expanded along the canal or river, while contracted elsewhere. He also considered the effects barriers or other constraints (e.g., impassable terrain or import restrictions) have upon the costs of moving goods. He concluded that distance should not be recorded in units of linear distance, but rather in broader economic terms. Accordingly, total cost incurred, and not merely the number of kilometers traveled, is the more important factor.

Von Thünen also applied his descriptive concepts to landscapes that contained multiple markets of varying sizes. He further discussed the role subsidies and taxes play in the formation of land-use patterns. All of these modifications influence the prices of goods to varying degrees, and therefore their locations of production.[13]

More recent scholars such as Benedict, Dunn, Lösch, Alonzo, Found, and Weber have discussed the modifications suggested by von Thünen and have also introduced improvements of their own.[14] None of the modifica-

---

[11] Chisholm, *Rural Settlement and Land Use*, pp. 19-21.
[12] Ibid., p. 21.
[13] Ibid., pp. 22-23.
[14] E.T. Benedict, ed., *Theodor Brinkman's Economics of the Farm Business* (Berkeley: University of California Press, 1935); Dunn, *The Location of Agricultural Production*; Lösch, *The Economics of Location*; W. Alonzo, *Location and Land Use: Toward a General Theory of Land Rent* (Boston: Harvard University Press, 1964); W.C. Found, *A Theoretical Approach to Rural Land-Use Patterns* (London: Edward Arnold, 1971); and A. Weber, *Theory of the Location of Industries*, trans. C.J. Friedrich (Chicago: University of Chicago Press, 1929). See

tions have affected the underlying principles of the model; rather they have increased its precision and accuracy. However, an in-depth analysis of modern modifications made to the basic model is beyond the scope of this monograph; they neither aid in its understanding nor are necessary for the discussion pursued in the succeeding sections.

Programming von Thünen's Theory of Agricultural Location

To establish an areal pattern of economic rent, given a demand for a number of agricultural goods, the von Thünen model may be written as an equation to be maximized subject to a number of constraints. Once again, the two most fundamental constraints are total cost of production and transport cost per hectare. Together, these must not exceed the net returns for any given area of land. This can be expressed in the form of both linear and quadratic equations.[15] Since the quadratic expressions were constructed to allow both yields and basic costs (production and transport) to vary, the simple linear case is more relevant to the original von Thünen model.[16]

The linear equation for the three crops–single market example is as follows:

$$\text{Maximize } Z = \sum_{i=1}^{3} \sum_{j=1}^{3} s_{ij} x_{ij} ; \qquad (2)$$

where s_{ij} is the net return per hectare of the jth crop in the ith zone, and x_{ij} is the area devoted to the jth crop in the ith zone. This maximization is subject to the following constraints:

$$\sum_{j=1}^{3} x_{ij} L_i ; \text{ and} \qquad (3)$$

$$\sum_{j=1}^{3} C_{ij} x_{ij} K_i \qquad (4)$$

where L_i is the total amount of land available in the ith zone; the total amount of land devoted to all crops cannot exceed the total land in the ith zone. In the second constraint, C_{ij} is the working capital required to cultivate

---

also: W.L. Garrison and D.F. Marble, "The Spatial Structure of Agricultural Activities," *Annals of the Association of American Geographers* 47 (1957): 137-144.

15 R.H. Day and E.H. Tinney, "A Dynamic von Thünen Model," *Geographical Analysis* 1 (1969): 137-151.

16 For a detailed discussion of both the linear and quadratic von Thünen programs see: B.H. Stevens, "Location Theory and Programming Models: The von Thünen Case," *Papers and Proceedings of the Regional Science Association* 21 (1968): 19-34; and W.D. Macmillan, "Some Comments on the Stevens Linear and Quadratic Programming Versions of von Thünen's Theory of Agricultural Land Usage," *Environment and Planning* A 11 (1979): 943-962.

one hectare of the jth crop in the ith zone; x_{ij} is the area devoted to the jth crop in the ith zone. K_i is the total capital available in the ith zone. These constraints apply to all three zones.

The constraints are written as inequalities because it may not be necessary to use all the available capital, or land, in order to maximize the first equation (2). This is a classic problem for linear programming—attempting to maximize one variable subject to numerous inequalities.[17]

Empirical Evidence for the von Thünen Model

The von Thünen model has been tested, at various scales of observation, in both developed and developing economies. Undoubtedly, no other agricultural land-use model has been so widely tested in the field. In general, the degree to which von Thünen-like agricultural landscapes exist, in either situation, is still being debated.

For more than a century, writers have reported finding examples of von Thünen rings in the economic landscape of what is called the developed realm. One of the first to affirm the statistical reality was Roscher, who claimed that both London and Capetown were encircled by belts of land use similar to those in von Thünen's estate at Mecklenburg.[18] A similar pronouncement was made by Buchanan and Hurwitz, who described the countryside around the South African port city of Durban as approximating a von Thünen land-use pattern.[19] Likewise, Chisholm noted similar gradation patterns around London in 1811.[20]

At the regional scale, Jonasson, Valkenburg, and Held have claimed that Europe as a whole exhibits, or has exhibited, a concentric von Thünen land-use pattern. In 1925, Jonasson proposed that Europe contained a gradation of five zones. Zone one, adjacent to the cities in the Northwest, was dominated by horticulture, whereas zone two contained fruit and vegetable truck gardening. Zone three included the intensive agricultural and dairying activities (dairy products, beef cattle, mutton sheep, veal, forage crops, oats, and flax for fiber). Zone four consisted of extensive general farming

---

[17] K. Williams, *Linear Programming: The Simplex Algorithm* (London: Longmans, 1969).

[18] W. Roscher, "Das von Thünensche Gesetz," in *Archiv der Politischen Oekonomie und Polizeiwissenschaft*, ed. Hermann et al., vol. 3: *Ideen zur Politik und Statistik der Ackerbausysteme* (Heidelberg, 1845), pp. 86-95; idem, *Nationalökonomik des Ackerbaus und der verwandten Urproductionen* (Stuttgart: Cotta, 1859), p. 187, cited by Gregor, *Geography of Agriculture*, p. 60.

[19] K. Buchanan and N. Hurwitz, "Land Use in Natal," *Economic Geography* 27 (1951): p. 236.

[20] Chisholm, *Rural Settlement and Land Use*, pp. 74-75.

(grain, hay, and livestock). Finally, the outermost peripheral area, zone five, was largely forest.[21] Similarly, Valkenburg and Held highlighted the fact that the average yield of Europe's eight major crops follows a consecutive pattern of decline with distance from the central market area.[22]

On a global scale, Peet applied a von Thünen-like analysis to the worldwide expansion of commercial agriculture during the nineteenth century. He utilized British import data to delineate and analyze these global zones of agricultural production. He concluded that the expansion of commercial agriculture was a direct response to an apparently ever increasing demand and rising prices of agricultural goods in the "Thünen world cities" of Western Europe and eastern North America.[23]

The von Thünen model has also been applied, with apparent success, to the contemporary United States. At a regional scale, Gottmann's study of the production intensity and fresh-market orientation of agriculture around the megalopolis of the northeastern seaboard is one example.[24] A second example is Durand's application of the model to the major milksheds of the United States.[25] At the national scale, both Muller and Jones have reported finding evidence of von Thünen-like landscapes. Muller, using the eastern megalopolis as a single national market, reported that the macroagricultural landscape of the United States approximated, to a significant degree, von Thünen-like land-use intensity patterns.[26] Likewise, Jones has claimed that the national zonation patterns of wheat and feed grains can be explained in the context of the von Thünen model.[27]

Although the list of affirmations is impressive, there is an equally large number of accounts that document deviations from the theoretical von Thünen pattern. Many geographers attribute the aberrations found in the developed countries to improvements in means of transportation. The economic advantage of proximity to markets diminishes at a decreasing rate as the efficiency of transportation increases. Accordingly, a common charac-

---

[21] O. Jonasson, "Agricultural Regions of Europe," *Economic Geography* 1 (1925): 277-314.

[22] S. Van Valkenburg and C.C. Held, *Europe*, 2d ed. (New York: Wiley and Sons, 1952).

[23] J.R. Peet, "The Spatial Expansion of Commercial Agriculture in the Nineteenth Century: A von Thünen Interpretation," *Economic Geography* 45 (1969): 283-301.

[24] J. Gottmann, *Megalopolis* (Cambridge, Mass.: Massachusetts Institute of Technology Press, 1961).

[25] L. Durand, "The Major Milksheds of the Northeastern Quarter of the United States," *Economic Geography* 40 (1964): 9-33.

[26] P.O. Muller, "Trend Surfaces of American Agricultural Patterns: A Macro-Thünian Analysis," *Economic Geography* 49 (1973): 228-242.

[27] R.C. Jones, "Testing Macro-Thünen Models by Linear Programming," *Professional Geographer* 28 (1976): 353-361.

teristic of a developed economic landscape is the regional specialization of agriculture. Therefore, other locational forces such as climate, soil, and terrain have replaced distance as the major land-use agent. Also, the emphasis in developed countries on economies of scale has reinforced areal specialization. This process of regional specialization is well documented by Baker in his study of land-use factors in the United States.[28]

Conflicting evidence concerning global von Thünen land-use patterns has been brought to light by Grotewold and Sublett. They disagree with Chisholm that the high agricultural intensities of northwestern Europe are mainly the result of proximity to market. They note a major inconsistency in Chisholm's argument insofar as farming is more intensive in West Germany than in the United Kingdom. Their assertion is that variations in European agricultural intensities can be attributed to the severity of agricultural import regulations by individual countries. They believe that trade barriers, rather than proximity to market, are responsible for the intensity of cropping in West Germany.[29]

At the micro level, a number of scholars have observed that the influence of distance relative to other factors has diminished. "From a pattern of intensity that was dictated primarily by the distance between field and farmstead has evolved another that reflects more the role of the physical environment."[30] De Garis De Lisle's analysis of farmstead cropping patterns in Manitoba supports this argument. His results show that the role the natural environment plays as a locational factor increases as the transport network improves.[31] A more extreme position is taken by Burton, who questions the postulate that distance was ever the major locational factor on American farmsteads. Like others, he points to the impact of environmental factors on agricultural decision-making.[32]

Another major deviation from the ideal von Thünen land-use pattern in developed economies is the apparent reversal of intensity gradation

---

[28] O.E. Baker, "The Increasing Importance of the Physical Condition in Determining the Utilization of Land for Agricultural and Forest Production in the United States," *Annals of the Association of American Geographers* 11 (1921): 17-46; for additional support concerning the increasing importance of environmental factors in the macroscale see: S. Visser, "Technological Change and the Spatial Structure of Agriculture," *Economic Geography* 56 (1980): 311-319.

[29] A. Grotewold and M.D. Sublett, "The Effect of Import Restrictions on Land Use: The United Kingdom Compared with West Germany," *Economic Geography* 43 (1967): 64-70.

[30] Gregor, *Geography of Agriculture*, p. 66.

[31] D. de Garis De Lisle, "Effects of Distance on Cropping Patterns Internal to the Farm," *Annals of the Association of American Geographers* 72 (1982): 88-98.

[32] I. Burton, *Types of Agricultural Occupance of Flood Plains in the United States*, University of Chicago Department of Geography Research Papers, no. 75 (Chicago: University of Chicago, Department of Geography, 1962), p. 26.

around major cities. Grotewold was the first to note this reversal gradation, and Sinclair subsequently constructed a more appropriate ring-type model.[33] This lack of intensive farming near cities has been attributed to high urban taxes, restrictive zoning, increasing competition from more distant areas with better production facilities, and the loss of casual labor to urban jobs.[34]

The results of two recent attempts to apply the von Thünen model to developed economic landscapes have concluded that, given the normative assumptions and static nature of the model, it does not accurately portray rural land-use patterns in advanced economies. Moran found no evidence of von Thünen land-use patterns around Auckland, New Zealand.[35] "Land use patterns on the urban periphery are heterogeneous, partly as a result of the variables that are treated as assumptions in land-use models, partly because they are constantly changing and adjusting, whereas most models are static."[36] Likewise, Kellerman, utilizing stepwise multiple regression procedures, found that only a small percentage of the variation in the national cropping patterns of the United States can be explained by the influence of local bid-rents.[37]

Although several authors have claimed that von Thünen's cropping and intensity theories are suitable to developing regions of the world, others contend that empirical evidence is lacking.[38] Several scholars have maintained that von Thünen-like landscapes are more likely to be present in developing regions because disruptive factors (e.g., sophisticated transport and marketing systems, and regional specialization) found in the developed countries are not present. In general, however, peasant farmers in developing countries operate in a more precarious physical and economic environment than their counterparts in the developed realm. As a result, the environmental and behavioral constraints inherent in the von Thünen model are even more inappropriate when applied to developing countries.

---

[33] A. Grotewold, "Von Thünen in Retrospect," *Economic Geography* 35 (1959): 346-355; R. Sinclair, "Von Thünen and Urban Sprawl," *Annals of the Association of American Geographers* 57 (1967): 72-87.

[34] Sinclair, "Von Thünen and Urban Sprawl," pp. 85-87; R.H. Best and R.M. Gasson, *The Changing Location of Intensive Crops* (London: Wye College, University of London, Department of Agricultural Economics, 1966), p. 63, as cited in Gregor, *Geography of Agriculture*, p. 67.

[35] W. Moran, "Spatial Patterns of Agriculture on the Urban Periphery: The Auckland Case," *Tijdschrift voor Economische en Sociale Geografie* 70 (1979): 164-176.

[36] Ibid., p. 175.

[37] A. Kellerman, "The Pertinence of the Macro-Thünen Analysis," *Economic Geography* 53 (1977): 255-264.

[38] J.D. Henshall, "Models of Agricultural Activity," in *Socio-Economic Models in Geography*, ed. R.J. Chorley and P. Haggett (London: Methuen and Co., 1968), pp. 444-445; Sinclair, "Von Thünen and Urban Sprawl," p. 72; J.R. Tarrant, *Agricultural Geography* (New York: John Wiley and Sons, 1974), p. 31.

It is true, however, that owing to the absence of sophisticated transport and marketing systems, distance does play a more significant role in determining agricultural land use in a developing economy.

Several geographers have reported finding some resemblance to von Thünen's general farming zones within developing countries. Among such reports, the farming pattern described by Horvath around Addis Ababa, Ethiopia, comes closest to approximating a von Thünian landscape. Apart from the absence of a timber zone, the land-use patterns around the capital city fit the von Thünen landscape moderately well. The author attributes the lack of a better fit to the inappropriateness of the profit maximization assumption.[39] The findings of Prothero and Mitchell support Horvath's observation concerning the unsuitability of this behavioral constraint. Although they found evidence of von Thünen rings at their respective sites, both noted a prevalent violation of the "profit maximizing peasant" assumption of the model.[40] It appears that the risk-aversion strategy of mixed cropping was widespread throughout both study areas.[41] This cropping pattern is inconceivable within a von Thünen framework, where it is assumed that a farmer will produce the crop, and only that crop, which maximizes the economic rent of a particular site. Kelly's historical account of cropping patterns in Hooghly, India, and my contemporary study in the Chandigarh region, India, provide further evidence that the customary practice of mixed-cropping hinders the development of a genuine von Thünian landscape.[42]

The presence of a von Thünen-like gradation of cropping intensity has been noted by several authors writing on land use in developing countries. For example, Fung in his study of suburban agricultural land use in China has noted both that vegetable production zones encircle China's cities, and that intensity of cultivation decreases with distance from an urban center.[43] Fung adds, however, that in the People's Republic, ideological

---

[39] R.J. Horvath, "Von Thünen's Isolated State and the Area around Addis Ababa, Ethiopia," *Annals of the Association of American Geographers* 59 (1969): 308-323.

[40] R.M. Prothero, "Land Use at Soba, Zaria Province, Northern Nigeria," *Economic Geography* 33 (1957): 72-86; W.A. Mitchell, "Turkish Villages in Interior Anatolio and von Thünen's Isolated State," *Middle East Journal* 25 (1971): 355-369.

[41] The term "mixed cropping" refers to cropping systems which involve a farmer growing two or more crops simultaneously within the same locality. While the notion of mixed cropping includes all types of intercropping (mixed, sow, strip, and relay) it differs in that there is not necessarily crop competition during all or part of crop growth.

[42] K. Kelly, "Agricultural Change in Hooghly, 1850-1910," *Annals of the Association of American Geographers* 71 (1981): 237-252; J.H. Astroth, Jr., "Cropping and Land Use Patterns in a Newly Developing Urban Fringe: A Case Study of the Chandigarh Region, India," paper presented at the annual meeting of the Missouri Academy of Sciences, Kirksville, Mo., April 1980.

[43] K. Fung, "Suburban Agricultural Land Use," in *China: Urbanization and National Development*, ed. C.K. Leung and N.S. Ginsburg, University of Chicago Department of

rather than strictly economic attributes contribute one of the most important determinants in agricultural location.[44] Katzman and Richardson also have commented that, with certain modifications, the intensity gradation is evident in their respective study areas.[45]

Although several authors have found at least modest evidence of von Thünian landscapes at the aggregated or regional level in developing countries, support for the existence of such land-use patterns at the disaggregated or village level is not as extensive. At the village level studies have highlighted the importance of cultural and environmental factors, rather than economic variables, in determining both intensity of cultivation and cropping patterns.[46] As Blaikie has stated: "There are many theoretical models in geography that predict patterns or locations from purely spatial factors (such as von Thünen's model based upon the distance factor as expressed by transport costs), but testing in the field usually calls for explanation other than that offered by location theory."[47]

Village-level observations in India by both Nair and Astroth support Blaikie's claim. This research adds weight to the theory that the values and beliefs associated with a particular culture group influence the degree to which economic factors will determine land-use patterns. It has been noted that there is often a significant differential response among culture groups to actual or potential opportunities in the economic sphere.[48] Blaikie's finding that distance was a key location factor in the village he studied in Rajasthan but not in those of Punjab seems to support this belief.[49]

Several authors have argued that because of the dissimilarity between nineteenth-century German agriculture and contemporary peasant farming systems, it is inappropriate even to attempt to apply the von Thünen model to developing economies. For example, Jackson maintains that the von

---

Geography Research Papers, no. 196 (Chicago: University of Chicago, Department of Geography, 1980).

[44] Ibid., p. 182.

[45] M.T. Katzman, "The von Thünen Paradigm, the Industrial-Urban Hypothesis, and the Spatial Structure of Agriculture," *American Journal of Agricultural Economics* 56 (1974): 683-696; R.C. Richardson, "Distance Regularities in Guyanese Rice Cultivation," *Journal of Developing Areas* 8 (1974): 235-256.

[46] E.g.: H.C. Darby, "Settlement in Northern Rhodesia," *Geographical Review* 21 (1931): 559-573.

[47] P.M. Blaikie, "Spatial Organization of Agriculture in Some North Indian Villages: Part II," *Transactions of the Institute of British Geographers* 53 (1971): 15-30.

[48] K. Nair, *In Defense of the Irrational Peasant: Indian Agriculture since the Green Revolution* (Chicago: University of Chicago Press, 1979); J.R. Astroth, Jr., "Influence of a Growth Center on Indian Rural Life" (M.A. thesis., University of Missouri, 1980).

[49] Blaikie, "Spatial Organization of Some North Indian Villages I," *Transactions of the Institute of British Geographers* 52 (1971): 1-40.

Thünen model is not appropriate where quasi-subsistence rather than cash cropping is dominant.[50] Stevens and Lee echo these sentiments and add that, even when physical factors are held constant, distance alone does not explain patterns of agricultural intensity. They contend that the perception of distance by farmers and the role of women in agriculture are more influential factors in peasant land-use systems.[51]

Summary and Evaluation of the von Thünen Model

The following statements summarize the von Thünen model in a normative economic framework:

1. An inverse relationship exists between location rent and transport costs.
2. An agricultural frontier exists on a homogeneous plain with a centrally located market town.
3. The value and intensity of land use decreases with distance from the market.
4. There is intercrop competition, with the location of each crop determined by the principle of highest economic rent.

Throughout the preceding discussion concerning the empirical testing of the model, several limitations have been noted. First, the von Thünen model assumes that variations in land rents are exclusively the result of differences that exist in costs of production. Second, the model is static and deterministic. It portrays an agricultural landscape at one point in time and therefore cannot forecast future rural land-use patterns. Furthermore, any change in technology, demand, or transportation cost is assumed to bring about instantaneous adjustments in land-use patterns. Third, the von Thünen model assumes a constant transport rate. In contrast, research has shown that transport costs increase with distance in a nonlinear fashion.[52] Fourth, the behavioral constraint of profit maximization is unrealistic, especially in peasant agricultural systems.[53] The von Thünen model characterizes farmers as optimizers (as opposed to "satisficers"), who have both perfect information and the ability to use it with complete rationality to maximize profits. As previously mentioned, studies have shown that farm-

---

[50] R. Jackson, "Some Observations on the Thünen Method of Analysis with Reference to South-East Ethiopia," *East African Geographical Review* 8 (1970): 39-46.

[51] R. Stevens and Y. Lee, "A Spatial Analysis of Agricultural Intensity in a Basotho Village of Southern Africa," *Professional Geographer* 31 (1979): 177-183.

[52] E.g., A.P. Jones, W.J. McGuire, and A.D. Witte, "A Reexamination of Some Aspects of von Thünen's Model of Spatial Location," *Journal of Regional Science* 18 (1978): 1-16.

[53] For a more in-depth evaluation of the von Thünen model see, e.g., ibid., pp. 1-16; W.B. Morgan, "The Doctrine of the Rings," *Geography* 58 (1978): 301-312.

ers, especially quasi-subsistence peasants, make suboptimal, in a purely economic sense, decisions. They do so because they possess less than perfect market information and they are subject to unpredictable weather and economic conditions. As a result, risk aversion rather than profit maximization is the behavioral norm.[54]

Despite these limitations, the von Thünen model still illustrates an important approach to studying agricultural land use. As Morgan stated: "The importance of Thünen's contribution to location theory is not in his actual model, nor in its applications in relation to reality, but in its attempt to develop the partial equilibrium method of analysis. Its importance lies also in its being the first model, however imperfect, and in its break away from contemporary methods of study and above all from contentment with description, simple comparison or vague generalization."[55]

Interregional Equilibrium Models

Through the use of marginal analysis, the von Thünen model, operating continuously over space, illustrates how types of land use blend into one another over a continuum. Other types of locational models are concerned with spatial equilibrium that may be derived by conceptualizing areas as points. This approach traditionally has been used in international trade theory. Producers, factors of production, products, and consumers are assumed to be located at a series of discrete points with zero transportation cost between them. Given the existence of trade, the concept of comparative advantage then explains the regional patterns of agricultural production. These models can be classified according to two basic types: input-output models and spatial equilibrium models.[56]

---

[54] E.g.: G.O.I. Abalu, "A Note on Crop Mixtures under Indigenous Conditions in Northern Nigeria," *Journal of Development Studies* 12 (1976): 212-220; G.H.M. Herath, "Crop Mixtures under Peasant Conditions: A Decision Theoretic Interpretation," *Journal of Development Studies* 16 (1980): 322-331; N.S. Jodha, "Intercropping in Traditional Farming Systems," Journal of Development Studies 16 (1980): 426-442; A.W. Johnson *Sharecroppers of the Serrtao* (Stanford: Stanford University Press, 1971): P.N. Junakar, "Do Indian Farmers Maximize Profits?" *Journal of Development Studies* 16 (1980): 48-59; D.W. Norman, "Rationalizing Mixed Cropping under Indigenous Conditions: The Example of Northern Nigeria," *Journal of Development Studies* 11 (1974): 3-21; and J.C. Scott, *The Moral Economy of the Peasant: Rebellion and Subsistence in Southeast Asia* (New Haven: Yale University Press, 1976).

[55] Morgan, "The Doctrine of the Rings," p. 311.

[56] For a more in-depth discussion of intraregional equilibrium models see: D. Harvey, "Theoretical Concepts and the Analysis of Agricultural Land-Use Patterns in Geography." *Annals of the Association of American Geographers* 56 (1966): 365-367; Found, *Theoretical Approach to Rural Land-Use*, pp. 83-105.

Input-Output Models

Leontieff originally developed this approach as an instrument for explaining the structural interrelationships within a national economy.[57] Subsequently, Isard, Moses, Chenery, and others have applied modified versions at the regional level.[58] Further, studies of this nature have been pursued by a group of agricultural economists at Iowa State University.[59] The focus of their work has been concerned mainly with the description of existing interrelationships in regional agricultural production. By assuming the temporal stability of interregional relationships, however, the model can be used to project the impact of economic changes on production patterns. The major drawback of this type of modeling is that a wide range of input data are needed. For the model to have any significant meaning, numerous regions and commodities must be specified. These types of data are scarcely available in developing countries and therefore have minimal application to the monograph.

Spatial Equilibrium Models

Linear programming is probably the most widely used operational technique for examining the spatial equilibrium of agricultural production patterns. When this methodology is applied, provided that sufficient data are available, it is possible to determine the location of agricultural production, while several other specified goals are also achieved. These goals might include that: (1) the model constructs an agricultural landscape where the average profit among all farmers is maximized, or (2) the cost of food for consumers is minimized. Among the most noteworthy pioneers of this methodology are Fox, Taeuber, Judge, Wallace, and Henderson.[60] Subse-

---

[57] W.W. Leontieff, *Studies in the Structure of the American Economy* (New York: Oxford University Press, 1953).

[58] W. Isard, *Methods of Regional Analysis* (New York: Wiley, 1960), chapter 8; H.B. Chenery, "Interregional and International Input-Output Analysis," in *Structural Interdependence of the Economy*, ed. T. Barnes, (New York, Wiley, 1954); L. Moses, "A General Equilibrium Model of Production, Interregional Trade, and Location of Industry," *Review of Economics and Statistics* 42 (1960): 373-397.

[59] G. H. Peterson and E. O. Heady, *Application of Input-Output Analysis to a Single Model Emphasizing Agriculture*; J. A. Schnittkar and E. O. Heady, *Application of Input-Output Analysis to a Regional Model Stressing Agriculture*; and H. A. Carter and E. O. Heady, *An Input-Output Analysis Emphasizing Regional and Commodity Sectors of Agriculture*, Iowa Agricultural and Home Economics Experiment Station Research Bulletin nos. 427, 454, and 469 (Ames, Ia.: 1956, 1958, and 1959).

[60] K. Fox, "A Spatial Equilibrium Model of the Livestock-Feed Economy in the United States," *Econometrica* 21 (1953): 547-566; K. Fox and R.C. Taeuber, "Spatial Equilibrium Models of the Livestock-Feed Economy," *American Economic Review* 45 (1955): 584-608; G.T. Judge and T.D. Wallace, "Estimation of Spatial Price Equilibrium Models," *Journal of Farm*

quent scholars have built upon their research to construct a model that predicts both agricultural production and distribution patterns.[61] It is beyond the scope of this monograph to summarize all the work that has been completed in regard to spatial equilibrium models, especially since the specifications of the various models are problem specific. It is beneficial, however, to describe two of the more applicable contributions. The first, a study completed by Heady and Egbert in the early 1960s, utilized linear programming techniques to allocate the production of field crops within 122 producing zones of the United States.[62] They allocated the crops based on two criteria: (a) the minimization of the overall supply cost, and (b) the satisfaction of the national demand for each commodity. Seven additional land constraints were added to the second criterion: the demand for each crop was to be met but not exceeded.

Therefore, in linear programming notation we minimize:

$$Sc = \sum_{i=1}^{n} \sum_{j=1}^{m} x_{ij} C_{ij} ; \quad (5)$$

where Sc are the total supply costs and x_{ij} is the level of the jth activity in the ith region and C_{ij} is the cost per unit of the jth activity in the ith region (in their example m = 7 and n = 122).

The minimization of this equation is subject to the following two inequalities:

$$\sum_{j=1}^{m} x_{ij} A_{ij} \leq S_i \quad (6)$$

where A_{ij} is the unit land requirement of the jth activity in the ith region, and S_i is the total amount of land available in the ith region. The second is:

$$\sum_{j=1}^{m} \sum_{i=1}^{n} x_{ij} = D_j ; \quad (7)$$

where D_j is the national demand for the commodity j.

There was a poor goodness-of-fit between the theoretical agricultural landscape produced by this model and the actual production patterns. The

---

Economics 50 (1958): 801-820; J.M. Henderson, "The Utilization of Agricultural Land: A Theoretical and Empirical Inquiry," *Review of Economics and Statistics* 41 (1959): 242-260.

[61] E.g.: A.C. Egbert and E.O. Heady, Regional Adjustments in Grain Production: A Linear Programming Analysis, U.S. Department of Agriculture, Technical Bulletin no. 1241 (Washington: U.S. Government Printing Office, 1961).

[62] E.O. Heady and A.C. Egbert, "Regional Programming of Efficient Agricultural Production Patterns," *Econometrica* 32 (1964): 374-386.

authors attribute the dissimilarity to deficiencies in both the data available and in the established relationships of the inequalities.

The other study was conducted by Howes for the United States Department of Agriculture.[63] It represents a more comprehensive land-use allocation model. Howes was concerned with the use of linear programming as a technique for allocating various types of agricultural production in the Susquehanna River basin. His objective was to minimize the total cost of producing and shipping agricultural commodities from each subregion of the basin to its respective market area. The inequalities are similar to those of the previous example: (1) the land used for any one particular crop cannot exceed the total available land within that region; (2) the ratios in which intermediate goods, such as fodder, can be combined to produce a final good are predetermined; (3) the shipments of goods from each region are greater than a limited threshold; and (4) all shipments are greater than or equal to zero.

The optimal solution produced by Howes's algorithm differed from the observed production patterns considerably. As a result, the author felt that the model, as is, had limited potential for widespread application. The difficulty is obtaining sufficient data; and the need to further quantify constraining relationships was once again singled out as a major obstacle. As a planning tool, however, the model does have a certain amount of usefulness. It can be used to illustrate how future resources should be allocated to maximize some defined function. It should be noted that spatial equilibrium models do not have to be linearly restricted, as in these two examples, but rather quadratic or more complex functions can be employed if the situation justifies their use.[64]

Like the von Thünen model, interregional equilibrium models are normative and therefore suffer from similar limiting assumptions: (1) that all individual farmers command complete information; and (2) that in the light of this perfect knowledge, they make rational decisions in order to maximize their net return. The extent to which these conditions are, or are not, met in any economic landscape is questionable. In response to the restriction of these questionable assumptions, many geographers, and other social scientists concerned with modeling the areal distribution of agriculture, have abandoned this normative economic approach to pursue the study of agricultural decision-making from a behavioral perspective.

---

[63] R. Howes, "A Test of a Linear Programming Model for Agriculture," *Papers of the Regional Science Association* 19 (1967): 123-140.

[64] Harvey, "Theoretical Concepts," p. 373.

The Behavioral Approach

By now it is evident that, owing to the existence of numerous causal factors, attempting to model agricultural land-use patterns is a difficult task. Ultimately, these patterns are the end result of decisions made by thousands of individual farmers, groups of farmers, and professional managers who are seldom motivated by economic considerations alone. As Harvey has stated: "If we recognize the all-important fact that geographical patterns are the result of human decisions, then it follows that any theoretical model developed to 'explain' agricultural location patterns must take account of psychological and sociological realities, and this can only be accomplished if the normative theories of agricultural location are made more flexible and blended with the insights provided by models of behaviour."[65]

A behavioral approach to the study of agricultural location involves the use of concepts from "decision theory." Proponents of decision theory have attempted systematically to describe those variables that influence entrepreneurial choices by farmers.[66] There are numerous types of decision-making, ranging from intentional problem-solving to unintentional, subconscious decision behavior. Ilbery claims that the majority of decision-makers tend to be of the latter type. This is due to both their inability to process large amounts of data, and the widespread desire to avoid burdensome work.[67]

Early attempts to model agricultural location patterns through a behavioral perspective revolved around the work of von Neumann and Morgenstern. They constructed the foundation of "game theory."[68] Game theory maintains a normative theory of behavior while recognizing the presence of uncertainty in the decision-maker's environment. This involves the construction of a payoff matrix. This matrix illustrates possible outcomes of various strategies available to the farmer, given a number of possible circumstances—the likelihood of which is uncertain.[69] The optimal decision, at least in the farmer's mind, may be selected according to various criteria. The two most familiar criteria contained in the geographic literature are Wald's "standards for judgment" and the Laplace criterion.[70] According

---

[65] Ibid.

[66] W. Edwards and A. Tversky, *Decision-Making* (Hammondsworth: Penguin, 1967).

[67] B.W. Ilbery, "Agricultural Decision-Making: A Behavioral Perspective," *Progress in Human Geography* 2 (1978): 448-466.

[68] J. von Neumann, and O. Morgenstern, *Theory of Games and Economic Behavior* (Princeton: Princeton University Press, 1944).

[69] For a more detailed account of the theoretical framework of game theory see: Tarrant, *Agricultural Geography*, pp. 38-48.

[70] For a discussion of these and other theories of choice under uncertainty see: J.L. Dillon and E.O. Heady, *Theories of Choice in Relation to Farmer Decisions.* Iowa Agri-

to Wald's standards, a farmer selects a strategy based on a pessimistic forecast and, accordingly, chooses the least risky farming practice. In contrast, under the Laplace criterion a farmer selects a strategy based on the assumption that each possible circumstance (e.g., weather or market conditions) is just as likely as the next. This latter criterion is commonly referred to as the "average approach." Depending on whether a short-term or long-term view is taken, each may be regarded as a basis for an optimal decision. For a quasi-subsistence farmer in a developing country, the luxury of long-term planning may not be realistic. Total crop failure in any year could be disastrous in terms of economic survival. As Norman has documented, short-term planning with maximization of security, rather than profit, is the primary goal of a quasi-subsistence farmer.[71] On the contrary, for a manager of a capital intensive farm in the United States, the long-term profitability measure may be better associated with optimality.

The assumption that farmers are optimizers has been questioned by numerous scholars. Simon and Dean, for example, each contend that the idea of profit maximization is unrealistic largely because it is impossible for a farmer to acquire complete knowledge.[72] Furthermore, it is doubtful that farmers examine all possibilities; on the contrary, they apparently select the first satisfactory outcome they encounter. Simon further introduced the idea that maximum utility could be acquired from many aspects of life (e.g., leisure time). As a result, Simon suggested that people will strive to obtain "subjective rationality" rather than "objective rationality."[73] It was this underlying premise that led Simon to develop the "satisficer" model, an alternative to optimizing models, such as those based on game theory.

In the satisficer model, farmers evaluate the various alternatives in their "subjective environment" according to whether or not the expected outcomes are satisfactory. If the elements of the set of satisfactory outcomes can be ranked, then the least satisfactory outcome of that set may be referred to as the level of aspiration adopted by the decision-maker for that problem. The theory suggests that aspiration levels tend to adjust to the attainable, to past achievement levels, and to levels achieved by other individuals.[74] The satisficer concept inherently recognizes the limitations placed on decision-

---

cultural and Home Economics Experiement Station Research Bulletin no. 485 (1960), pp. 906-908.

[71] D.W. Norman, "Economic and Non-Economic Variables in Village Surveys," *Rural Africana* 8 (1969): 18-24.

[72] H.A. Simon *Models of Man: Social and Rational* (New York: Wiley and Sons, 1957); G.W. Dean, "Firm Theory Incorporating Growth and Risk: Integration into Farm Management Research," *International Journal of Agrarian Affairs*, Supplement 1974-1975 (1975): 110-120.

[73] Ibid.

[74] J. Wolpert, "The Decision Process in Spatial Context," *Annals of the Association of American Geographers* 54 (1964): 545.

makers, whose perceptions will be constrained by age, education, urban influence, attitudes, and beliefs, as well as the realities of the socioeconomic world in which they exist.

In a satisficer model, decision-makers select farming practices, which are in turn reflected in land-use patterns, that yield satisfactory rather than optimal outcomes. Hart points out, however, that the inability of such an approach to identify specific factors that influence a farmer's final decision is a major drawback.[75] In other words, given that farmers will be aware of more than one satisfactory option, on what specific criteria are their final decision based? Simon implies that they merely select the first satisfactory strategy that comes along, in which case agricultural land-use patterns are largely a product of chance. Alternatively, a farmer, in order to determine which is the "most satisfactory," may compare all outcomes. But this transforms the model into nothing more than a modified version of game theory. It is evident therefore, that neither game theory nor satisficer concepts, alone, provide an adequate explanation of agricultural decision-making. Game theory provides no indication of why one criterion for resolving the payoff matrix is selected over another.[76] Satisficer models, on the other hand, do not explain how, out of a number of satisfactory strategies, one is selected.

Alternative Behavioral Approaches

A shortcoming of the behavioral models so far discussed is their failure to take into account the entire range of behavioral factors that may be present when a land-use decision is made. The indicator technique offers an alternative approach toward the conceptualization of this extensive array of characteristics. In geography, this technique has mainly been employed to facilitate judgments concerning levels of social welfare.[77] As Knox has stated, social indicators "are generally designed to facilitate concise and comprehensive judgments about levels of social welfare."[78] Wolpert's contention that behavioral characteristics may suggest similar judgments that affect agricultural decision-making behavior has provided much impetus for

---

[75] Hart, "Problems and Potentialities of the BehavioUral Approach," p. 100.

[76] P. Gould, "Man against His Environment: A Game Theoretic Framework," *Annals of the Association of American Geographers* 53 (1963): 290-297.

[77] E.g.: E. Carlisle, "The Conceptual Structure of Social Indicators," in *Social Indicators and Social Policy*, ed. A. Shonfield and S. Shaw (London: Heinemann, 1972): D.M. Smith, *The Geography of Social Well-Being in the United States* (New York: McGraw-Hill, 1973); P.L. Knox, *Social Well-Being: A Spatial Perspective* (London: Oxford Clarendon Press, 1975).

[78] Knox, *Social Well-Being*, p. 8.

study.[79] A partial list of these sociopersonal characteristics includes age, culture group, level of education, achievement motive, and socioeconomic status.[80] There is little doubt that the relationship between behavioral characteristics and agricultural decision-making is very complex. Correspondingly, if models are to be constructed upon a behavioral framework, they must be flexible enough to fit a wide array of socioeconomic and cultural environments.

Two additional weaknesses have plagued decision-making behavioral models: their static nature, and the lack of a common methodological approach. In regard to their static nature, Edwards has noted that a relationship exists between decisions made at one point in time, and decisions—and also their outcomes—made in a preceding time.[81] Furthermore, he and his associate, Tversky, have shown that an individual is capable of making different decisions at different times, even though identical conditions exist.[82]

The lack of a common methodological approach has been addressed by several authors. Both Henshall and Hart have suggested that principal component and factor analyses could be used as a standard approach for certain types of behavioral studies. For example, such an inquiry might lend itself to situations where the main objective is to identify groups of significantly associated variables (e.g., those related to the attitudes, decisions, and sociopersonal characteristics of farmers).[83] Comparisons between such

---

[79] Wolpert, "The Decision Process," p. 553.

[80] Some of the more noteworthy studies concerning the influence of sociopersonal characteristics on decision-making in agriculture are: D.C. McClelland, "The Achievement Motive in Economic Growth," in *Development and Society: The Dynamics of Economic Change*, ed. D.E. Novack and R. Lekachman (New York: St. Martin's Press, 1964); M. Moerman, *Agricultural Change and Peasant Choice in a Thai Village* (Berkeley: University of California Press, 1968); K. Nair, *The Lonely Furrow: Farming in the United States, Japan, and India* (Ann Arbor: University of Michigan Press, 1969); F.F. Caucian, *Change and Uncertainty in a Peasant Economy* (Stanford: Stanford University Press, 1972); S.L. Shah, G.S. Bhatnagas, S.C. Agrawal, and D.K. Singh, *Agricultural Production Potential and Cultivators Decision-Making as Influenced by Environmental Factors in North India* (Nainital: Pant University of Agriculture and Technology, 1973); B. Falusi, "Multivariate Probit Analysis of Selected Factors Influencing Fertilizer Adoption among Farmers in West Nigeria," *Nigerian Journal of Economic and Social Studies* 16 (1974): 3-16; M.H. Choi, "An Analysis of Factors Associated with the Adoption of Rice Farm Practices and Yields," *Journal of Korean Agricultural Education* 6 (1974): 1-30.

[81] W. Edwards, "The Theory of Decision-Making," in *Decision-Making*, ed. W. Edwards and A. Tversky (Hammondsworth: Penguin, 1967).

[82] Edwards and Tversky, eds., *Decision-Making*, pp. 76-75.

[83] J.D. Henshall, "The Demographic Factor in the Structure of Agriculture in Barbados," *Transactions of the Institute of British Geographers* 338 (1966): 183-195; P.W.E. Hart, "Geographical Aspects of Contract Farming, with Special Reference to the Supply of Crops to Processing Plants," *Tijdschrift voor Economische en Sociale Geographie* 69 (1978): 205-215.

studies are difficult, however, unless the input variables, situations, and decisions being compared are extremely similar.

In contrast, Ilbery has offered the technique of point-score analysis as a standard methodology for behavioral studies in agricultural location.[84] This methodology entails recording farmers' opinions concerning whether or not a selected list of decision-making factors has influenced their choice of farming practices. They are also asked to rank the influential factors according to some given graduated scale. The overall importance of each factor is determined by totaling up its point scores for all farmers interviewed. Based on these totals, factors can be ranked by order of importance, and three indices can be calculated to determine: (1) percentage of applicability, (2) total percentage, and (3) percentage of importance.[85]

Heretofore, studies utilizing point-score analysis have been confined to developed economies. Results of these studies indicate that a widespread objective among farmers is to obtain a secure and stable form of income. It appears that even in developed economies farmers strive to achieve a goal that is below the level of profit maximization. This safety-first strategy is based on a combination of sociopersonal, economic, and environmental considerations.[86] Ilbery adds a cautionary note in regard to utilizing techniques that rely merely on perceptual data: "Human decision-making is a very complex process and it must be realized that land-users may be unaware of the bases of their decisions, being unknowingly influenced by factors they never recognized."[87]

Summary

This chapter has highlighted the problems and potentialities of the two approaches that have dominated agricultural location theory. Although research aligned with an economic approach has highlighted the role of transport costs, comparative advantage, and market demand, it has failed to produce a model that accurately portrays contemporary agricultural landscapes in developing economies. This inability to replicate existing landscapes is due largely to the constraints within which such models operate. Among these, the most inappropriate assumptions are that a peasant farmer

---

[84] B.W. Ilbery, "Point Score Analysis: A Methodological Framework for Analyzing the Decision-Making Process in Agriculture," *Tijdschrift voor Economische en Sociale Geografie* 68 (1977): 66-71.

[85] %A = the number of cases where the factor was regarded as influential, expressed as a percentage of the total number of cases investigated; %T = the total score, expressed as a percentage of the maximum possible score; %I is expressed as a percentage of the maximum possible score for all those cases where the factor was applicable.

[86] Ilbery, "Point Score Analysis," p. 460.

[87] Ibid., p. 461.

operates in a sphere of perfect information and makes land-use decisions based solely upon the principle of profit maximization. In contrast, proponents of the behavioral approach have clearly illustrated that sociopersonal characteristics influence the decision-making process of quasi-subsistence farmers and also that risk aversion, rather than profit maximization, is the norm. They too, however, have failed to provide a successful operational alternative. As Harvey has stated: "Unfortunately many of the (behavioral) models discussed above are either just a system of conceptual notions, or they are specified to be operational in a nonspatial context.... [B]ehavioral models show how decision-making on the part of individuals and groups can be studied scientifically, but models that specify these processes as operating over space are rare."[88]

In conclusion, therefore, I contend that what is needed is an integrated model of agricultural location, one that not only rests upon a sound foundation of economic principles, but also recognizes that agricultural land-use patterns are ultimately formed by farm practices employed by thousands of individual farmers, who may or may not be motivated primarily by economic forces. In this regard, only Hart has employed such a comprehensive approach. Incorporated in his model are conditional probability statements based on aspects of both economic and behavioral approaches. These conditional probabilities are constructed by incorporating both farm and farmer characteristics as decision-making indicators (e.g., farm size, tenure status, and membership in a cooperative group).[89]

Through such an approach, one can model the likelihood that a farmer will adopt or reject a specified farming practice. Although this methodology is useful in that it provides a more comprehensive approach to the study of the diffusion of innovations, it does not necessarily lay the groundwork for a more appropriate and functional agricultural location model. Furthermore, it would be extremely difficult to use this methodology to construct a theoretical pattern of agricultural land use within a less developed country. First, the type of data required for Hart's model could be obtained only from an exhaustive field survey, the logistics of which would be significantly greater than those he faced in the United Kingdom. Second, given the nature of the data, the model would be virtually site-specific. There is, in my opinion, an alternative integrated approach that offers greater potential for providing a comprehensive agricultural land-use model; it is one that utilizes maximum-likelihood principles. It is with the intro-

---

[88] Harvey, "Theoretical Concepts," p. 374.
[89] Hart, "Problems and Potentialities of the Behavioural Approach," pp. 102-107.

duction and empirical testing of this type of model that the remainder of this monograph is concerned.

Chapter 3

MAXIMUM-LIKELIHOOD MODELING AND PEASANT AGRICULTURAL LAND USE

Maximum-likelihood modeling (often referred to as entropy maximization modeling) can provide an integrated approach to agricultural location theory. Such models inherently include situational characteristics and movement costs as expressed in a von Thünen-like model, and site characteristics, risk aversion, and minimum marketplace competition as outlined in behavioral-type models. It is my contention, therefore, that a maximum-likelihood approach to modeling peasant agricultural land-use patterns offers a viable alternative to the traditional, linearly constrained, cost-minimization models.

The Basic Model

The concepts and formulations of that family of models known as maximum-likelihood spatial interaction models were first introduced into studies of a geographic nature by Wilson.[1] Until now, this approach has been confined to modeling urban journeys to work and commodity flows over a highly developed transport net.[2] However, it is becoming apparent that this approach has a particular relevance to the modeling of the movement of agricultural goods in a developing economy, and by extension to the underlying agricultural land-use patterns.[3]

---

[1] A.G. Wilson, *Entropy in Urban and Regional Modelling* (London: Prior, 1970); idem, *Urban and Geographical Models in Geography and Planning* (London: John Wiley and Sons, 1974).

[2] A.G. Wilson et al., "Calibration and Testing of the SELNEC Transport Model," *Regional Studies* 3 (1969): 337-350.

[3] J.H. Astroth, Jr., and J.T. Meyer, "A New Approach to Modeling the Interregional Trade Flows of Foodgrains in a Developing Economy: The Case of Wheat and Pulse Flows between Trade Blocks in India, 1975," paper presented at the 78th annual meeting of the Association of American Geographers, San Antonio, Tex., 28 April 1982; Idem, "Maximum

Recent geographical research has firmly established the relationships between maximum-likelihood models and spatial interaction on a geographic scale.[4] As the name implies, through a maximum-likelihood approach, one models the most likely state of a system, under the constraint of minimum information about the behavior of an individual in the system (i.e., under the constraint of maximum entropy or uncertainty). Since the attributes of uncertainty and of the equiprobability of microstates are utilized in an maximum-likelihood model to estimate spatial interaction, it is profitable to examine the concept of the most probable state in detail.

In a given system of interaction, the number of ways (W) in which n elements (e.g., molecules, human beings, or units of grain) may be arranged at any one time is given by:

$$W\{T_{ij}\} = \frac{\sum_i \sum_j T_{ij}!}{\prod_{ij} T_{ij}!} ; \qquad (1)$$

where $T\{_{ij}\}$ indexes flows between subregions i and j.

Equation (8) assumes that each and every microstate that is the result of $\{T_{ij}\}$ is equally probable. Accordingly, no distinction is made between individuals. Intuitively, this concept is defensible on the basis that, in the absence of any specific information concerning the feasibility of any particular microstate(s), an unbiased position must be adopted; therefore each arrangement of individuals comprising one microstate is equally likely to occur. This interchangeability of microstates is essential to the minimum information approach.

When the concept of maximum entropy is applied, the maximum number of microstates associated with the macrostate $\{T_{ij}\}$ may be calculated. According to Cesario, the distribution that has maximum entropy produces "minimally prejudiced estimates of probabilities consistent with a given amount of information."[5] Maximum entropy is determined by maximizing:

Likelihood Models and Agricultural Landscapes in a Developing Economy: The Case of Kharar Tehsil, Punjab, India," Association of American Geographers, Annual Meeting, Washington, D.C., April 1984.

[4] Thomas and Huggett, *Modelling in Geography;*; Y. Medvekov, "Entropy : An Assessment of Potentialities in Geography," *Economic Geography* 46 (1970): 306-316; Baxter, "Entropy Maximizing Models"; J.C. Lowe, and S. Moryadas, *The Geography of Movement* (Boston: Houghton Mifflin Co., 1975).

[5] F.J. Cesario, "A Primer on Entropy Modelling," *Journal of the American Institute of Planners* 41 (1975): 46.

$$S = \text{Ln} \frac{\sum_i \sum_j T_{ij}!}{\prod_{ij} T_{ij}!} \quad (2)$$

or any other monotonic equivalent of equation. The above equation, however, is subject to a number of constraints. Wilson has demonstrated that if the constraints on the overall system are:

$$\sum_i T_{ij} = D_j, \quad (3)$$

$$\sum_j T_{ij} = O_i, \quad (4)$$

$$\sum_i \sum_j T_{ij} c_{ij} = C, \quad (5)$$

where D_j = quantity demanded at destination zone j,
O_i = quantity supplied by origin zone i,
c_{ij} = cost of movement between zones i and j, and
C = observed total cost of transport in the system,
it follows then that the distribution that maximizes entropy is:

$$T_{ij} = O_i A_i D_j B_j e^{-\beta c_{ij}} \quad (6)$$

where

$$A_i = (\sum_j D_j B_j e^{-\beta c_{ij}})^{-1} \text{ and} \quad (7)$$

$$B_j = (\sum_i A_i O_i e^{-\beta c_{ij}})^{-1}; \quad (8)$$

where ß is the parameter associated with the friction of distance. A_i and B_j are Lagrangian multipliers balancing the system; A_i ensures that the origin constraint (equation 4), is met, while B_j ensures that the destination constraint (equation 3), is satisfied.

Equations (3), (4), and (5), therefore, represent an attraction constraint, a production constraint, and a total cost of interaction constraint respectively. In other words, these three constraints require that all goods available for shipment are shipped; that each area's demand is met, and that the total transport cost of the most likely state is equal to the total cost available in the system. The total cost available to the system is defined as the difference between the market return for the entire production and the total production costs (including normal profit but excluding transport costs). These three basic constraints are interrelated and allowed to operate simultaneously. Therefore, the model operationalizes what is probably the key concept in general systems theory—that everything is related to everything else.

Equations (6), (7), and (8) define "the most probable state of the system, consistent with all the known information, but maximally uncommitted in relation to what is unknown."[6] Origin and destination values are known, as are the costs of movement. These quantities are ensured by the operation of the constraints and no other assumptions are necessary in order for the model to operate.

Despite the apparent complexity of the formulations above, it is not difficult to obtain an intuitive understanding of what is happening. The model simply says that the most likely state of the system, expressed as probabilities or frequency distributions, is described by that flow matrix for which the combinatorial possibilities are the largest. Also, by seeking to maximize $W(T_{ij})$ and trying to find that flow matrix that has the greatest number of microstates associated with it, the model is also explicitly recognizing individual behavior. However, this is accomplished without recourse to studying individuals as such, or by means of a behavioral approach. Irrational behavior (from some given norm) by a farmer can be explained or predicted in this model by systems concepts rather than by recourse to a micro level of observation.

Maximum Likelihood and Mathematical Programming Models

Several authors have shown that the cost-minimizing solution of the transportation problem in linear programming is an extreme solution, on a continuum of possible solutions derived from maximum-likelihood techniques.[7] The transportation problem is usually expressed by the system of equations:

$$\text{Minimize} \quad C = \sum_i \sum_j t_{ij} c_{ij}, \qquad (9)$$

$$\text{subject to} \quad \sum_j t_{ij} = O_i, \qquad (10)$$

---

[6] Ibid., p. 48.
[7] Ibid., p. 50.

$$\sum_i t_{ij} = D_j \quad \text{and} \tag{11}$$

$$t_{ij} \geq 0 \tag{12}$$

Wilson and Senior have demonstrated this system of equations to be equivalent to the solutions of equation (6) subject to (7) and (8), when ß=>∞. Beta is the distance-deterrence function associated with movement costs. They further demonstrate that the dual of the transportation problem:

$$\text{Maximize} \quad C' = \sum_i \alpha_i O_i + \sum_j u_j D_j \;, \tag{13}$$

$$\text{subject to} \quad c_{ij} - \alpha_i - u_j \geq 0 \;,$$

also approaches the solution of the equivalent entropy-maximization problem as ß=>∞.[8] The significance of this realization is that the Lagrangian multipliers in equations (7) and (8) can be rewritten as:

$$A_i = e^{-\lambda^{(1)}} \div O_i \quad \text{and} \tag{14}$$

$$B_j = e^{-\lambda^{(2)}} \div D_j \;; \tag{15}$$

and evaluated as:

$$-\lambda_i^{(1)} \div \beta \quad \text{and} \tag{16}$$

$$-\lambda_j^{(2)} \div \beta \;, \tag{17}$$

respectively.[9]

The multipliers, therefore, may be interpreted as location rents or as measures of comparative advantage in the same way that the dual variables

---

[8] S.P. Evans, " A Relationship between the Gravity Model for Trip Distribution and the Transportation Problem of Linear Programming," *Transportation Research* 7 (1973): 39-61; A.G. Wilson and M.L. Senior, "Some Relationships between Entropy Maximizing Models, Linear Programming Models, and Their Duals," *Journal of Regional Science* 14 (1974): 207-215.

[9] Wilson and Senior, "Some Relationships," p. 213.

are normally interpreted as shadow prices or location rents. From such discussions, it follows that "any model which can be formulated as either a programming model or an entropy maximization model can be related to this scheme and alternative programming models, respectively, may then be of interest."[10]

Wilson and Senior provide some suggestions as to the potential of such comparisons. As they have shown, a corresponding linear program is a useful aid in the interpretation of the terms for the maximum-likelihood model under construction. In contrast, it is the maximum-likelihood equivalent of a particular linear program that is of special interest to the main objective of this monograph—the introduction of a new methodology for the study of agricultural location in a developing economic landscape. An entropy-maximizing version of a linear program is suggested where "real-world behavior is not optimal because of imperfect markets, imperfect availability of information, and so on."[11] As the following comment from Geertz illustrates, this is precisely the case within a developing economy. "Information is poor, scarce, maldistributed, inefficiently communicated, and intensely valued. Neither the rich concreteness nor reliable knowledge that the ritualized character of nonmarket economies makes possible, nor the elaborate mechanisms for information generation and transfer upon which industrial ones depend, are found in the [peasant market]."[12]

Maximum Likelihood and Agricultural Land Use

In formulating macroscale von Thünen models via linear programming, Jones has noted that the resultant cropping pattern is a function only of transport costs and supply and demand constraints.[13] Given that these are the major factors, a direct relationship exists between Jones's von Thünen model and a maximum-likelihood approach to agricultural location. The relationship centers around the major role the distance-deterrence parameter, ß, plays in a maximum-likelihood model. In fact, a point exists (when ß approaches infinity) where a von Thünen land-use pattern may be replicated by a specific maximum-likelihood formulation. As information is reduced (when ß moves further away from infinity), the maximum-likelihood solution moves away from this extreme. A major challenge in constructing an agricultural land-use model based on maximum-likelihood principles was finding a way to incorporate crop types and their differential transportation

---

[10] Ibid., p. 214.
[11] Ibid., p. 214.
[12] C. Geertz. "The Bazaar Economy: Information and Search in Peasant Marketing," *American Economic Review* 68 (1978): 29.
[13] Jones, "Testing Macro-Thünen Models," pp. 360-61.

costs into a general equation that would allow the condition of maximum entropy to be maintained.

This challenge was met by recognizing the analogy between modal split and route selection, in Wilson's urban and regional models, and crop selection in an agricultural land-use framework.[14]

Modal Split and Crop Types

When the maximum-likelihood approach is used to model the distribution of person-trips, as for example in urban journey-to-work models, the model may be modified to include a direct specification of trips by various available transportation modes.[15] The total number of person-trips will be divided up among the available modes of transportation (e.g., cars, buses, and trains). In general, the modeling of the mix of transportation types is known as the problem of the "modal split." In a model involving such a modal split, the performance of each transport mode is seen to involve its own specific movement costs, as well as its own specific impedance parameter ß. Such costs and parameters are, in general, different for different transportation types.

Wilson has shown that the proportion of trips by each transportation type, i.e., the modal split, may be found in a straightforward manner, assuming that movement costs and the impedance parameters are known in some exogenous fashion.[16] The number of trips between zones i and j by transport mode k is given by:

$$T_{ij} = O_i \, A_i^k \, D_j \, B_j \exp(-\beta^k c_{ij}^k) \qquad (18)$$

Clearly one such equation is required for each of the k distinctive transportation types. The modal split is the proportion of all trips between i and j that take place by mode k. That is, the modal split is given by:

$$M_{ij}^k = T_{ij}^k \div T_{ij} \Sigma k = \exp(-\beta^k c_{ij}^k) \div \Sigma k \exp(-\beta^k c_{ij}^k) \text{ for all k.} \qquad (19)$$

In the agricultural location model presented in this monograph there is a direct analogy between crop type and modal split. Each crop type has its own cost of distance and spatial-deterrence parameter β. In the simplest modeling instances, such as the examples below, the actual movement-cost matrix may be constant between crop types, representing, for example, a distance metric, which represents an existing road network. In such a case the

---

[14] Wilson, *Entropy in Urban and Regional Modelling;* idem, *Urban and Geographical Models.*
[15] Ibid.
[16] Ibid.

cost-of-movement matrix for mode k would be equal to the cost of movement for any other mode. That is,

$$C_{ij}^k = C_{ij}^k, \text{ for all i and j.} \qquad (20)$$

In that case, only the deterrence parameter, ß, varies between crop types.

It should be noted that a maximum-likelihood formulation is not being applied here in the more direct application as an agricultural goods distribution model, with known production amounts being distributed to zones having a known demand.[17] Instead, the demand for the various crops at the market, and the impedance functions associated with each crop type, are allowed to interact so as to produce an agricultural landscape that will meet demand in the most likely fashion. Therefore, the market demand and the spatial-deterrence functions determine where, on a von Thünen-like homogeneous plain, and in what proportions, the various crops need to be grown in order to produce the most likely landscape.

Some Illustrative Concepts

The following illustrative examples will clarify how a maximum-likelihood approach might be employed to model the areal distribution of agriculture in a developing economic landscape. The number of both crop types and markets are the same as in the previous von Thünen example; this will facilitate a direct comparison of the resultant landscapes.

The problem approached in the application of maximum-likelihood techniques to the modeling of agricultural land use in developing economies may be stated succinctly: given the initial conditions of the classical von Thünen model, subject to two qualifications, what is the most likely pattern of agricultural production around a single market (or in a field of such markets) having a specified demand for a mix of crop types? The qualifications to the traditional von Thünen model are: (1) the substitution of a class of spatial-deterrence functions (e.g., negative exponential functions of distance) for the von Thünen assumption of constant transport costs per unit distance; and (2) the replacement of the von Thünen assumption that the crop chosen for production will be confined to that one providing the farmer with the highest return—the so-called behavioral assumption—with a risk-averting strategy of mixed cropping at all locations from the market. Hence, the problem may then be generally restated as the following:

• given the assumption that transport costs are a monotonic increasing, but nonlinear, function of distance;

---

17 Astroth and Meyer, "A New Approach to Modelling Interregional Trade Flows."

- given that these nonlinear transport costs vary between crops; and
- given that farmers will mix crops to reduce their risk, what agricultural land-use pattern is most likely to be found around a market in a developing agricultural landscape?

Multiple Crops–Single Market Case

In order to operationalize the model presented here, a version of R.S. Baxter's widely available FORTRAN routines for the solution of problems associated with trip distribution have been employed. In this example, a three crops–single market scenario has been constructed. These crops, vegetables, wheat, and cotton, are demanded at the market in the ratio of 2:7:1 respectively. Field evidence has indicated that these proportions are representative of actual production ratios in northern India.[18]

The spatial-deterrence functions utilized within this example are of a negative exponential nature, and are shown in figure 6. Note that these are not themselves cost curves, but rather interaction curves over distance. Clearly the closer parameter ß is to zero, the flatter is the interaction function over distance. In this case the simple example, ß = -.05 has been assigned to the movement of cotton, a relatively durable product over distance; ß = -.25 is associated with the movement of wheat over distance; and ß = -.50 is delegated to vegetables, the least hardy of these three commodities.

In this simple scenario it is assumed that a homogeneity of production capacity exists for each crop throughout the agricultural field, that is, there are no site advantages accruing to locations in the plain. Unlike the von Thünen model, however, movement to the market is not linear; rather it is a monotonic increasing, nonlinear function of distance. If the demand for these three crops at the market is some nonnegative amount in the proportion 2:7:1, the land-use intensity surfaces for each of the crops would resemble those shown in figure 7. The demand for each of the three crops is met at the market, but the agricultural intensity in the landscape is controlled by each crop's proportional demand interacting with that crop's spatial-deterrence function.

Clearly the most radical departure of the maximum-likelihood procedure from the von Thünen formulation is the relaxation of the so-called behavioral assumption—i.e., that farmers will produce only that crop that will provide them with the greatest return at any specific location. However, it is interesting to note that, even with the relaxation of this assumption, as in the case of mixed cropping, the linear nature of the von Thünen cost func-

---

[18] Astroth, "Influence of a Growth Center on Indian Rural Life," pp. 77-108.

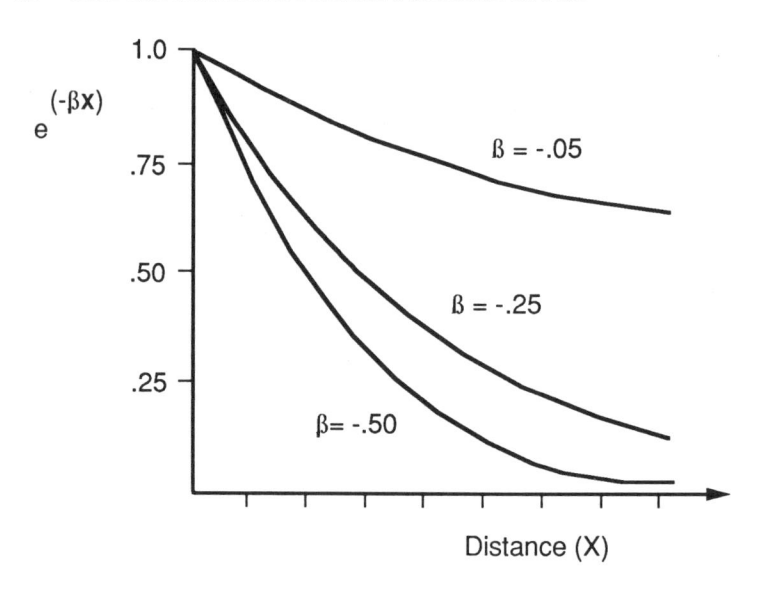

Fig. 6. Negative Exponential Spatial-Deterrence Functions.

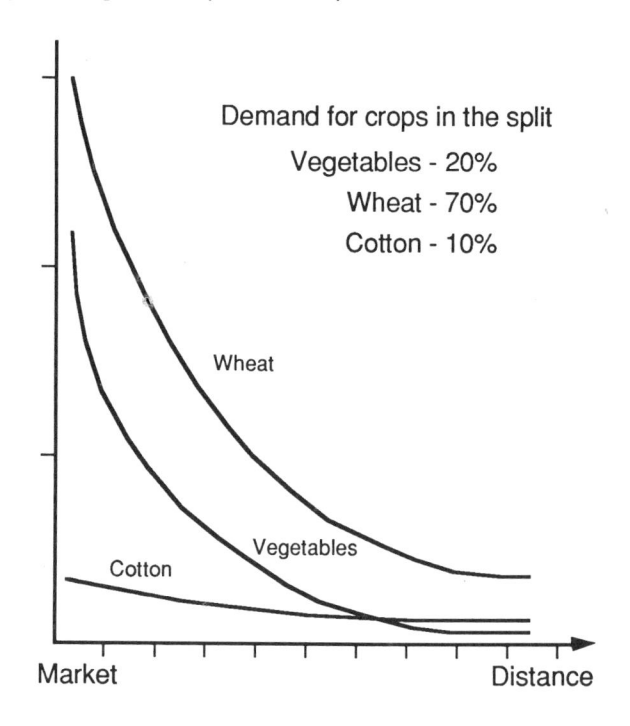

Fig. 7. Land-Use Intensity and Modal Split.

tions produces a landscape having portions characterized by the absence of one or more of the mix of crops at various distances from the market (figure 8). This figure represents the proportion of land devoted to each of the three crops in a scenario in which the behavioral assumption is relaxed, but the linear cost functions are retained. Notice that at some short distance from the market the proportion of land devoted to vegetables drops to zero, and likewise, at a further distance, land is no longer devoted to wheat.

In contrast, figure 9 illustrates the proportion of land devoted to each crop (given the same 2:7:1 mix) at various distances from the isolated market, under the maximum-likelihood assumptions. Unlike the von Thünen mixed-crop case shown in figure 8, a proportion of the land at all locations is devoted to each of the crops in the mix. However, as one would expect, the proportion of land devoted to less perishable crops of wheat and cotton increases with distance from the market. It is evident from the empirical findings previously discussed that figure 9 more adequately represents the cropping landscape in a developing agrarian economy. Furthermore, it would seem from figure 8 that the relaxation of the behavioral assumption is insufficient for the adequate modeling of such a landscape. Therefore, an approach incorporating nonlinear transport costs and their effect on production levels better fits the reality of an agrarian peasant landscape.

Multiple Crops–Multiple Markets Case

The second brief example models a landscape containing two markets. In this scenario a mix of three crops—vegetables, wheat, and cotton—is again demanded in the proportion of 2:7:1, and the demand at market B is arbitrarily made to be two-thirds that of the demand at market A. Utilizing the same spatial-deterrence functions as for the previous example, and again assuming the homogeneity of production throughout the landscape, we can determine the production required at all locations in order to meet the demand for these crops at the two markets. Figure 10 represents a transect between markets A and B and shows the proportion of land devoted to each of these crops at various distances from the two markets. Notice that because the overall demand at each of the two markets is not equal, the proportional production in the landscape is not symmetrical across the transect, although it is very nearly so for cotton, the crop with the flattest spatial-deterrence function. Figure 11 shows the land-use intensity for each of the crops along the transect between the two markets. As expected, steep peaks of production intensity for the perishable crop having the steepest spatial-deterrence function appear near each of the markets.

It is important, but perhaps unnecessary, to note that under the minimum-information assumptions of the maximum-entropy formulation used here, some of each of the three crops is produced for each market at all

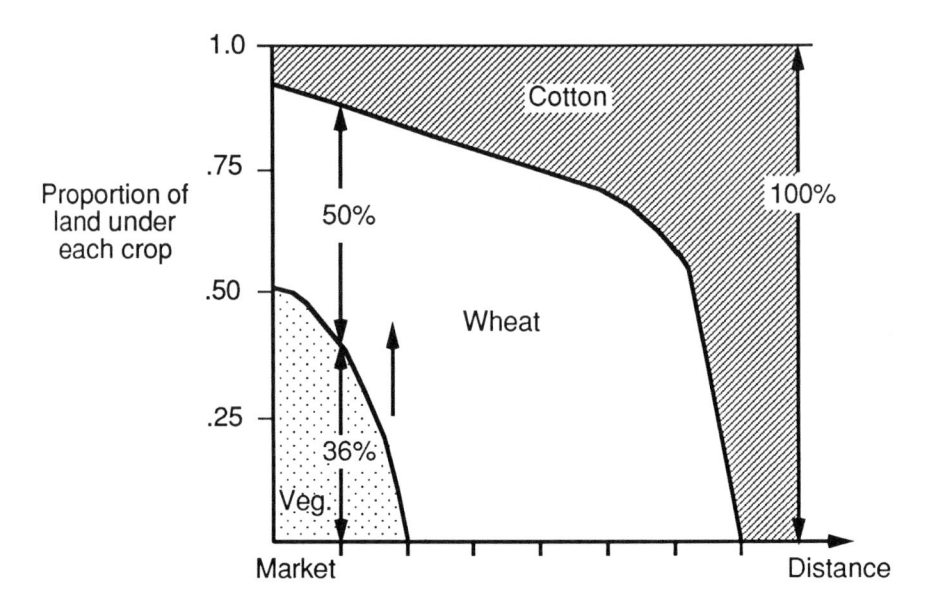

Fig. 8. Land-Use Patterns: Von Thünen and Mixed Cropping.

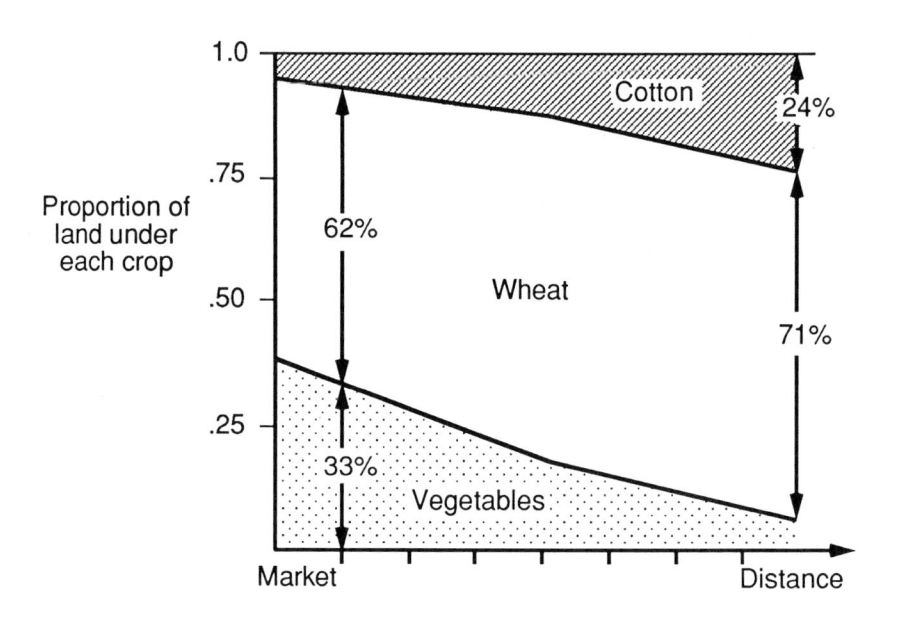

Fig. 9. Land-Use Patterns: Minimum Information and Mixed Cropping.

locations in the agricultural landscape. Thus the production profile of location i in the landscape is determined by three factors: (1) the profile of demand at all the markets; (2) the distance of location i from all markets; and (3) the nature of the spatial-deterrence functions for each of the crops. To require that a producer ship to the nearest (or any other specified) market is, of course, to depart from the minimum-information formulation of the problem. The reader need only recall the relationship between entropy models and mathematical programming formulations to realize that as information is added to the system—as for example, by requiring that shipments go to the nearest markets—the model becomes increasingly similar to a classical transportation problem in linear programming.[19]

Summary

Throughout this chapter, the argument has been made that agricultural land-use patterns in less developed countries are the byproduct of a system lacking in information and dominated by uncertainty. Peasant farmers know little about market conditions and forces and have little knowledge concerning the production behavior of their competitors, aside from their immediate village peers. Uncertainty embodies the peasant farming operation. Costs of necessary agricultural inputs such as seed, fertilizer, pesticides, electricity, and fuel increase substantially without either notice or indication. Market prices fluctuate unpredictably, making one season a profitable venture, rendering another a total loss.

In most semiarid agricultural regions of less developed countries adequate irrigation is the exception rather than the rule. Given the scarcity of irrigation facilities and the unpredictable arrival intensity and duration of rainfall, the assurance of a profitable harvest is always uncertain. Under such conditions, peasant farmers as a rule practice mixed cropping and other risk-averting strategies in order to avoid sharp fluctuations in total yields, and therefore income.

On the basis of the discussion throughout this chapter, it should be evident that entropy formulations and maximizing models represent two different approaches to modeling peasant agricultural land use. Owing to their constraints, maximum-information models, such as linear programs, have only a limited number of acceptable solutions. Likewise, at the other extreme, random production patterns that meet the demand of the markets represent at best a minimal number of feasible production patterns. The trade-off is between information and the total likelihood of occurrence of a particular production pattern. When our information concerning the behavior and constraints of a system is valid, the trade-off is acceptable. Yet

---

[19] See chapter 4.

48 UNDERSTANDING PEASANT AGRICULTURE

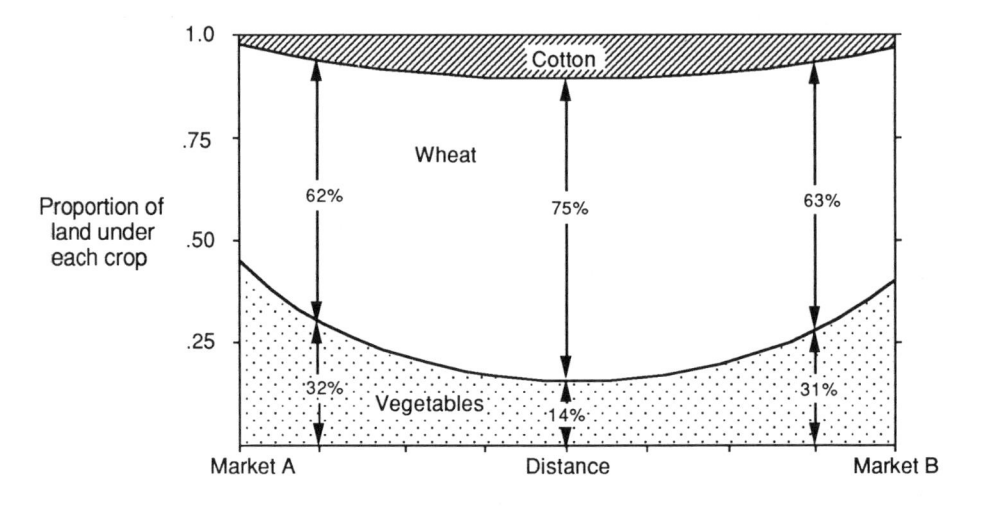

Fig. 10. Land-Use Patterns: Mixed Cropping and Two Markets.

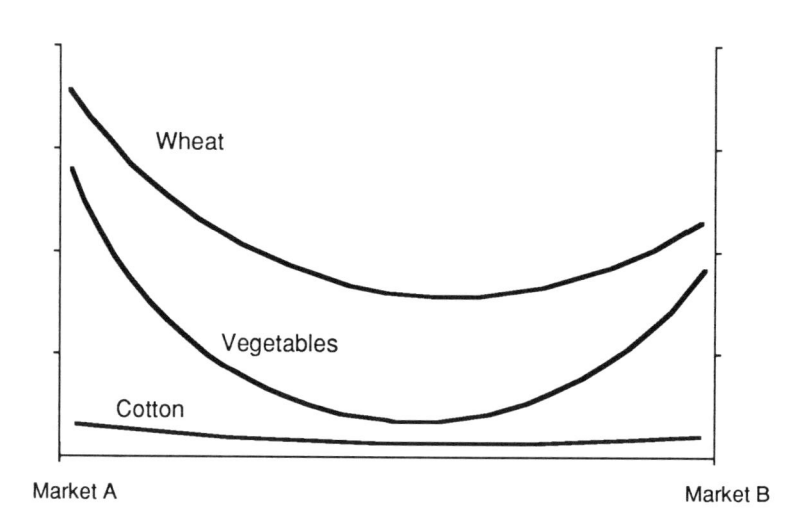

Fig. 11. Land-Use Intensities around Two Markets.

valid information is precisely what is missing in peasant agricultural systems. The extent to which peasant producers are ignorant of, and have no control over, those factors that affect their output and the general success of their operations, is the extent to which they cannot perform as economic maximizers. Logically it seems more useful to model a low-information system by utilizing entropy-like formulations than by applying a more highly constrained approach—such as linear programming techniques.

In order to evaluate the validity of this assertion, a test-case application of a maximum-likelihood agricultural land-use model was carried out in Punjab, India. It is with the formulation and results of this test case that the next two chapters are concerned.

Chapter 4

THE STUDY AREA AND
RESEARCH METHODOLOGY

Location and Character of the Study Area

The study area is located within the state of Punjab, in northwest India (figure 12). More specifically, it is confined to the market areas [*umlands*] of two government regulated agricultural markets (*mandi*), Kharar and Kurali.[1] Over 80% of their combined market area lies within the boundaries of Kharar tehsil, in Rupnagar district.[2] The remainder of the study region falls within the tehsil boundaries of Rupnagar, Rajpura, and Fatehgarh Sahib (figure 13). The study area is bounded by the rugged Shivalik Hills to the northeast (figure 14), a rapidly expanding city and Union Territory (U.T.) of Chandigarh to the east, and a crescent of small market towns to the west (figure 15).[3]

As discussed in the introductory chapter, the study area has attained a level of agricultural development more similar to India as a whole rather than to the extremely productive Punjab-Haryana region within which it is

---

[1] A *mandi* is a government regulated and supervised wholesale agricultural marketplace. The effort to regulate agricultural markets dates back to the Patiala Agricultural Produce Markets Act of 2004 BK. This law, which governs the purchase and sale of farm produce, has been subsequently consolidated and amended by both the Punjab Agricultural Produce Markets Act of 1939 and the current Punjab Agricultural Produce Markets Act of 1961.

[2] In terms of the Indian administrative hierarchy, a district is comparable to a county in the United States. A tehsil is a subdivision of a district for administrative and land revenue purposes. In general, a district is subdivided, depending upon its size, into three to five such subdivisions.

[3] The provisional total for the 1981 population of the city of Chandigarh stands at 450,061 (D.N. Dhir, *Census of India, 1981: Provisional Population Totals, Paper-1 of 1981, Supplement, Series-17, Punjab* [Chandigarh: Government Press, 1981]).

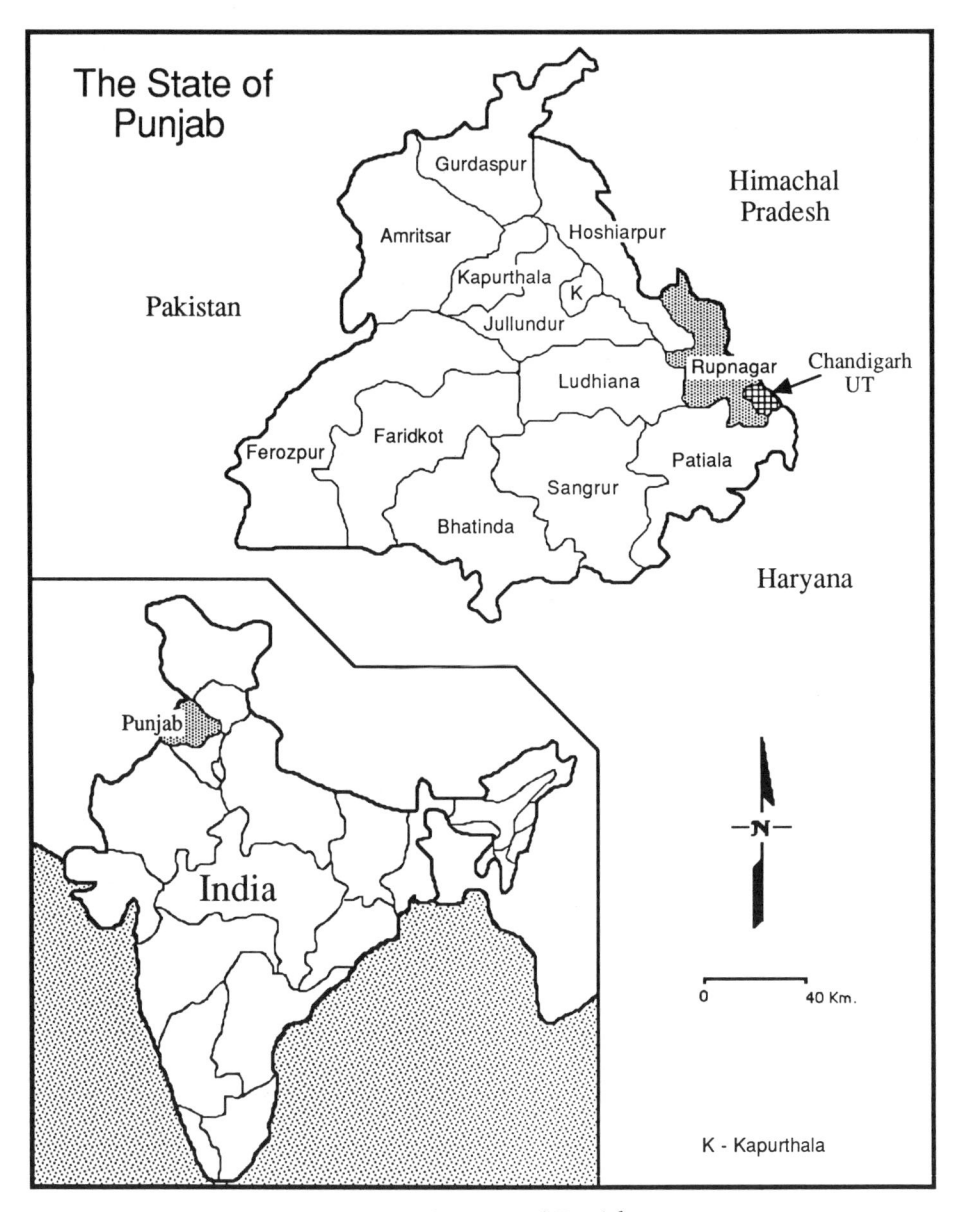

Fig. 12. *The State of Punjab.*

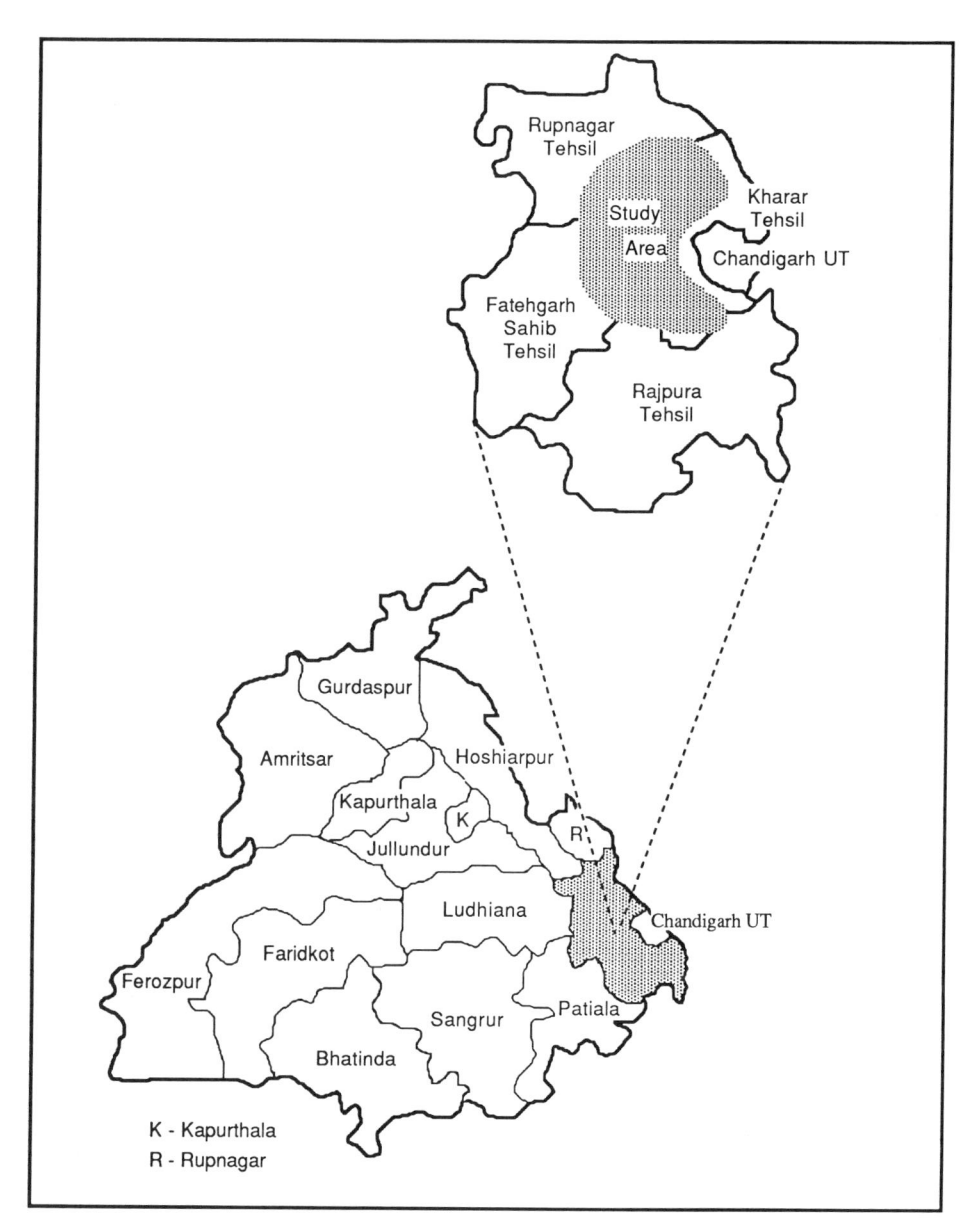

Fig. 13. Location of the Study Area within Rupnagar District.

Fig. 14. Shivalik Hills.

found. According to various agricultural development indices, such as the proportion of irrigated land, intensity of cropping, degree of farm mechanization, and level of fertilizer consumption, Kharar consistently occupies one of the lowest rankings in Punjab. However, in spite of its inferior state wide ranking, Kharar either exceeds or approaches the national mean in each category (tables 1-4).[4]

Table 1. Percentage of Net Area Irrigated to Net Area Sown, 1978-79

Kharar Tehsil	35%
Punjab State	78%
India	27%

SOURCES: *Statistical Abstract of Punjab,* 1982; and *District Statistical Abstract of Rupnagar,* 1978-79.

---

[4] These indices are commonly accepted as reliable indicators of regional levels of agricultural development. See for example: Bina Agarwal, "Tractors, Tubewells and Cropping Intensity in the Indian Punjab," *Journal of Development Studies,* (January 1982): 115-126.

THE STUDY AREA AND RESEARCH METHODOLOGY 55

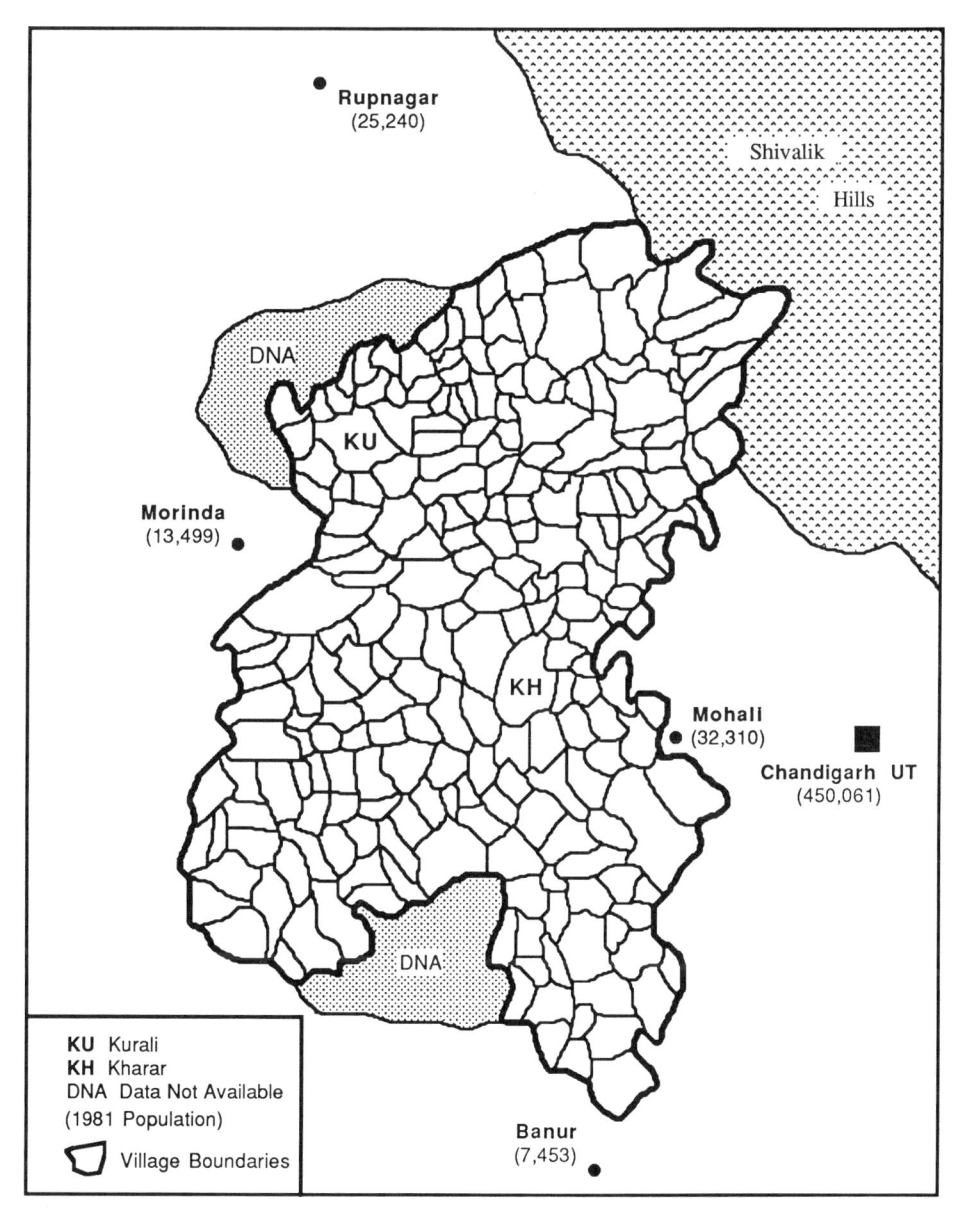

Fig. 15. Market Towns and Villages of the Study Area and Surrounding Region.

Table 2. Percentage of Net Area Sown More Than Once, 1978-79

Kharar Tehsil	39.58%
Punjab State	58.73%
India	22.55%

SOURCES: *Statistical Abstract of Punjab*, 1982; and *District Statistical Abstract of Rupnagar*, 1978-79.

Table 3. Tractors, 1977

	Net Area Sown (Ha)	# of Tractors	Hectares/Tractor
Kharar Tehsil	48,000	640	75
Punjab State	4,171,000	64,307	65

SOURCES: *Statistical Abstract of Punjab*, 1982, and *District Statistical Abstract of Rupnagar*, 1978-79.

Table 4. Chemical Fertilizer Consumption in Punjab, 1981-82

Punjab District	Net Area Sown (000 ha)	Total (NPK) Consumption (000 nutrient tonnes)	Tonnes/ha
Amritsar	418	84	0.20
Bhatinda	503	56	0.11
Faridkot	526	117	0.22
Ferozpur	495	95	0.19
Gurdaspur	260	60	0.23
Hoshiarpur	252	27	0.11
Jullundur	299	62	0.21
Kapurthala	148	37	0.25
Ludhiana	327	89	0.27
Patiala	393	85	0.22
Rupnagar	129	18	0.14
Sangrur	460	82	0.18

SOURCES: *Statistical Abstract of Punjab*, 1982; and *District Statistical Abstract of Rupnagar*, 1978-79.

There are two major reasons why agriculture in Kharar tehsil has not developed as rapidly as in other regions of Punjab. The foremost inhibiting factor is the unfavorable natural environment. The most limiting of these environmental constraints is the region's rainfall pattern. Like most of northern India, the study area is plagued by an unequal distribution of rainfall throughout the year. Approximately 80% of the total annual rainfall is confined to the four summer months of June through September. This feast-or-famine situation in regard to yearly rainfall is depicted by figure 16; as illustrated, only three months enjoy the benefit of a water surplus. During these months the positive water balance is the byproduct of heavy monsoonal rainfall, the onset, intensity, and duration of which are all highly unpredictable. This unreliability of rainfall during the summer months makes cultivating the two chief economic *kharif* crops, maize and rice, a risky proposition.[5] As figure 17 demonstrates, despite tube-well irrigation, rice yields are noticeably dependent upon adequate monsoonal rainfall. Just as yields of the important *kharif* crops are related to the heavy summer rains, likewise, a successful *rabi* harvest depends to a large degree upon the occurrence and timing of the lighter winter rains. The association between the annual yields for wheat, the most prominent *rabi* crop, and winter rainfall is portrayed by figure 18. One must bear in mind, however, that what figures 17 and 18 do not show is the element of timing associated with rainfall. In this region, which is characterized by predominantly rain-fed agriculture, timing is just as important as amount of total precipitation.

A second major limiting environmental constraint is the scarcity of affordable groundwater supplies for single-family irrigation systems. In order to obtain sufficient and dependable groundwater supplies, some farmers are forced to drill to depths of 300' or more. The costs associated with such an endeavor are well beyond the means of most farmers in the region.

The scarcity of readily available groundwater is the result of both the adverse climate and the geological structure of the region. The problematic nature of the region's climate, in regard to availability of groundwater, is evident from the preceding discussion of rainfall. During the eight to nine month dry season, there is a significant increase in the depth of the region's water table. This drop in the water table can place the upper aquifer out of reach for many of the area's shallow tube wells. Also, peasant farmers who are fortunate enough to be able to operate their tube wells during these arid

---

[5] Throughout India agriculture is characterized by two annual harvest seasons, the *kharif*, or autumn harvest, and the *rabi*, or spring harvest. The *kharif* crops are the monsoon crops, sown after the onset of the heavy summer rains in June and July and are harvested throughout September and October. The *rabi* crops are sown after the autumn harvest and reaped during the months of March and April.

58 UNDERSTANDING PEASANT AGRICULTURE

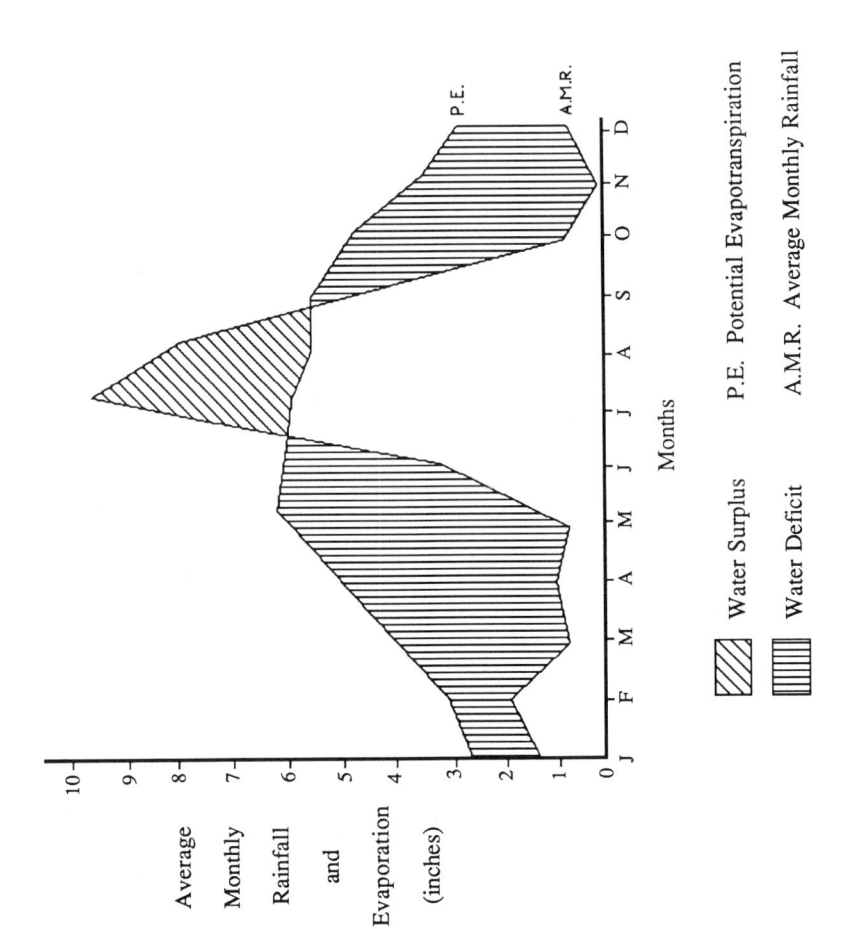

Fig. 16. Average Water Balance for Rupnagar District.
SOURCE: Meteorological Office, Civil Secretariate, Chandigarh, India, 1982.

months see their rate of extraction decrease significantly. In some cases, this decrease can double the time and cost necessary to irrigate a plot of land adequately.

With regard to geologic structure, the entire study area is situated in a region of unconsolidated alluvial deposits. In such alluvial formations, water-bearing strata are often found at more than one depth.[6] In the study area, there appear to be two water-bearing strata: one 25'-80' deep, and a second 150'-300' beneath the surface. As one moves toward the Shivalik Hills in the east, the depth of both aquifers increases quite noticeably. Given that the shallow aquifer is believed to be unconsolidated, the depth of the water table throughout the test site can fluctuate dramatically from one village to the next.[7] This irregularity in the depth of available water supplies can also be observed at the village level. A 30'-50' difference in the water table depth between two plots of land within the same village is not uncommon. The fluctuation in depth of the shallow aquifer can render private tube wells uneconomical in certain regions of the test site, and also in specific areas within a single village (figure 19).

The costs associated with single-family irrigation systems are substantial. For example, the cost of a 25´-80´ shallow tube well was approximately 10,000 rupees in 1983; 4,000 of which went toward the purchase of the engine alone.[8] Furthermore, the average daily operating cost of such a well is approximately 65 rupees per acre per day.[9] The cost of tube-well irrigation increases sharply when a farmer is forced to drill to depths of over 100'. The average cost of a 200´ tube well, for example, is approximately 50,000 rupees. Due to these almost insuperable costs, all but a few of the deep tube wells in the study region are owned and operated by the government. Farmers receiving water from these wells pay a flat monthly rate that is significantly less than the monthly operating expenses of a private well.

The end result of the prohibitive costs of single-family irrigation is that only 35% of the area sown in the study region is irrigated (table 1). As a

---

[6] International Land Development Consultants, *Agricultural Compendium for Rural Development in the Tropics and Subtropics* (New York: Elsevier Scientific Publishing Co., 1981), pp. 286-90.

[7] Even among the hydrologists at the Department of Agriculture, Punjab, there exists a degree of uncertainty about whether or not the deep aquifer is consolidated or unconsolidated.

[8] At the time of the study, one rupee was equal to approximately nine cents of a 1983 American dollar. It is fairly accurate, however, to think of a rupee as having the same purchasing power in the Indian economy as the dollar has in the American economy.

[9] This figure represents the cost of enough diesel fuel (20 liters) to operate the pump for six to eight hours. Given the soil and climatic conditions of the test area, this is long enough to irrigate one acre of land properly. The daily operating cost of a tube well with an electric pump would be somewhat less. The initial outlay for an electrical motor, however, would be greater.

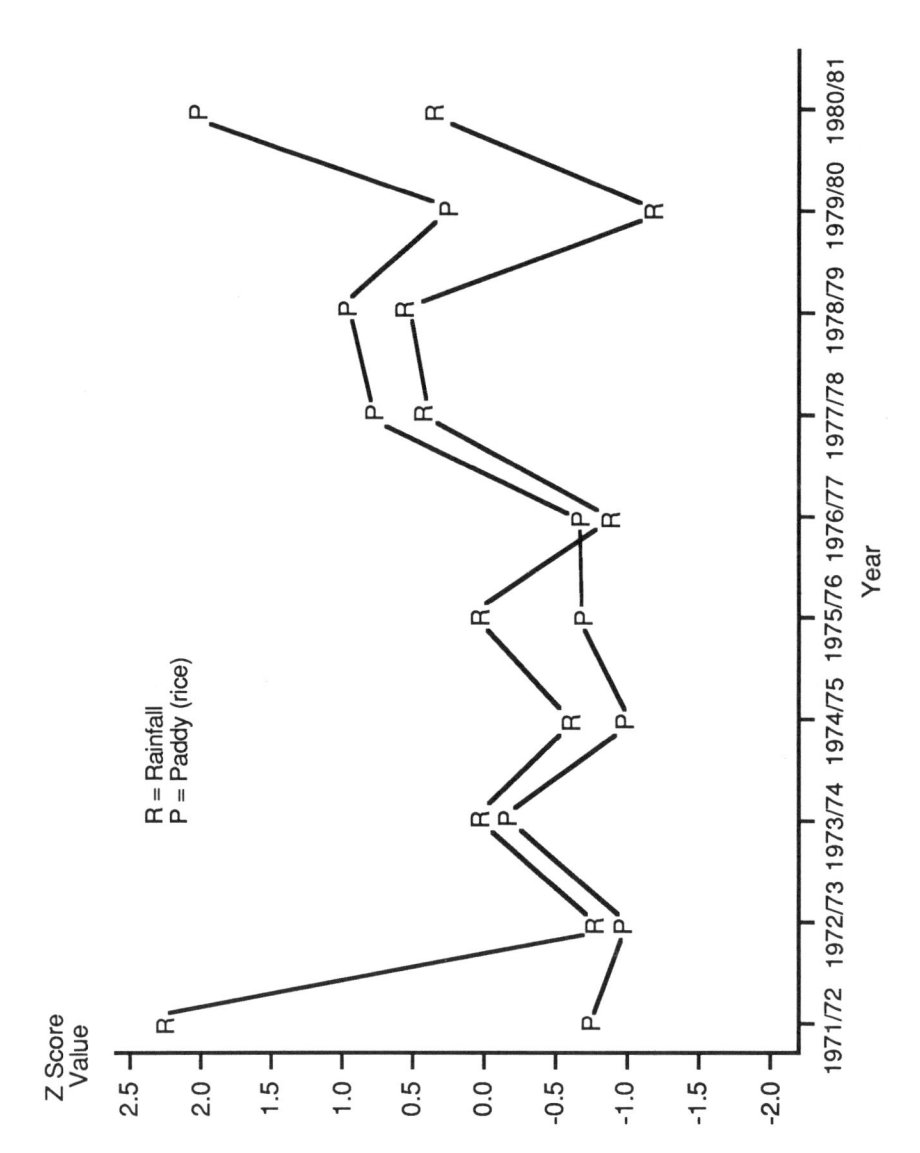

Fig. 17. *Relationship between Rainfall and Yield: Paddy.*
SOURCES: Director of Land Records, Punjab; Department of Agriculture, Punjab.

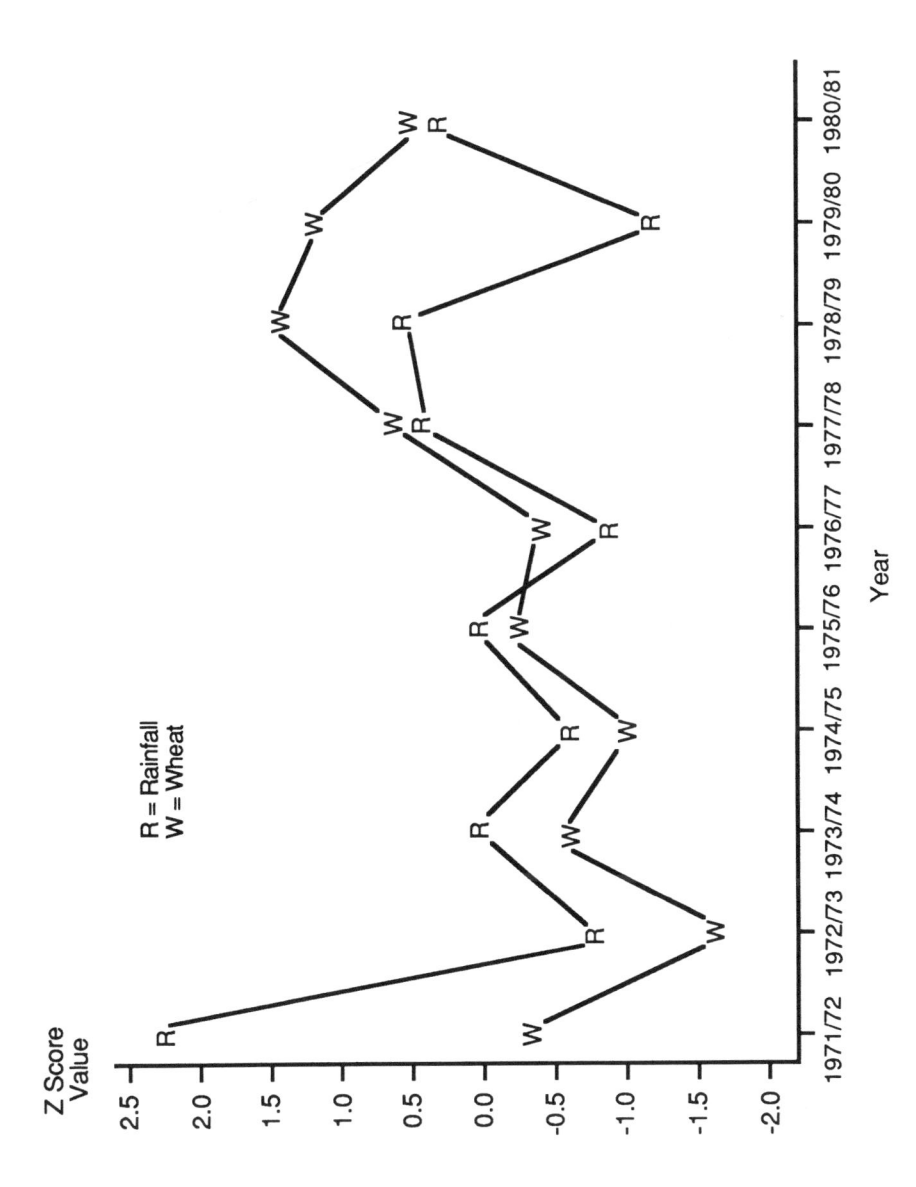

Fig. 18. *Relationship between Rainfall and Yield: Wheat.*
SOURCES: Director of Land Records, Punjab; Department of Agriculture, Punjab.

62   UNDERSTANDING PEASANT AGRICULTURE

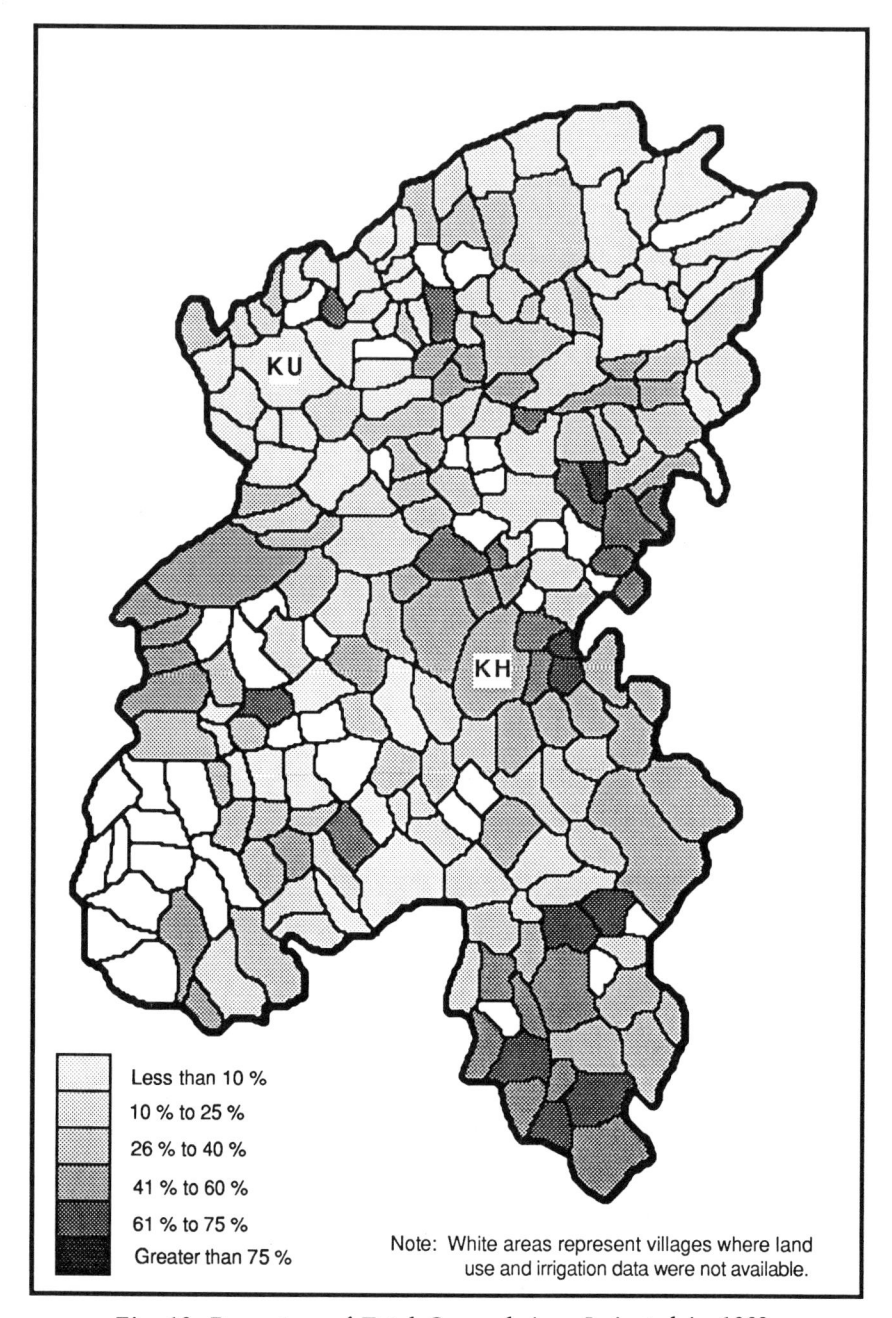

Legend:
- Less than 10 %
- 10 % to 25 %
- 26 % to 40 %
- 41 % to 60 %
- 61 % to 75 %
- Greater than 75 %

Note: White areas represent villages where land use and irrigation data were not available.

Fig. 19. Percentage of Total Cropped Area Irrigated in 1982.
SOURCE: Village Land Revenue records (*lal kitab*).

result, yields per hectare are more highly variable from year to year in the study region than in the other, more heavily irrigated, districts of Punjab (tables 5 and 6).

Table 5. Patterns of Rice Yields* and Rainfall,** 1971-72 through 1980-81

Punjab District	Arithmetic mean	Standard Deviation	Coefficient of variation (%)
Amritsar	2218.20	341.38	15.39
Bhatinda	2532.50	512.19	20.22
Faridkot	3126.22	343.65	10.99
Ferozpur	2594.30	253.95	9.79
Gurdaspur	1906.30	483.31	25.35
Hoshiarpur	2033.60	216.87	10.66
Jullundur	2725.00	388.89	14.27
Kapurthala	2688.70	257.67	9.58
Ludhiana	3229.50	591.80	18.32
Patiala	2553.50	472.82	18.52
Rupnagar	2009.20	580.72	28.90
Sangrur	2843.10	676.94	23.81
Punjab State	2476.10	351.90	14.21

* Kgs/ha
** Cms

SOURCES: Department of Agriculture, Punjab. *Agricultural Statistics of Punjab*, 1971-72 to 1980-81; and Economic Advisor to Government, Punjab, *Statistical Abstract of Punjab*, 1971-82.

For a significant portion of the study region, a third physical constraint is the seasonal arrival of flood waters and, therefore, large-scale erosion (figure 20). The topography of the area susceptible to annual inundation is characterized by the existence of numerous seasonal dry river beds (*choe*). These intermittent streams have their origins in the nearby Shivalik Hills. During periods of heavy monsoonal rainfall, they become raging rivers. At flood stage, they transport large loads of suspended sand and pebbles that are deposited over large areas adjacent to their course (figure 21). The area of deposition is extended by annual lateral swing shifts in the stream's path. Over time, these yearly changes in course destroy numerous acres of productive farmland.

Table 6. *Patterns of Wheat Yields* and Rainfall, 1971-72 through 1980-81*

Punjab District	Arithmetic mean	Standard deviation	C.V. (%)
Amritsar	2488.70	249.14	10.01
Bhatinda	2317.60	318.33	13.74
Faridkot	2549.89	178.49	7.00
Ferozpur	2496.20	294.18	11.78
Gurdaspur	2124.00	123.14	5.80
Hoshiarpur	1886.60	216.97	11.50
Jullundur	2484.50	157.25	6.33
Kapurthala	2226.30	314.01	14.10
Ludhiana	3149.90	224.31	7.12
Patiala	2436.90	354.12	14.53
Rupnagar	2068.40	320.78	15.51
Sangrur	2659.10	265.91	10.00
Punjab State	2483.40	205.29	8.27

*D.N.A. for 1971-72, X based on 9 years.
SOURCES: Department of Agriculture, Punjab, *Agricultural Statistics of Punjab*, 1971-72 to 1980-81; and Economic Advisor to Government, Punjab, *Statistical Abstract of Punjab*, 1971-82.

In an attempt to reclaim the land rendered unsuitable for cultivation, and also to prevent further loss of farmland, over the last decade the Indian government has undertaken several dam and channelization projects in the region (figure 22). In order to finance these costly but much needed projects, the government has received financial assistance from several international development and lending institutions. The most recent (and still ongoing) of these erosion control and reclamation projects is the Khandi Watershed and Area Development Project.[10] The extreme eastern portion of the study area is included in this scheme.

---

[10] The Khandi Watershed and Area Development Project is a World Bank funded scheme with two main objectives. The primary objective is to reverse the human-induced ecological degradation that has taken place in this region of the Shivalik Hills for generations. A secondary objective is to protect, reclaim, and develop the agricultural land below the hills, widely regarded as the most backward farming region in Punjab (Government of Punjab, *Khandi Watershed and Area Development Project: Patiala-ki-Rao Watershed Feasibility Report, Volume I* [Chandigarh: Government Press, 1981]). By 1983, numerous small-scale dam and irrigation projects, along with a livestock development scheme, were well underway throughout the region.

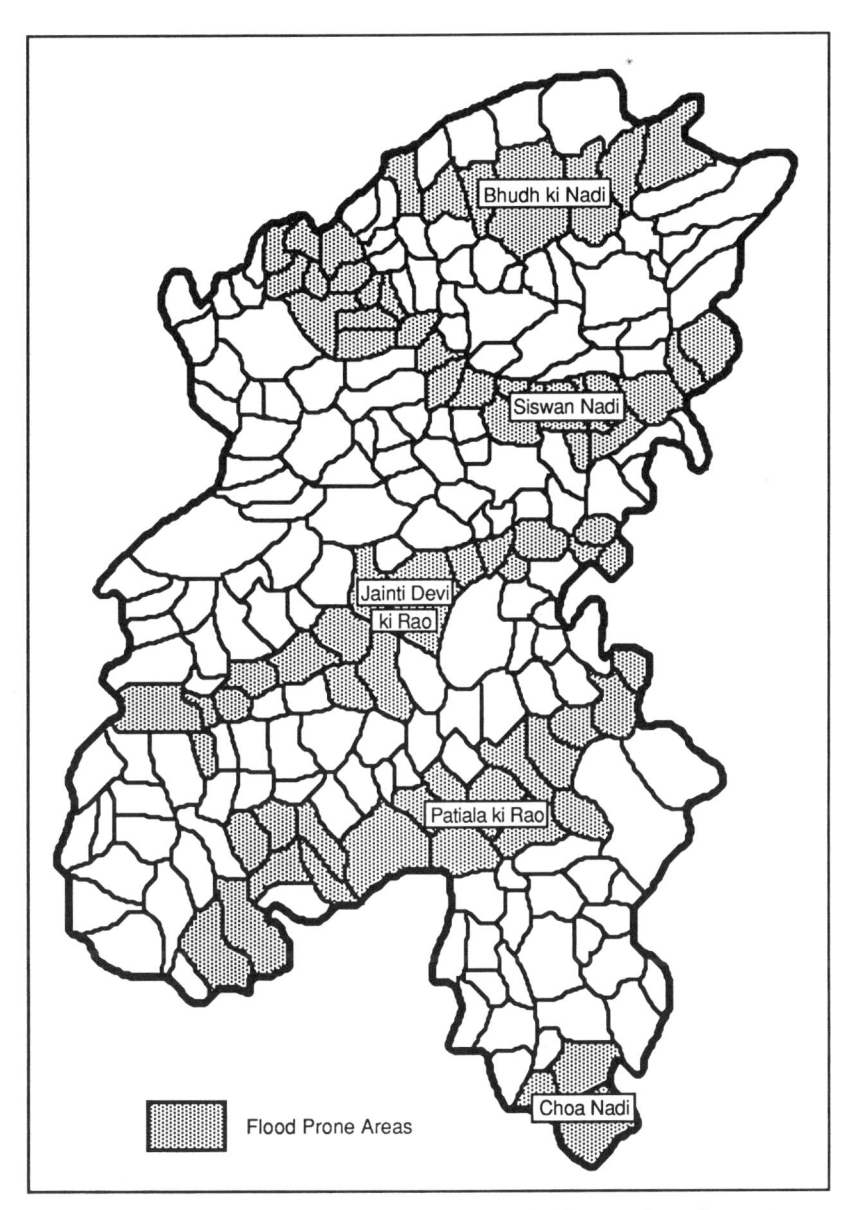

Fig. 20. Villages Susceptible to Seasonal Flooding and Soil Erosion.
SOURCES: Department of Town and Country Planning, Punjab, 1983; Field survey, 1983.

Fig. 21. Dry Channel of a Choe.

Fig. 22. Channelization Project for Erosion Control.

In addition to environmental constraints, a second principal factor contributing to the low level of agricultural productivity in Kharar tehsil, when compared to other areas of Punjab, is the predominance of small landholdings throughout the region. As table 7 illustrates, nearly 50% of the operational holdings within Rupnagar district are less than one hectare.[11] A closer examination of the distribution of size of landholdings reveals that approximately 30% of all parcels of land are less than one-half hectare (table 7). It is interesting to note that the agricultural department of Punjab did not include such landholdings in its 1980 agricultural census; they omitted the category from their 1980 survey because "no household can afford to be a viable operational holder with such a small amount of land."[12]

Table 7. Percentage Distribution of Operational Holdings, 1970-71

District	% < 0.5 ha	% < 1.0 ha
Amritsar	29.2	46.9
Bhatinda	11.5	23.6
Faridkot	15.8	29.3
Ferozpur	18.7	33.4
Gurdaspur	28.4	46.2
Hoshiarpur	38.3	55.5
Jullundur	25.1	40.9
Kapurthala	26.2	43.7
Ludhiana	15.2	27.9
Patiala	13.0	25.4
Rupnagar	32.4	48.4
Sangrur	10.9	22.5
Punjab State	22.4	37.6
India	32.2	50.6

SOURCES: Government of India, *All India Report on Agricultural Census 1970-71* (New Delhi: Government Press, 1975); Government of Punjab, *The Third Decennial World Agricultural Census, 1970-71*, Punjab State (Parts 1 and 2) (Government Press: Chandigarh, 1974).

---

[11] Kharar tehsil is located within the district of Rupnagar. Data concerning the distribution of size of landholdings is not available below the district level.

[12] Department of Agriculture, Punjab, "Preliminary Report on the Agricultural Census of Punjab, 1980-81," Chandigarh, 1983 (Typewritten.)

The positively skewed distribution of landholding sizes is not representative of the state of Punjab. On the contrary, the proportion of landholdings less than one-half hectare in Rupnagar is nearly 20% higher than in the majority of remaining districts. The study region, however, does accurately reflect the nationwide distribution (table 7).

The relationship between size of landholding and level of agricultural productivity in the region is threefold. First, farmers with less than one hectare of land were, and to a large extent remain, unable to take full advantage of the new technologies associated with the Green Revolution. The new technologies of the late sixties and early seventies include the high response varieties (HRVs) of crops, petrochemical fertilizers and pesticides, and electric and diesel tube-well irrigation systems. Small farmers in the study region are unable to obtain credit and lack sufficient cash funds for the purchase of these costly inputs. In Punjab, as in other regions of India, the Green Revolution was not neutral toward scale of farming operation.[13] As Chinnappa has stated, "The much discussed scale-neutrality of the new technology is therefore belied by the greater access which the larger cultivators have to the crucial factors of production involved—cash, pump sets and fertilizers."[14]

Second, a delicate balance exists between small landowners and the precarious natural environment of the region. Floods, droughts, or other natural calamities have an immediate and severe impact upon the economic survival of the small landowner. Large landowners are able to minimize the risk of natural disasters by cultivating a greater diversity of crops, in several distinct environmental zones that may exist within a single village. In contrast, the small landowner is usually confined to a specific farming location and a limited variety of crops. Furthermore, these sites are more often than not located within the most marginal lands of the village. Within the study region it is not uncommon to encounter a village land-use pattern where the landholdings of the smaller cultivators are confined to the areas that, owing to either physical or economic constraints, are unavailable for irrigation (*baaraanii zamiin*).[15] This trend is evident at the

---

[13] For further support of this argument see: B.H. Farmer, ed., *Green Revolution?: Technology and Change in the Rice-growing Areas of Tamil Nadu and Sri Lanka* (Boulder, Colo.: Westview Press, 1977).

[14] B. Nanjamma Chinnappa, "Adoption of the New Technology in North Arcot District," in *Green Revolution?: Technology and Change in the Rice-growing Areas of Tamil Nadu and Sri Lanka*, ed. B. Farmer (Boulder, Colo.: Westview Press, 1977), pp. 70-85.

[15] *Baaraanii zamiin* is a local Punjabi term used to describe a plot of land which the farmer perceives the forces of nature to have rendered unsuitable for irrigated agriculture. This usually means that either the land is adjacent to an intermittent stream, and therefore characterized by sandy soil, or the water table is at such a depth that shallow tube well irrigation is not possible.

tehsil level as well, where only a limited number of holdings below one-half hectare are irrigated (table 8). Therefore, given the unpredictability of the onset, intensity, and duration of the summer and winter rains, the small farmer operates under greater risk than the large landowner.

Table 8. Percentage of Irrigated Operational Holdings in Rupnagar District by Size of Holding, 1970-71

Hectares	Percentage
< 0.5	27.6
0.5-1	42.0
1-2	51.8
2-3	61.8
3-4	67.4
4-5	69.8
5-10	72.4
10-20	69.4
20-30	54.6
30-40	63.5
40-50	51.5
> 50	50.0

Note: Includes both wholly and partially irrigated land.
SOURCE: Government of Punjab, *The Third Decennial World Agricultural Census, 1970-71, Punjab State* (Parts 1 and 2) (Government Press: Chandigarh, 1974).

Third, small farmers are severely affected by fluctuations in the agro-economic climate. A lower-than-expected market price for their produce, or even a minimal increase in the cost of seeds, fertilizer, or other agricultural inputs can threaten the livelihood of small farmers. Those who go deeply into debt at the time of sowing face the real possibility of having to sell all or part of their land in order to repay loans at harvest time. In the last several years, for example, the government support price for wheat has come close to, or even fallen below, the production costs per quintal.[16] Although the

---

[16] In 1983, it cost the farmers in the study region between 160 to 175 rupees to produce a quintal of irrigated and chemically fertilized wheat. The government support price for wheat, however, was only 151 rupees per quintal. Three to four months after the initial harvest, a farmer could expect to receive over 200 rupees per quintal for wheat in the same marketplace. Only the large farmer, however, is able to wait several months for the market

price of wheat will rise substantially higher than the support price in later months, the small farmer is forced to sell immediately, for the lowest possible rate, because the lender typically demands prompt repayment at the time of harvest. This is not surprising; the moneylender and grain merchant are often one and the same person. Because of their lack of land for collateral, small farmers are forced to secure loans from grain merchants, rather than from government or private lending institutions. Within the study area there are a significant number of tenant-cultivators who were, not long ago, owner-cultivators.

In response to the high level of risk associated with the natural and economic environment within which the peasant farmers of the region operate, many small landowners have developed a "safety first" attitude toward agriculture.[17] Operating under such a strategy, the foremost goal of small farmers is to insure that all household requirements for agricultural produce are met. They produce to fulfill family needs first, and respond to the perceived market demand second. This means that the small farmer generally avoids cultivating risky but highly profitable crops such as fruits and vegetables. Throughout the region, risk-aversion techniques such as mixed cultivation and intercropping are evident.[18]

In summary, the unfavorable physical environment and the large number of small holdings have inhibited the agricultural productivity of the region. If one examines the districtwide yields for the six major crops of Punjab, the relatively backward nature of the study area becomes evident. For each of the six crops, the yield per hectare is significantly lower in Rupnagar than the statewide mean (table 9). It should be noted, however, that these yields are noticeably greater, with the minor exception of gram, than the national average.

The Market Town of Kurali

Although the exact date of the establishment of Kurali as an agricultural market town is difficult to discern, some speculate that it dates to the

---

rate to rise substantially above his total production cost. It is interesting that during the same year, the price of milled wheat flour (*atta*) in the marketplace was 270 rupees per quintal.

[17] The term "safety first" was first used in this context by James Scott in *The Moral Economy of the Peasant: Rebellion and Subsistence in Southeast Asia* (New Haven: Yale University Press, 1976).

[18] The term "mixed cultivation" refers to cropping systems that involve a farmer growing two or more crops simultaneously within the same locality. While the notion of mixed cultivation includes all types of intercropping (mixed, row, strip, and relay), it differs in that there is not necessarily crop competition during all or part of crop growth.

Table 9. Mean Yield of Important Crops, 1979-80 and 1980-81

	Region	Rice	Maize	Groundnut	Cotton**	Wheat	Gram
1979-80	Amritsar	2,202	1,698	*	146	2,773	822
'80-81		1,774	1,698	*	152	2,715	302
1979-80	Bhatinda	2,622	1,366	890	328	2,653	656
'80-81		3,542	1,018	1,245	339	2,753	660
1979-80	Faridkot	2,690	1,293	*	366	2,711	686
'80-81		3,107	1,269	1,245	324	2,829	539
1979-80	Ferozpur	2,640	831	*	376	2,843	702
'80-81		2,547	1,180	*	310	2,928	415
1979-80	Gurdaspur	2,116	1,104	*	156	2,248	758
'80-81		2,050	1,475	*	151	2,186	93
1979-80	Hoshiarpur	2,046	1,843	890	156	2,114	751
'80-81		2,416	1,541	1,245	151	2,041	720
1979-80	Jullundur	2,935	2,071	861	156	2,886	686
'80-81		2,951	1,737	1,106	151	2,456	582
1979-80	Kapurthala	2,595	1,815	1,165	156	2,798	686
'80-81		2,984	2,091	1,416	151	2,781	*
1979-80	Ludhiana	3,443	1,798	981	236	3,436	653
'80-81		3,790	1,871	1,113	292	3,163	673
1979-80	Patiala	2,669	1,643	648	219	2,939	626
'80-81		3,054	1,800	1,321	215	2,633	653
1979-80	Rupnagar	2,155	1,557	510	255	2,533	472
'80-81		3,297	1,290	992	151	2,190	314
1979-80	Sangrur	3,062	1,661	951	274	2,962	828
'80-81		3,665	1,388	1,473	281	3,067	722
1979-80	Punjab State	2,606	1,723	890	326	2,797	686
'80-81		2,736	1,601	1,245	808	2,730	582
1979-80	India	*	*	*	*	*	*
80-81		1,338	1,137	*	*	1,650	692

* Data not available
** Kg/ha (lint)
SOURCES: Economic Advisor to Government, Punjab, *Statistical Abstract of Punjab*, 1982; and Department of Agriculture, Punjab, *Report on Crop Estimation Surveys in Punjab*, 1979-80 and 1980-81.

Mogul period.[19] During this early period, it functioned as a relatively small agricultural market town, serving only a handful of villages. With the

---

[19] Personal conversations with various officials of the Punjab Agricultural Marketing Board and Professor A.B. Mukerji, Department of Geography, Punjab University.

building of a railway under British rule, however, the *mandi* of Kurali grew in importance. A second stimulus for growth was the loss of numerous large agricultural markets in western Punjab upon the independence and partition of India in 1947. Unlike other rapidly expanding grain markets of eastern Punjab, however, the main agricultural commodities bought and sold in Kurali were *gur* and *shukr*.[20] Because of this its prominent standing and growth as an important regional market center was diminished by the construction of a state cooperative sugar mill at Morinda in 1962 (figure 15). In accordance with state law, all sugarcane within a notified area, approximately a ten-to-fifteen-mile radius of Morinda, must be sold to the so-called farmer's cooperative mill. Because the mill has operated at a loss throughout most of its history, the state from time to time has also placed a ban on the production and sale of *gur* and *shukr* within any village of the notified area. In addition to the sugar mill, branches of the State Bank of India and the Punjab National Bank were opened in Morinda in the early 1960s.

Despite the infusion of these important facilities, and contrary to projections made by state planning agencies in the middle 1960s, Morinda has had a limited impact upon the agricultural land-use and marketing pattern of the region. Morinda has not absorbed a large amount of the general agricultural market area of Kurali. Due to inertia, the railway line, superior marketing facilities, and the existence of several large grain merchants and moneylenders, Kurali to this day continues to maintain a larger agricultural *mandi* than Morinda.[21]

The major crops of the *mandi* today are wheat, maize, and paddy. Secondary crops include groundnuts, other oilseeds, *gur* and *shukr*, several sorghums and millets, cotton, gram, and numerous types of fruits and vegetables. The market area of Kurali consists of approximately 100 villages villages. Its market area is restricted to the west-southwest by the *mandi* in Morinda and it is constrained to the north by the large market town of Rupnagar (figure 23).

The Market Town of Kharar

The rapidly growing town of Kharar is located fourteen kilometers west of the Union Territory of Chandigarh. In the period between the 1971

---

[20] *Gur* is a heavy brown sugar produced by boiling off the excess water from the juice extracted from stalks of sugarcane. When it is allowed to cool, it crystallizes into a crude grade of sugar. A more refined grade of cane sugar is *shukr*. Instead of permitting the boiled cane juice to cool and solidify, this lighter grade of sugar is separated by either a hand-operated or machine-driven centrifuge. The market price for *shukr* is significantly higher than that commanded by *gur*.

[21] Walter C. Neal, Harpal Singh, and Jai Pal Singh, "Kurali Market: A Report on the Economic Geography of Marketing in Northern Punjab," *Economic Development and Cultural Change* 13 (January 1965): 129-68.

and 1981 censuses of population, Kharar experienced the highest growth rate among all Punjab towns, more than doubling in size. As a result of this period of rapid growth, Kharar now contains nearly twice the population of the town of Kurali (table 10).

Table 10. *Population of Kharar and Kurali Market Towns, 1951-81*

	1951	1961	1971	1981
Kharar	6,317	8,216	10,686	23,154*
Kurali	N.A.	6,390	9,776	12,638*

*Provisional population totals
SOURCES: Economic and Statistical Organization, Government of Punjab, India, *Statistical Abstract of Punjab*, 1982 (Chandigarh: Government Press, 1983), pp. 56-62.

Like Kurali, Kharar was established sometime during the late Mogul period. Unlike Kurali, however, during its early stages of development Kharar contained a comparatively obscure agricultural market, and the lowly status of its market remained unchanged until the 1970s. Until that time, Kharar *mandi* was always considered the poorer sister of the market in Kurali. Several events over the last three decades have led to the reversal of these traditional roles. Today, the *mandi* of Kharar overshadows the declining market of Kurali.

One factor that stimulated growth of the agricultural market of Kharar was the construction of new market facilities under a state government sponsored *mandi* development scheme.[22] The newly built agricultural market is located on the western edge of town and contains all the modern facilities, including several large warehouses, for the Food Corporation of India, PUNSUP, and MARKFED. These three organizations are the major state and national procurement agencies for agricultural goods. Under this *mandi* development scheme, Kharar received a disproportionately large amount of funds when compared to Kurali. One might speculate that the reason for the inequality is due to Kharar's role as the administrative headquarters for the tehsil.

A second force behind the impressive growth of the agricultural market in Kharar was the Green Revolution. The introduction of high response varieties (HRVs) of wheat and paddy transformed a somewhat subsistence

---

[22] Government of Punjab, *Fourth Five Year Plan* (Chandigarh: Government Printing Press, 1970). For an in-depth discussion concerning government investment in the construction and upgrading of market facilities in Punjab, as part of the "growth centre theory" for rural development, see: Barbara Harriss, "The Role of Punjab Wheat Markets as Growth Centres," *Geographical Journal* 140 (1974): 52-71.

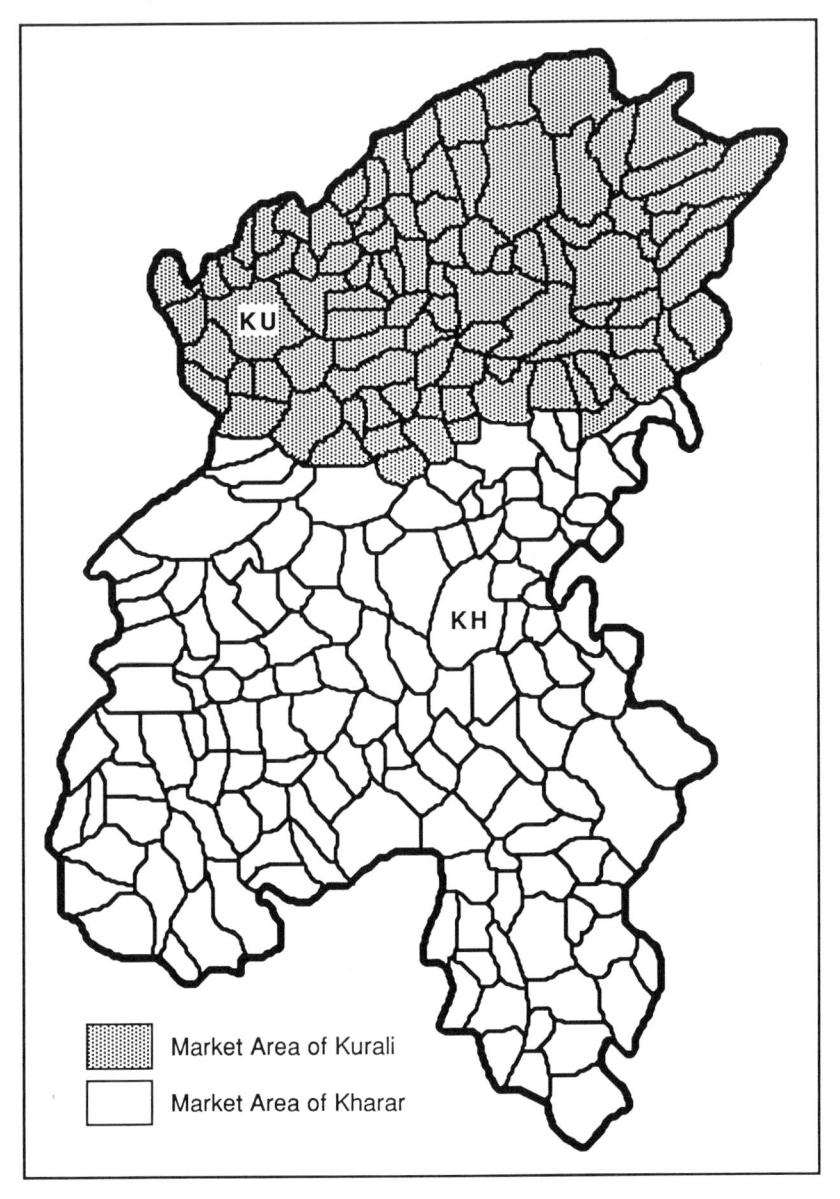

Fig. 23. Kurali and Kharar Market Areas (umlands), *1982.*
SOURCE: Field survey, 1982.

agricultural area into a surplus-producing region. Although the transformation was not as spectacular as in other tehsils across the state, at least the majority of farmers are now able consistently to produce a marketable surplus.

A third component involved in the recent growth of the agricultural market in Kharar is its location. Kharar is at the intersection of two major roadways leading into the city of Chandigarh. All of the major highway traffic originating from Rupnagar and beyond in the north, and the majority of movement in and out of the city from the rich farming district of Ludhiana and beyond in the west-northwest, funnels through Kharar (figure 24). Over the past ten to fifteen years, these two major arteries, along with numerous feeder roads, have been greatly improved. Not only have they been widened to facilitate bus and truck traffic, but several new bridges have been constructed over the two large intermittent rivers that border the town. Historically, these two rivers, impassable during the monsoonal rains, have isolated the town of Kharar. This isolation was a formidable obstacle to the development of agricultural trade in the region.

A fourth and somewhat obvious factor behind the recent growth in the agricultural market of Kharar is that the town's population has more than doubled in the last fourteen years. Kharar had the highest growth rate among Punjab towns over the last census period, 1971-81 (table 10). Accompanying this rapid population growth has been an increased local demand for agricultural goods.

The rapid expansion of the nearby town of SAS Nagar (Mohali) during the 1970s is a fifth causal factor behind the recent ascent of the agricultural market in Kharar. Owing to its locational advantage in reference to the large urban market of Chandigarh, the rapidly sprawling township of Mohali is quickly becoming the industrial center of Kharar tehsil (figure 14). With a population of over 32,000, Mohali has had a positive impact upon the local demand for agricultural goods, especially fresh milk, fruit, and vegetables.[23] Because there is neither a *mandi* in Mohali nor any plan to build one, the growth and survival of the market in Kharar is not threatened. The present market area of the Kharar *mandi* is noted in figure 23.

The continued growth of Kharar *mandi* has also been insured by the recent arrival of several large commissioned agents, or grain merchants (*arthiya*). The arrival of these large buyers has, in a very short period of time, actually increased the number of villages in the market area. One *arthiya* in particular can claim that the addition of more than twenty villages is due to his presence alone. The reasons why these large grain

---

[23] Government of Punjab, *Census 1981: District Census Handbook, Rupnagar District* (Chandigarh: Government Printing Press, 1983).

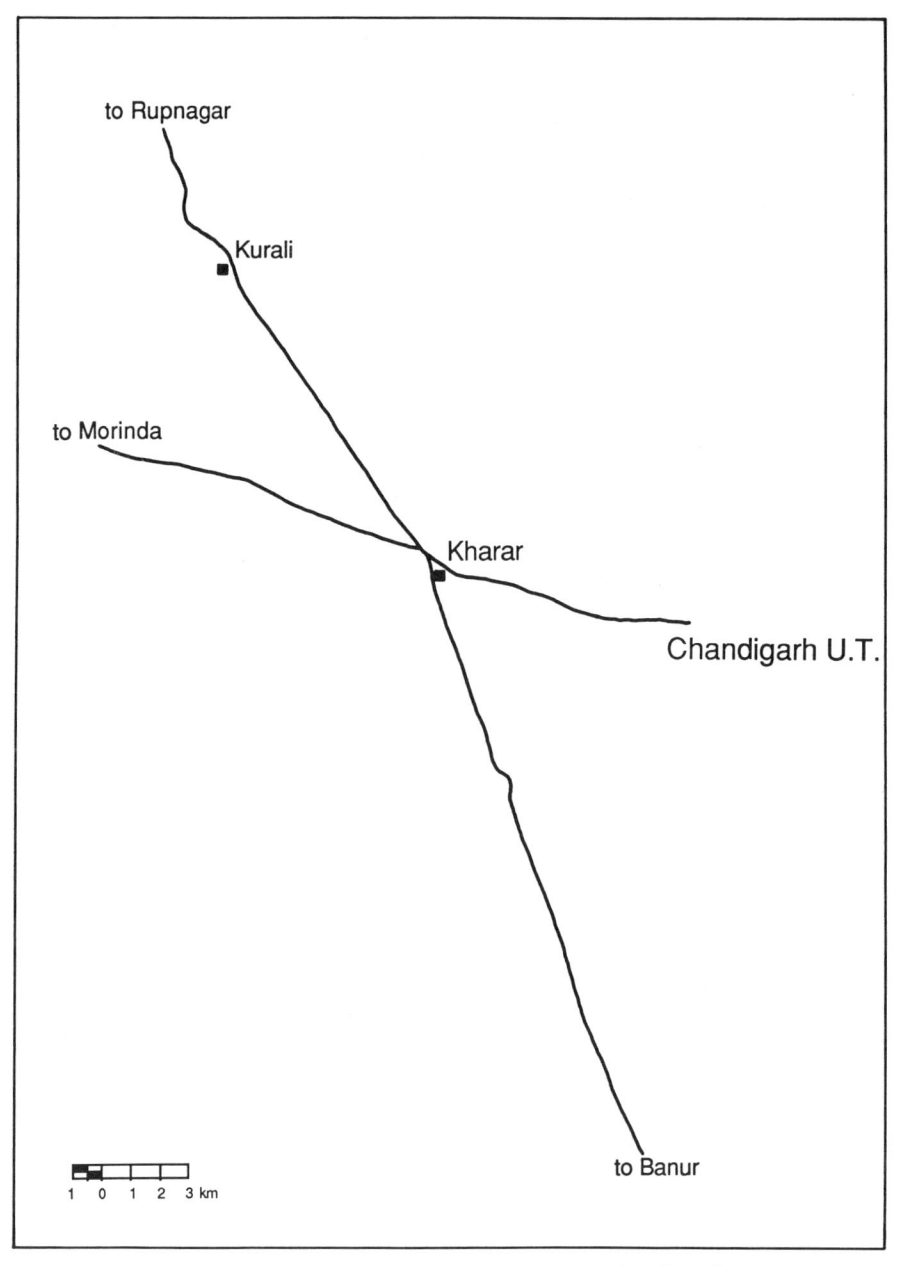

Fig. 24. Major Roadways to and from Chandigarh.
SOURCE: Department of Town and Country Planning, Punjab, 1982.

merchants are able to draw more farmers into the market are threefold. First, from the beginning of the harvest season large grain merchants are able to offer a slightly higher price than the established government procurement rate. Second, they pay cash in full the same day the sale is made. It is not unusual for farmers to be paid a week, ten days, or even a month later for their produce from a smaller *arthiya*. Third, they are able to issue a greater number of loans at the time of sowing. It should be noted that these large agricultural merchants, along with the majority, if not all, of the smaller *arthiya* as well, are involved in the sale of goods beyond the scope of local demand. Indeed, the larger merchants are involved in both statewide and interstate trade of agricultural commodities.

Influence of Chandigarh

The city of Chandigarh, a completely planned new town, was built on a sparsely populated tract of land at the foot of the Shivalik Hills during the late 1940s and early 1950s.[24] After a modest growth rate during the 1951-61 census period, Chandigarh quickly became one of India's most rapidly growing cities. In fact, it recorded the highest population growth rate among all Indian metropolitan areas during the 1961-71 census period.[25] Although its growth rate has slowed somewhat, owing to political and physical constraints, it remains one of India's most rapidly expanding urban centers.

Despite its rapid growth since the 1960s, Chandigarh has had a surprisingly limited influence on the surrounding agricultural land-use and marketing patterns of Kharar tehsil. As figure 25 illustrates, only a small number of immediately adjacent villages are selling the majority of their agricultural produce in Chandigarh. It is estimated that only one-tenth of the total marketable surplus of paddy from Kharar tehsil is sold in Chandigarh. Likewise, no more than one-quarter of the total wheat sales originating from Kharar villages are made to commissioned agricultural merchants in Chandigarh.[26]

The most notable impact that this rapidly growing urban center has had on the agricultural landscape of the study area is an increase in the amount of land devoted to fodder, fruits, and vegetables. The increase in fodder cultivation is the result of the large urban demand for fresh milk. The growth of commercial dairy activity in the region, however, has been

---

[24] Chandigarh was officially declared opened by the first president of India, Dr. Rajendra Prasad, on 7 October 1953. The city presently serves as a dual capital for the states of Punjab and Haryana.

[25] Government of India, *Census 1971: Primary Census Abstract, Chandigarh Union Territory* (Chandigarh: Government Printing Press, 1972).

[26] These estimates are based on discussions with various marketing officials and commissioned agricultural merchants in the Chandigarh *mandi*.

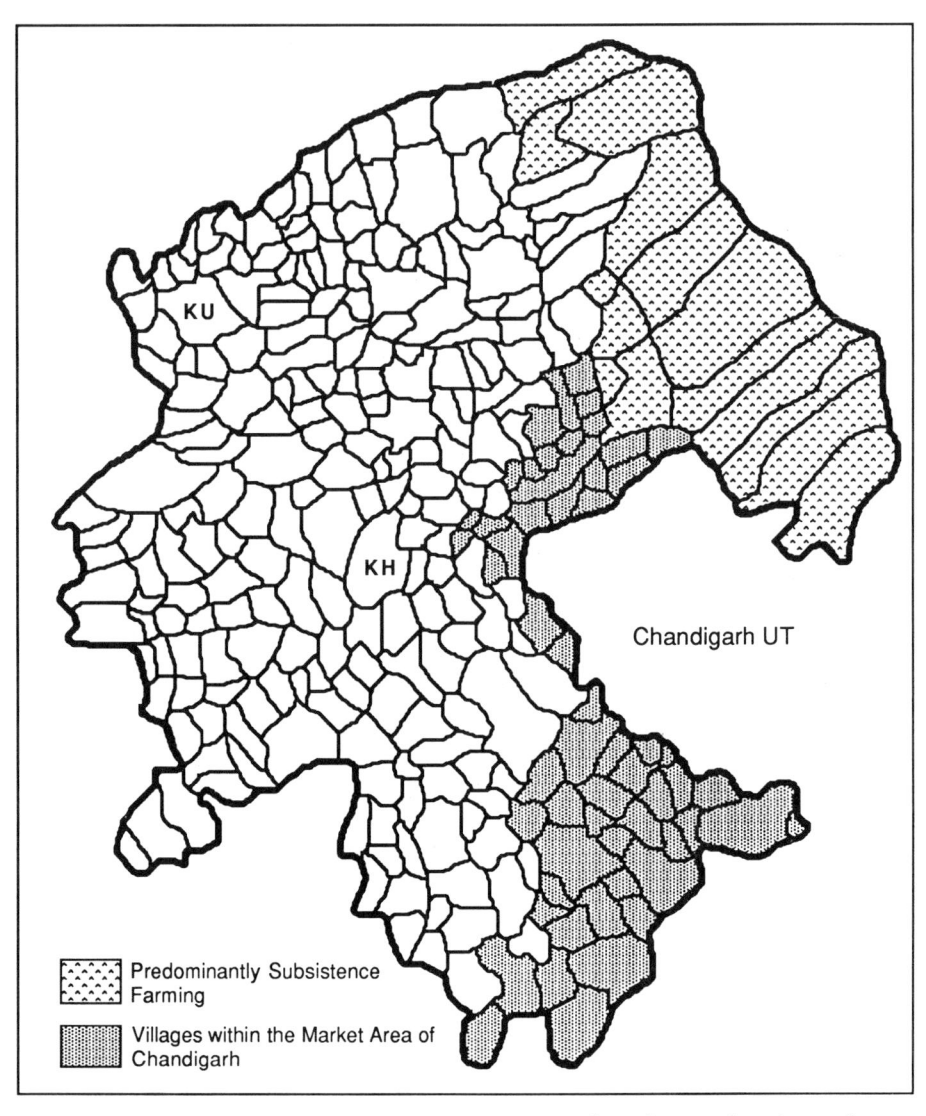

Fig. 25. Villages in Kharar Tehsil Located within the Market Area of Chandigarh.
SOURCE: Field survey, 1982.

less than impressive given the large local demand (figure 26). In fact, in order to satisfy the urban demand for milk, a sizable amount must be brought in from other nearby areas in the state.

The lagging growth of commercial dairy farming in the study region can be attributed to two main factors. First, the state dairy cooperative, Milkfed Punjab, has been unsuccessful in generating widespread support among the local farmers. The failure in the cooperative movement can be attributed largely to low cooperative milk prices, delinquent payments, and distrust of local Milkfed officials.[27] Second, the lack of refrigerated, and in most cases even motorized, means of transportation limits the distance one can deliver such a perishable good. Although motorcycles are becoming more widely used, the overwhelming majority of milk is still transported to the city on overladen bicycles.

The second major impact, namely an increase in fruit and vegetable production, has been confined to an even smaller number of villages. As figure 27 illustrates, the spatial distribution of commercial fruit and vegetable production geared toward the urban markets of Chandigarh and Mohali is limited to a small number of villages in the eastern portion of the study area. As in the case of dairying, a major obstacle to the development of this type of specialized agriculture is the limited means of personal transport. Once again, the bicycle is the major means of transportation utilized by the individual farmer. This holds true even in the case of the few large farmers who own tractors. In general, the local scale of production is not large enough to produce sufficient daily quantities to make tractor transport economically feasible.

Transportation by bullock cart is also not usually a workable alternative. Fruits and vegetables are harvested daily for an extended period of time; a farmer could not possibly use his bullocks, given that their primary use is for plowing, to transport his produce to market. A twenty-kilometer round trip to market and back renders even a strong pair of bullocks useless for plowing for one to two days. In recent years, hiring a horse cart to transport vegetables to the city has become more common. Cost is a problem, however, in using this method of transport, and a farmer cannot always rely on the hired cart showing up every day. In summary, given that (a) a farmer must arrive at the *mandi* at dawn to insure immediate sale of

---

[27] The price a farmer receives from the cooperative society is dependent upon the fat content in his animal's milk. The percentage of milk fat is tested twice, once at the village by the local cooperative official, and a second time at the milk processing plant. Numerous farmers in the study area have complained that the local Milkfed representative purposely underestimates the fat content of their milk. Therefore they allege that the price they receive is below the fair market rate. There are other accounts circulating throughout the countryside that several of the local cooperative officials have disappeared from the area, taking with them the monthly payments of all the farmers in a village.

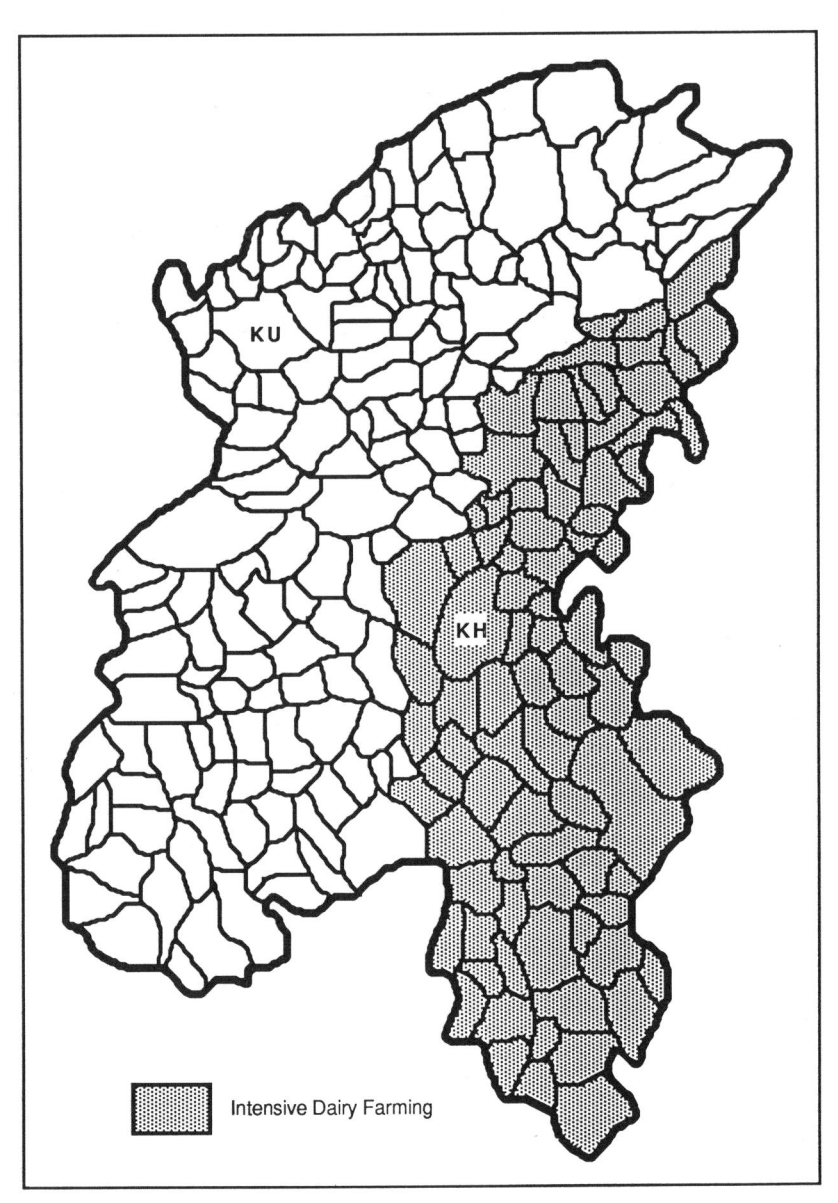

Fig. 26. Villages in the Study Area in which Farming Households are Involved in Commercial Dairying for the Chandigarh Market, 1982.
SOURCE: Field survey, 1982.
Note: This map does not include those farming households that sell milk to the village collection center of MILKFED, which produces bottled mik for sale in Chandigarh.

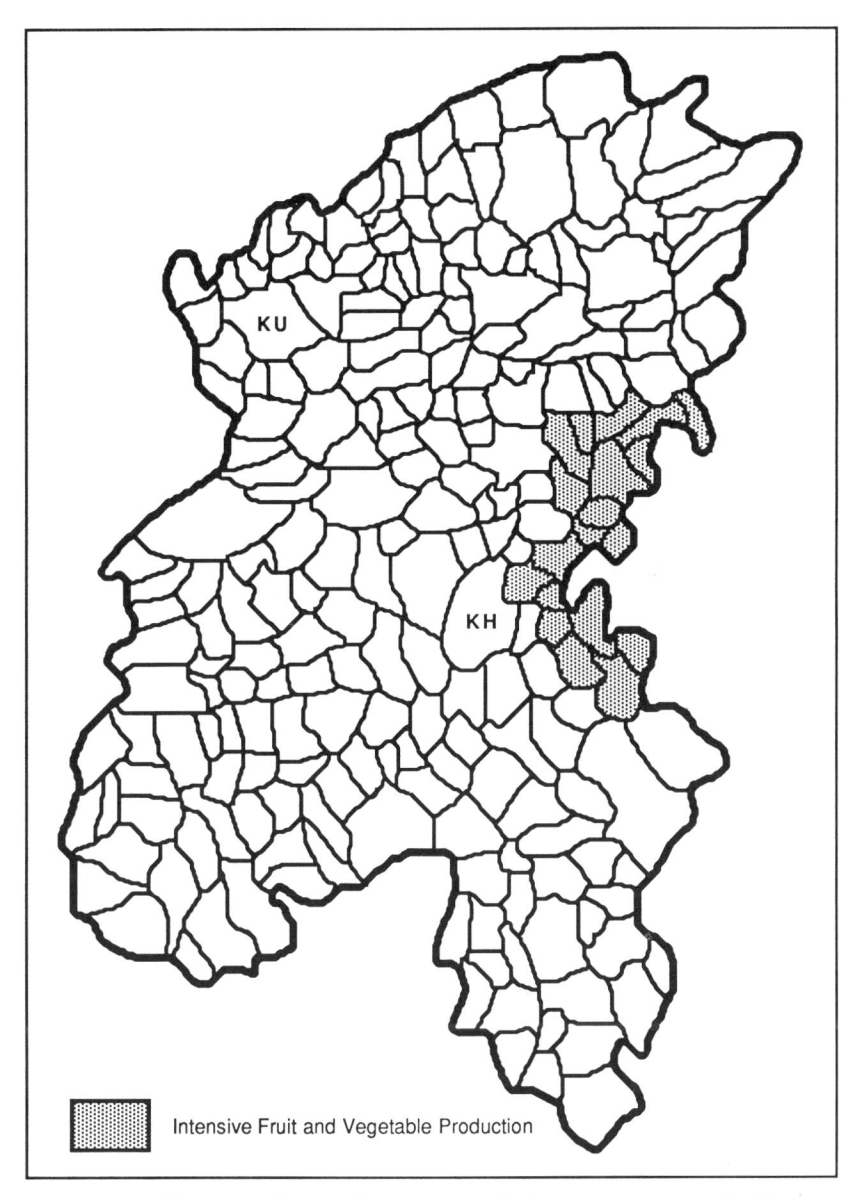

Fig. 27. Villages in the Study Area in which Farming Households are Involved in Fruit and Vegetable Production for the Chandigarh Market, 1982.
SOURCE: Field survey, 1982.

his produce at a high price, which means traveling at night on unlit roads, and that (b) the main means of transportation is by bicycle, it is not surprising that vegetable farming in the study region is restricted to an eight-to-ten-kilometer radius around the Chandigarh-Mohali urban area.

One factor that would upset the confined spatial pattern of commercial vegetable farming would be the existence of extensive contract farming. With the exception of potatoes, however, very little contract vegetable farming occurs in the study area. In the case of potatoes, the buyer contracts, or purchases, the entire production from a certain field at a price usually set before harvest. It is the buyer's responsibility to make arrangements for, and assume the cost of, all labor and transportation. Accordingly, the spatial distribution of the commercial production of potatoes is not determined largely by distance from market but rather by soil and other local environmental conditions.

There are other constraints more closely aligned with the general conditions of peasant agricultural systems that limit the extent of vegetable farming around the Chandigarh-Mohali urban cluster. These additional constraints include: (1) a larger labor and capital investment than is required in the cultivation of the traditional food crops; and (2) a much greater risk of losing a large sum of money in such an endeavor. The cultivation of fruits and vegetables demands large quantities of costly physical inputs such as irrigation water, chemical fertilizers, and pesticides. In addition, they are the most labor intensive of all possible crops the peasant farmer could grow. The greater degree of risk involved is related, in part, to the susceptibility of fruits and vegetables to crop damage as a result of disease, pests, or adverse weather conditions. Also, since there are no guaranteed government support prices for nonstaples, their market price can fluctuate dramatically from day to day. Wide price fluctuations and the necessity of selling produce on a given day, regardless of the going market rate, make specializing in the production of fruits and vegetables a potentially very profitable but highly uncertain and risky enterprise.

The three main reasons why Chandigarh has not played a larger role in determining the agricultural land-use and marketing patterns of Kharar tehsil are: (1) restriction of agricultural trade across Union Territory boundaries; (2) the lack of traditional or economic ties between the farmers of the region and the grain merchants of Chandigarh *mandi* ; and (3) the fact that is dangerous for farmers to travel by bullock cart along the roadways into the city.

With regard to the restriction of agricultural trade across either state or Union Territory boundaries, the following clarification should be made. At the present time, the central government prohibits the interstate trade only of paddy. Intermittently during the 1970s, however, the sale of wheat across state boundaries was also outlawed. In order to monitor interstate trade, the state government has erected checkpoints along all roadways leading into Chandigarh (figure 28). These checkpoints are manned by armed Punjab police officers who go one step beyond enforcing the law. In addition to paddy, they also prevent large quantities of other agricultural goods, mainly wheat, from leaving the state. Whenever farmers approach the city limits with loads of agricultural produce they are immediately stopped by the border guards. If they are transporting wheat, for example, the guards will misinform them that, like paddy, it is illegal to transport wheat across state lines. Most farmers will believe that it is illegal; others who challenge the existence of such a law will be threatened with physical harm if they attempt to pass through the checkpoint. Of course, for a substantial amount of money, the guards can be persuaded to look the other way while a farmer enters the city. Small farmers can rarely afford to pay the sum of money that is required to enter the city "illegally," so they turn their bullock carts around and head toward Kharar *mandi*.

Some farmers and grain merchants feel that the border police are under orders from high-ranking state government officials to prevent the movement of wheat across state lines. The theory is that the state does not want to lose the tax revenue generated from the sale of this important commodity, and also that it wants to be assured of meeting its target contributions to the central wheat pool. There is a great deal of pride among state agricultural officials that Punjab is the breadbasket of India. As stated earlier, this obstruction to the free movement of wheat across state lines has been successful in preventing large quantities of it from leaving the study area and entering the market in Chandigarh.

The lack of traditional or economic ties between the farmers of the region and the grain merchants in Chandigarh is another reason why the city has not been a greater force in the development of the agricultural land-use and marketing patterns in the study region. One related factor is that the agricultural market in Chandigarh is dominated by a few large merchants from outside the region. There are only eight to ten merchants who deal directly with farmers; others buy from them and sell milled flour to consumers. Only the very large farmers of the region are able to secure loans from these few large merchants. Small farmers are looked upon as bothersome and an unnecessary risk. Most small farmers of the region are intimidated by these large dealers and fear, even if they were able to secure a loan from them, drastic reprisals if they failed to repay them on time. Their greatest fear is the loss of their land.

The interest rates on loans from the merchants in Chandigarh are usually several percentage points higher than those offered by the dealers in Kharar and Kurali. In fact, in many cases loans are given out at sowing time

Fig. 28. Checkpoint at the Chandigarh Union Territory Boundary.

by the grain merchants in Kharar and Kurali interest-free, if the loan is paid in full at harvesttime. This practice is unheard of among the merchants of Chandigarh. Also, it is difficult to secure a loan from these large dealers for crops other than wheat and paddy. Since, for the most part, these two commodities are successfully prevented from entering the urban market of Chandigarh from the study area, the number of loans issued to local farmers from these large grain merchants is minimal.

Among the more important traditional barriers to trade between the farmers of Kharar tehsil and the grain merchants of Chandigarh is the innate fear and distrust the local small farmers have of outsiders, and the lack of family ties with these dealers. In some instances, familial relations with local merchants date back three or four generations. When farmers are asked why they sell produce to a particular grain merchant a common response is, "I go to the same *arthiya* my father went to and my father's father went to." The relationship between a farmer and a grain merchant traditionally goes beyond strictly business concerns into personal matters. The *arthiya* not only lends the farmer money for his farming enterprise but also for family needs. It is, for example, the *arthiya* in many cases who lends the farmer money for his daughter's dowry and other wedding expenses. In exchange for his financial help with nonfarm expenses, the grain merchant secures a long-lasting loyalty from the farmer and his sons.

THE STUDY AREA AND RESEARCH METHODOLOGY 85

The end result of these traditional, economic, and governmental barriers to free trade is that only a small number of large farmers from the study area sell their agricultural produce in Chandigarh. Even among these few large farmers, most of them store their grain and come to Chandigarh long after the harvest season, when the prices are sufficiently high enough to warrant all the risk and trouble involved in coming to this *mandi*. Therefore, the majority of agricultural goods sold in Chandigarh *mandi* come from the rich, and some cases distant, agricultural areas of Punjab and Haryana. It should be noted, however, that it is highly probable that in time, as Chandigarh continues to grow in population and industrial base, it will exert a greater influence over the agricultural land-use and marketing patterns of Kharar tehsil.

The growth of Chandigarh has already instilled new life into the regional economy in several ways. The Chandigarh region, once labeled as the most backward area in the state, has made significant progress in terms of economic development. One obvious economic advantage the city has to offer the surrounding region is in the area of nonfarm employment opportunities. Within a fourteen-kilometer radius, about one out of every ten village families have at least one member employed in Chandigarh. The income this family member receives from his or her city job is more often than not invested into the family farm.[28]

In the study area, this urban income is commonly invested in one of three ways: (1) the money may be used to keep up with the ever escalating costs of agricultural inputs, such as diesel fuel, chemical fertilizers, pesticides, new varieties of seeds, and electricity; (2) the funds may be spent on increasing the amount of land under tube-well irrigation; or (3) this additional capital may allow a family to move toward a specialized type of commercial agriculture.

A move toward specialization in agriculture may take several forms. A family farming operation might devote most of its efforts toward the cultivation of the more risky and capital-intensive crops of fruits, vegetables, and paddy. Although the cultivation of these crops entertains greater risk and investment, it also gives the potential for a much greater return. A second regional type of specialized commercial agriculture is the cultivation of fodder, or livestock feed crops. The cultivation of these crops can be extremely profitable but they require a large capital investment in the form of extensive irrigation facilities. In the study area, farms that specialized in this type of commercial agriculture had several family members working in Chandigarh for better than average wages. A third form of farming specialization is the move toward dairying and away from the commercial pro-

---

[28] The joint, or extended, household is still the common family unit throughout the study area, and for that matter, throughout most of rural India.

duction of food crops at all. Once again, dairy farming can be a lucrative business, but it requires a large capital investment. The investment is not confined to the purchase of livestock but also involves the high costs of caring for the animals. In order to secure the large amounts of green fodder required, extensive irrigation facilities are needed. Also, because of the climatic extremes of the region, enclosed shelters are a must for the milch cattle. It should be noted that the overwhelming majority of specialized commercial farms in the region are not owned by farming families who antedate Chandigarh, but rather by retired high-ranking military officers and other senior pensioned government employees.

The added resources from city employment can be spent on mechanizing the farm operation. Granted, the degree of mechanization is marginal when compared to the more advanced areas of Punjab, but nevertheless it is significant on a local scale. This increased mechanization can be in the form of electric/diesel engine tube wells, tractors, combine harvesters (usually rented), or motor-driven grain threshers and fodder cutters.

The need to mechanize has become more pronounced throughout the region since the rise of Chandigarh. The supply of local agricultural labor has declined dramatically since the city was established. A substantial number of workers belonging to the traditional agricultural labor castes (*jati*) of the region have secured menial labor jobs in Chandigarh. Almost all of the seasonal agricultural labor now comes from other north Indian states such as Bihar and Uttar Pradesh.

Market Crops

This study is concerned with modeling land-use patterns stimulated, in a large measure, by market demand. It is important, therefore, to clarify what is meant by the term "market crops," and how they differ from the remaining crops, which might be labeled "household crops." In this monograph, the term "market crops" simply refers to those crops whose extent of cultivation is significantly related to market demand. In contrast, household crops are those crops grown strictly for household consumption.

Insofar as the amount of land devoted to each crop in a peasant agricultural system is determined mainly by household needs first and market demand second, strictly speaking, with the exception of several specialized fruits and vegetables, there are no purely market crops. Also, not every crop so labeled commands the same degree of market orientation.[29]

Only those crops in the study region identified as market crops have been incorporated into the test case of the maximum-likelihood land-use

---

[29] This difference in market sensitivity will be discussed at greater length in chapter 5 in the context of distance-deterrence functions assigned to each crop.

model introduced in this monograph. Local household crops excluded from the model include fruits, vegetables, and other specialty crops grown in garden plots for household consumption, and all animal fodder crops. Given that the sorghum and millet crops of *jowar* (*Sorghum vulgare*) and *bajra* (*Pennisetum typhoides*) are grown for both human and animal consumption, a distinction was made when compiling the data for the model between land under cultivation of these two crops that would be used solely for fodder, and that grown for the market and destined for human consumption. *Jowar, bajra,* and other fodder crops are sometimes grown for commercial sale. In the study region, however, there was an insignificant amount of this type of commercial activity.

One additional market crop was not incorporated into the model because of special local marketing circumstances. That crop is sugarcane (*Saccharum officinarum*). It was excluded because, by law, all raw sugarcane in the study area must be sold to the cooperative sugar mill in Morinda. Furthermore, a farmer does not necessarily have to take his cane directly to the mill; he may choose to bring it to any one of the numerous collection centers dispersed throughout much of the region. Although the two crudely refined byproducts of *gur* and *shukr* are sold in both Kurali and Kharar, the sale of these two commodities, as mentioned earlier, has been outlawed from time to time in an attempt to insure that the mill runs at full capacity and at a profit.

In order to incorporate the identified market crops into the model they were divided into five groups. All crops cultivated during either of the two major agricultural seasons were included in the analysis. In other words, the total cropped area for a year was divided among five distinct crop groupings. These five general crop types are: (1) cereals and millets, (2) pulses, (3) oilseeds, (4) fiber crops, and (5) fruits and vegetables.

Cereal and millet crops included:
paddy (*Oryza sativa* L.)
maize (*Zea mays*)
bulrush millet (*Pennisetum typhoides*)
sorghum (*Sorghum vulgare*)
finger millet (*Eluisine coracana*)
barley (*Hordeum vulgare* L.)
oats (*Avena sativa* L.)
wheat (*Triticum aestivum*)

Pulses included:
black gram (*Phaseolus mungo* var. *radiatus* L.)
field pea (*Pisum arvense* L.)
Bengal gram (*Cicer arietimum* L.)
green gram (*Phaseolus aureus* Roxb.)
kidney bean (*Phaseolus aconitifolius* Jacq.)
lentil (*Lens esculenta* Moench.)

pigeon pea (*Cajanus cajan* Milsp.)

Oilseeds included:
brown *sarson* (*Brassica campestris* L. var. *dichotoma*)
groundnut (*Arachis hypogaea* L.)
rapeseed (*Brassica campestris* L. var. *sarson* Prain.)
Indian mustard (*Brassica juncea* Coss.)
Indian rape (*Brassica campestris* L. var. *toria* Dath.)
linseed (*Linum usitatissinum* L.)
sesamum (*Sesamum indicum* L.)

Varieties of cotton:
American cotton (*Gossypium hirsutum* L.)
desi cotton (*Gossypium arboreum* L.)

Fruits and vegetables included:
watermelon (*Citrullus vulgaris* Sohrad.)
grapes (*Vitis vinifera* L.)
mango (*Mangifera indica* L.)
muskmelon (*Cucumis melo* L.)
eggplant (*Solarnum melongena* L.)
cabbage (*Brassica oleracea* L.)
carrot (*Daucus carota* L.)
cauliflower (*Brassica oleracea* L. var. *botrytis* L.)
cucumber (*Cucumis sotivus* L.)
okra (*Hibiscus esculentus*)
onion (*Allium cepa* L.)
potato (*Solarnum tuberosum* L.)
tomato (*Lycopersicum esculentum* Mill.)
turnip (*Brassica campestris* L. var. *rapa*)

The groupings basically follow those outlined in the *Handbook of Agriculture*.[30] In addition, however, transportation costs, market orientation, and groupings that the farmers themselves perceived were taken into account. With these concerns in mind, cereals and millets were combined into the same group. A more detailed discussion in regard to the role transportation costs and degree of market orientation played in the categorization scheme follows.

Data Sources

Land Use and Cropping Data

Comprehensive land-use and cropping data were obtained, with the assistance of the *tehsildar* and his staff, from the village land revenue rec-

---

[30] Indian Council of Agricultural Research, *Handbook of Agriculture* (New Delhi: ICAR, 1980), pp. 1236-79.

ords (*lal kitab*). The village land revenue official (*patwarii*) is required to record what crops are grown on each and every hectare of land in the village, for both *rabi* and *kharif* agricultural seasons. This very detailed information was collected for every village in that portion of the combined market areas of Kharar and Kurali that fell within the boundaries of Kharar tehsil. Only a limited number of villages in the combined market areas were located outside the tehsil boundaries. Land use data for those villages were unavailable.

The land-use and cropping data from the village land revenue records were double-checked for accuracy and were compared to similar data collected by the agricultural extension agents of the Department of Agriculture, Punjab. Their reliability was further estimated by a survey of 163 villages located throughout the study area (Appendix A). The end result of the double checking was that, although the land revenue records were not 100% accurate, they were well within an acceptable margin of error (10-15%).

Transportation Costs and Road Network

Information regarding costs of transporting agricultural goods to market were obtained from estimates given by the farmers in the study region. Both time and monetary expenditures were recorded. This information was collected for each mode of transportation the farmer had available to him, regardless of whether or not he utilized all of them (Appendix A).

Owing to the lack of an accurate map of the secondary and tertiary feeder roads in the study area, one was created from information in several sources. The primary data sources for the exact location of roads and cart paths were the appropriate topographical sheets (scale 1:50,000) from the Survey of India. Since these topographical sheets were last field checked in the middle to late 1960s, more recent information had to be added from maps available from the Office of Town and Country Planning, Punjab, and the Public Works Department, Punjab. After discovering that some roadways were still missing, or inaccurately drawn, a personal road survey of the entire study area was completed. The end result of this procedure is the detailed road map represented in figure 29.

Agricultural Land Use in the Study Area

In order to identify the main economic, legal, political, and/or physical factors that affect land-use and marketing decisions made by local farmers, and to aid in the delimitation of the formal market areas of Kharar and Kurali, discussions were held with various government, cooperative society, and market officials.[31] Similar information was gathered, by use of a

---

[31] Officials from the following government and cooperative bodies were interviewed: Department of Agriculture, Punjab; Punjab State Marketing Board; Punjab State

survey questionnaire, from a sample of 500 farmers in 163 villages dispersed throughout the study area (Appendix A).

Marketing information was acquired through informal interviews with grain merchants and from the *Heap Disposal Records* kept by the Secretary of the *mandi*. The data contained within these registers are extremely detailed. Information such as the type of produce, quality of grade, selling price, purchaser, and village of origin is noted for each and every sale. This last disclosure was useful in delimiting the combined market area utilized in this test case.

Summary

Although the study region is located in Punjab, the most advanced agricultural state in India, owing to several local natural and economic constraints the area actually ranks close to the national average for nearly all indices of development. Given that the study area is more representative of the nation in terms of agricultural development than first appears, I would argue that the model presented here has the potential for wider application beyond the state of Punjab.

Furthermore, although Chandigarh, which is adjacent to the study area and also one of India's most rapidly growing urban areas, has had some influence on the agricultural land-use patterns of the region, the city's impact on the actual test site was limited to the degree of intensity of fruit, vegetable, and fodder cultivation. This has been accounted for in the formulation of the model. Attempting to model the agricultural land-use patterns associated with the market towns of Kharar and Kurali is one of the major objectives of this monograph; with the conclusion of this chapter, the stage is set for an analysis of the procedures and results of the initial test case of the maximum-likelihood model.

Cooperative Supply and Marketing Federation (MARKFED); Food Corporation of India (FCI); PUNSUP; and Office of Town and Country Planning, Punjab.

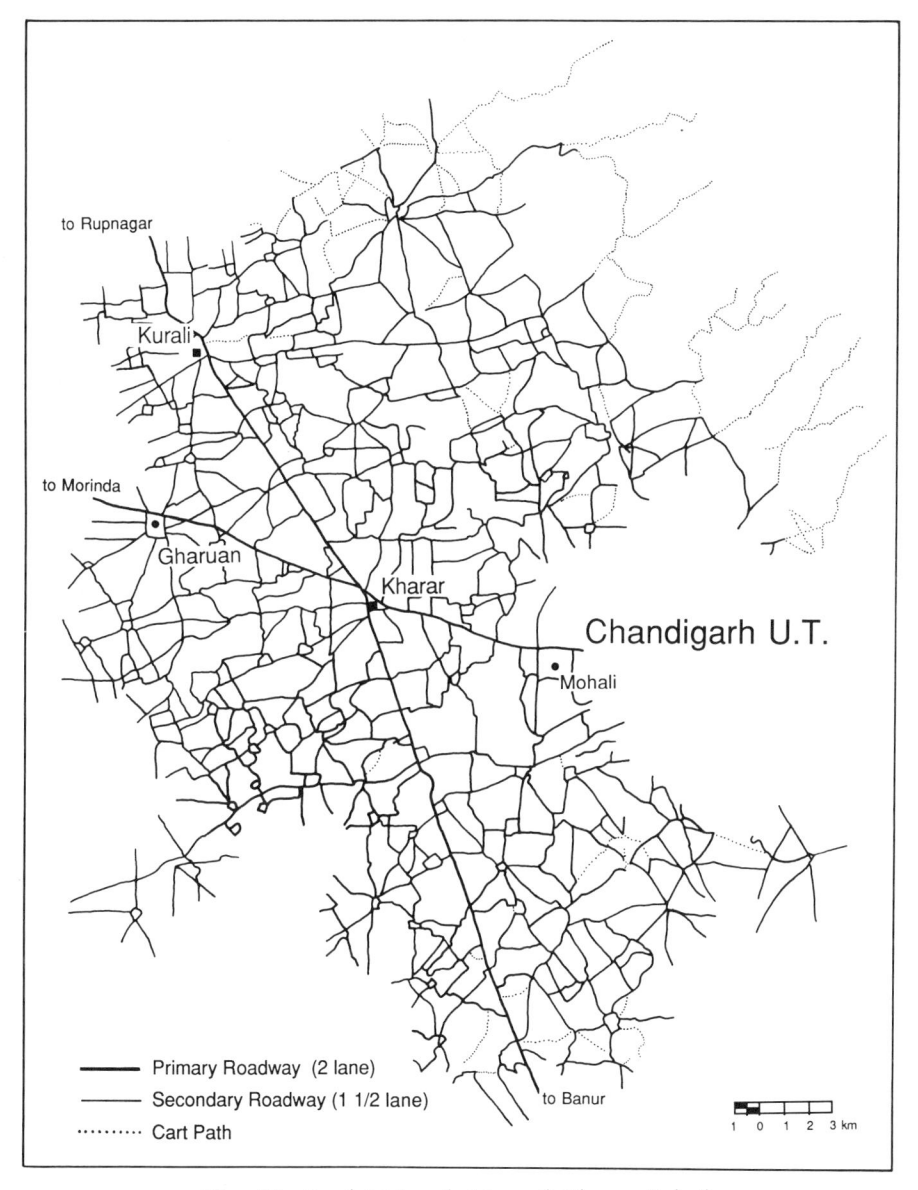

Fig. 29. Road Network Map of Kharar Tehsil.
SOURCES: Department of Town and Country Planning, Punjab, 1982; Field survey, 1982.

Chapter 5

PROCEDURE AND RESULTS OF THE TEST CASE

A General Maximum-Likelihood Agricultural Land-Use Model

The general maximum-likelihood model introduced in chapter 3 can be restated in a concise manner utilizing several of Wilson's basic equations.[1] A model of this type requires one to maximize the value of entropy (W)

$$W\{T_{ij}\} = \frac{\sum_i \sum_j T_{ij}!}{\prod_i \prod_j T_{ij}!} \quad ; \qquad (1)$$

subject to an origin constraint

$$\sum_j^n T_{ij} = O_i \, , \qquad (2)$$

a destination constraint

$$\sum_j^n T_{ij} = D_j \, , \qquad (3)$$

and a cost constraint

$$\sum_i^n \sum_j^n T_{ij} \, c_{ij} = C \qquad (4)$$

Given these constraints, it follows that the maximum-likelihood solution of W can be found by solving the general equation

---

[1] Wilson, *Entropy in Urban and Regional Modelling*, pp. 4-5.

where
$$T_{ij} = O_i A_i D_j B_j \exp(-\beta c_{ij}) \qquad (5)$$

and
$$A_i = 1 / [\sum_{j}^{n} B_j D_j \exp(-\beta c_{ij})] \qquad (6)$$

$$B_j = 1 / [\sum_{i}^{n} A_i O_i \exp(-\beta c_{ij})] ; \qquad (7)$$

To this general equation a modal-split constraint is sometimes added to accommodate a mix of transportation types. As a result, the modified equation now takes the general form

$$T_{ij}^k = O_i^k A_i^k D_j^k B_j^k \exp(-\beta c_{ij}^k) \qquad (8)$$

In the manner in which the model was employed in the test case, this modification requires the assignment of one such equation to each transport mode (k). Therefore, each equation will produce a subordinate predicted trip matrix $(t_{ij})^k$, in this case more appropriately labeled a subordinate land-use matrix. These subordinate matrices will become part of the final predicted land-use matrix T_{ij}, which contains the results of k individual runs by crop type.

When a maximum-likelihood approach is utilized to model an agricultural landscape, the individual components of equation (8) take on the following meaning: O_i^k is the amount of the total cropped area in village i under the cultivation of crop type k. A_i^k is a scalar (i.e., Lagrangian multiplier) that ensures that the origin constraint (equation 2) is met, meaning that all the available crop type k to be shipped from village i to market j will be shipped. D_j^k is the total demand at market j for the kth crop type. B_j^k, like A_i^k, is a scalar that ensures that the destination constraint (equation 3) is met. In reference to the present application, B_j^k makes certain that the demand for crop type k at market j is satisfied. The negative exponential function - β^k is the spatial-deterrence parameter for crop type k.

In the land-use model presented here the value of the deterrence parameter, $-\beta^k$, is related to three factors: (1) the cost, in terms of both man hours and money, of transporting crop-type k to market, (2) the perishability/durability of crop type k, and (3) the degree of market orientation crop type k possesses. The nature of the β parameter in the model will be analyzed in greater detail in the next section.

The last term in equation (5), c_{ij} represents the movement-cost matrix. In the test-case application of the model the matrix is a distance metric held constant between crop types. Therefore, with regard to movement costs, only the deterrence parameter, $-\beta^k$, varies between crop types. This is justifiable in the agricultural land-use application of the model because all crop types are transported over the same road network; this is what the cost-of-movement matrix, c_{ij}, actually represents. What may be unrealistic about this approach is that individual farmers, although traveling the same road network, might be using various modes of transport. To incorporate such an additional constraint into the equation, however, would demand a much more sophisticated reformulation of the basic equation, which is beyond the scope of this initial test case.

Test-Case Version of the Model ENT-3

Previous studies conducted by Wilson and others concerning urban journey-to-work applications of a maximum-likelihood approach have utilized a fully constrained model.[2] In certain cases, even a fourth modal-split constraint has been added to the general model.[3] It should be made clear that the maximum-likelihood formulation used in this test case is not the more analogous application as an agricultural goods distribution model. In such an application, known production amounts are being distributed to zones, or markets, having a known demand. In this test-case application, the demand for various crop types at two markets (D_j^k) and the impedance parameter assigned to each crop type ($-\beta^k$) are allowed to interact so as to produce an agricultural landscape that will meet market demand in the most likely, i.e., least unbiased, fashion. In other words, the market demand at Kharar and Kurali, along with the spatial-deterrence parameter assigned to each of the five crop types, determines where in a physically homogeneous countryside, and in what proportions within each village, the various crops need to be cultivated in order to produce the most likely agricultural landscape.

In this particular application, therefore, it is not possible to operate under an origin and destination-constrained model. It is obvious that doing so would force the model merely to replicate the observed landscape. Consequently, in an agricultural land-use application, one must operate under a singly constrained formulation.

To do so, ENT-3, a destination constrained subroutine of Baxter's widely available FORTRAN computer algorithm with minor bookkeeping

---

[2] See for example: Wilson et al., "Calibration and Testing of the SELNEC Transport Model"; Wilson, *Urban and Geographical Models in Geography and Planning;* and Gregory A. Elmes, "Modeling Spatial Interaction of Utility Coal in Pennsylvania," *Annals of the Association of American Geographers* 75 (June 1985): 212-226.

[3] Wilson, *Entropy in Urban and Regional Modelling,* pp. 7-9.

modifications, was employed.[4] The resultant output from the computer algorithm ENT-3, after the five individual runs, one for each crop type, are completed is a predicted land-use matrix T_{ij} with 207 rows and 5 columns. The individual cells of the matrix represent the percentage of the total cropped area (TCA) in a village devoted to a specific crop type.

The only required inputs in a destination-constrained model of this type are: (1) an estimate of total market demand at each market for each crop type (D_j^k), (2) a cost of movement matrix (c_{ij}), and (3) a specific distance-deterrence parameter for each crop type ($-\beta^k$). This minimal number of required inputs is a distinct advantage in utilizing a maximum-likelihood approach to modeling peasant agricultural landscapes.

Operationalization of the Model

In order to operationalize the model used in this test case, the following procedure was followed. The first step was to delimit the areas of the two markets in the test case, Kharar and Kurali. From discussions with various marketing and agricultural officials, I learned that these two particular markets commanded approximately an eight-to-ten-kilometer range. Based on this information, I conducted a separate field survey in all villages situated at a radius of ten kilometers from each town. The major objective of each survey was to determine whether or not the majority of agricultural produce from these villages was being sold in either of the two markets, or elsewhere. If the surplus production was being marketed in Kharar or Kurali, then the next farther village was surveyed, until an "agricultural frontier" village had been identified. Likewise, if the farmers in the initial village were not sending most of their goods to Kharar, then the next village closer in was examined. This procedure continued until the outer limit of the individual market areas of Kharar and Kurali had been determined. Based on this methodology, two irregularly shaped market areas containing 242 villages were delimited. The market area of Kharar contains 140 villages, whereas that of Kurali incorporates 102 villages. Of these 242 villages, land-use data were available for 207 (figure 23).

The second step of the procedure was to estimate a total market demand (TMD) for each market by crop type (i.e., the determination of the D_j^k values for equation 9). Since this is neither a trip generation nor commodity distribution form the maximum-likelihood model, the demand is expressed in terms of land area and not in units of grain. In this case, the TMD for cereals in Kharar market is equal to the amount of land devoted to commercial cereal production in the market area of Kharar. One can readily see that a problem arises concerning this definition. How does one differentiate

---

[4] Baxter, "Entropy Maximizing Models of Spatial Interaction."

a hectare of land in a village that is under commercial production of a particular crop, from another hectare of that same crop, the harvest from which will be set aside for household consumption? Given that the proportion of land devoted to commercial production will vary between, and within, crop types from one farming household to the next, it is difficult to justify the assignment of some arbitrary percentage to the amount of land under the commercial cultivation of each crop type for all villages in the study area. One way to circumvent this problem of calculating a value for TMD, which represents the appropriate number of hectares in the study area under the commercial cultivation of a particular crop, is to assume that the total amount of land devoted to a specific crop type in the market area is the amount required to satisfy both household and market demand. In that case, the TMD for any crop type is equal to the total cultivated area in the market area under that particular crop. It should be noted that in the test case, actual areal units have replaced the demand ratios employed in the illustrative examples in chapter 3 for estimating market demand by crop type. Table 11 summarizes the TMD for each crop type in Kharar and Kurali.

Table 11. *Total Market Demand for Kharar and Kurali Markets by Crop Type, 1982*

Crop type	Kharar	Kurali
Cereals and millets	22,373	8,889
Pulse	1,044	827
Oilseeds	715	690
Cotton	717	324
Fruits and vegetables	1,262	243
Total	26,111	10,973

Note: Total Market Demand (TMD) is expressed as the total number of hectares of cultivated area in each market's area.
SOURCES: Land revenue records (*lal kitab*) of the individual villages.

The third step in the operationalization of the model was to construct a cost, or distance, matrix (c_{ij}). This task entailed measuring actual road distances for all villages to both markets by the shortest or least hazardous route. If a road was known to be in poor condition or impassable during a portion of the marketing season because of flooding, a longer but more reliable path was recorded. The road network map described in chapter 4 was used as the source of information for this cost matrix (figure 29).

The fourth and final step in the preparation of the model was the assignment of an initial set of distance-deterrence parameters ($-\beta^k$). The value of the assigned beta was determined by the cost, as measured in both man-hours and money expended, of transporting the crop type to market, the perishability of goods within the individual crop type, and the degree to which the crop is market oriented. A strong market orientation implies that the crop is grown mainly for commercial production. The allocation of resources, including land, is determined largely by market forces rather than household demand. As a result, the negative exponential beta functions are not cost curves, but rather interaction curves over distance. In other words, in the test case the betas represent the degree of market interaction, which is determined by transportation cost, perishability, and market orientation.

The assignment of a single deterrence parameter for each crop type assumes that all the individual members of that crop group possess approximately the same value for each of the three market interaction characteristics mentioned above. For example, the millets were combined with cereals rather than pulses to form a distinct group. In this case, their degree of market orientation was the deciding factor in the assignment of millets to a specific crop type. In the study area, millets such as *jowar* and *bajra* are grown for commercial production rather than household consumption. Millets are consumed mainly by the lower castes and not by the more wealthy farming households. The opposite is true of pulses, where most of the harvest is consumed by the farmer and his family and a very small amount is sold in the market.

Based on the three market interaction factors discussed above, the following initial set of distance-deterrence parameters were assigned to the five crop types. Owing to their perishability and high transport costs, fruits and vegetables were given a steep spatial-deterrence function, $\beta = -0.70$. In recent years, throughout the study region, store-bought materials have largely replaced homespun cotton cloth. Accordingly, although cotton production has declined throughout the region, the remnants are increasingly becoming market oriented. Given that cotton has a strong market orientation but also keeping in mind that it is a highly durable good, cotton was assigned a β value of -0.50. The next strongest distance decay function was allotted to the crop group consisting of cereals and millets. Although wheat and paddy, which command by far the largest portion of total land area in this group, are the two leading crops in both agricultural markets, they also rank among the top in household consumption. Given that the peasant farmer produces for the household first and the market second, a β of -0.35 was initially assigned to this crop type. Both oilseeds and pulses are primarily household crops; most farmers in the region sell approximately five to ten quintals of each crop type in the market annually. Of the two, oilseeds are marketed more frequently, so they were delegated a somewhat larger β of -0.20. The pulses accordingly were allotted the smaller β of -0.10, a spatial-deterrence function that produces a nearly flat interaction curve.

Calibration of the Model

Calibration of a maximum-likelihood model as it is being employed in an agricultural land-use framework entails selecting the most appropriate set of distance-deterrence parameters for each of the five crop types. When operating under a fully constrained version, as one traditionally does in a trip-distribution application, this is not a concern, because the computer algorithm is set up to select the most appropriate β for each transportation mode. In a partially constrained model, however, the "best" values for the distance-deterrence parameters are commonly estimated by utilizing an appropriate goodness-of-fit statistic to find optimal conformity between the matrix of predicted and observed land use.[5]

It has been shown by Ayeni that significant problems exist with the conventional methods of comparing interaction matrices, namely mean trip costs and chi-square.[6] As he has demonstrated, the deficiency in using mean trip costs is to be found in their insensitivity to distributions that have relatively high values on the main diagonals of the matrix.[7] This insensitivity could lead to the situation where two significantly different trip matrices have exactly the same mean trip costs. One drawback of the chi-square statistic is the requirement of collapsing adjacent cells of a contingency table if in more than five categories there are fewer than five observations. The appropriateness of collapsing cells in an interaction matrix has been questioned by several authors.[8] In addition, Pitfield has shown an additional problem in the application of the chi-square statistic in a trip distribution application as represented by equation (11).[9]

$$\chi^2 = \sum_{i=1}^{k} \sum_{j=1}^{l} \frac{(T_{ij} - P_{ij})^2}{P_{ij}} , \qquad (9)$$

---

[5] D.E. Pitfield, "Algorithm 6: The X Test for Predicted Trip Matrices." *Environment and Planning*, A 10 (1978): 1201-6; B. Ayeni, "The Testing of Hypotheses on Interaction Data Matrices," *Geographical Analysis* 14 (1982): 79-84; idem, "Algorithm 11: Information Statistics for Comparing Predicted and Observed Trip Matrices," *Environmental and Planning* A 15 (1983): 1259-66.
[6] Ayeni, "Algorithm 11," pp. 1260-1261.
[7] Ibid., p. 1261.
[8] Pitfield, "Algorithm 6," p. 1202; P.G. Hoel, *Introduction to Mathematical Sciences* (New York: John Wiley and Co. 1971); J.A. Black and R.J. Salter, "A Statistical Evaluation of a Family of Gravity Models," *Proceedings of the Institution of Civil Engineers* 59 (1975): 1-20.
[9] Pitfield, "Algorithm 6," p. 1201.

100 UNDERSTANDING PEASANT AGRICULTURE

where T_{ij} is the observed number of trips between zones i and j; P_{ij} is the predicted number of trips between zones i and j; k is the zone of origin; and l is the number of destination zones. The degrees of freedom are found by

$$v = N - m - 1 \qquad (10)$$

where $N = kl$ and m is the sum of the number of estimated parameters and the number of constraints. Pitfield highlights the fact that whereas equation (11) refers to trip numbers, it should really be expressed in terms of trip frequencies. The difficulty here lies in the fact that the resulting χ^2 is compared to a χ^2 derived from v. The value of v is not sensitive to the scale of the entries in the trip matrices, whereas the value of χ^2 is. As a result, the test might initially suggest the rejection of a model, but after the data have been scaled downward the test may suggest the acceptance of the null hypotheses. As Pitfield has stated, "This difficulty limits the usefulness of the test as a means of comparing the efficiency of a model between a number of T matrices, and also limits the usefulness of the test in judging whether a model is statistically significant."[10]

In light of the deficiencies associated with the mean trip costs and chi-square approaches, Ayeni has introduced an apparently more appropriate test statistic, the minimum discrimination information statistic (MDIS), for testing goodness of fit between observed and predicted trip matrices.[11] MDIS has its origins in testing the null hypotheses of homogeneity on contingency tables $2\Psi(H_o)$[12]. In testing for the same property on interaction matrices, MDIS is defined as

$$2\Psi(*:H_o) = 2 \left[N_1 \sum \sum P_{ij}^{(1)} \ln \left(\frac{P_{ij}^{(1)}}{P_{ij}} \right) + N_2 \sum \sum P_{ij}^{(2)} \ln \left(\frac{P_{ij}^{(2)}}{P_{ij}} \right) \right] \qquad (11)$$

where the least biased estimate of the population probability, P_{ij}, is expressed as

$$P_{ij} = X_{ij}^{(1)} + X_{ij}^{(2)} / N_1 + N_2 \qquad (12)$$

MDIS 2Ψ is known to approximate the chi-square distribution with $(m - 1)(n - 1)$ degrees of freedom.[13] In the test case, since the model was run separately for each of the five crop types, and given that there are 207 villages, the appropriate number of degrees of freedom is 206.

---

[10] Ibid., p. 1202.
[11] Ayeni, "Algorithm 11."
[12] Ibid., p. 1260.
[13] Ibid.

PROCEDURE AND RESULTS OF THE TEST CASE 101

Before the model could be calibrated utilizing MDIS as the "best-fit" statistic, the observed and predicted land-use matrices, T_{ij}^* and T_{ij}, were proportioned across the rows, that is, the individual cells of the matrices were expressed as a percentage of the total cropped area (TCA) of the village. For example, the row in the predicted land-use matrix that represents village 110 reads as 84.01% of TCA under the cultivation of crop type 1 (cereals and millets); 4.28% of TCA under the cultivation of crop type 2 (pulses), etc. In comparison, the row in the observed land-use matrix that represents village 110 reads as 78.17% of TCA under the cultivation of crop type 1 (cereals and millets); 11.97% of TCA under the cultivation of crop type 2 (pulses), etc. Because of the absence of an origin constraint in the maximum-likelihood equation of the test case (equation 10), this proportioning technique is required before applying the statistic MDIS. In this test case, therefore, the proportional observed and predicted matrices described above are being tested for goodness of fit.

While calibrating the model through the use of this methodology, a problem associated with MDIS arose. It appears that MDIS is overly sensitive either to a few large residuals, like those associated with the fruit and vegetable crop type calibration results, or to numerous small residuals, like those found in the pulses subordinate land-use matrix (Appendix B).[14] As a result, it was possible to select a final set of distance-deterrence parameters, $-\beta^k$, which placed only two of the MDIS values between upper and lower critical values at alpha = 95% (table 12).

Table 12. *Distance-Deterrence Parameter by Crop Type as Selected by MDIS*

Crop type	MDIS	df	Beta
Cereals and millets	198.18	206	-0.25
Pulses	532.40	206	-0.10
Oilseeds	858.62	206	-0.10
Cotton	223.90	206	-0.35
Fruits and vegetables	676.75	206	-0.80

Note: The lower critical value of MDIS at alpha = 95% is 168.14.
The upper critical value of MDIS at alpha = 95% is 247.64.

---

[14] This is, to a degree, mere speculation based upon my experience of working with MDIS in the computer runs associated with this test case. There is no doubt that the use of MDIS as a goodness-of-fit measure requires further examination.

Test-Case Results

In general, the model was able to replicate the observed agricultural land-use patterns of the study region with notable accuracy. This claim is supported by the following series of residual maps (figures 30-34). These maps highlight those villages where the difference between predicted and observed land-use quantities represents a significant portion of the total cropped area (TCA). For cereals and millets, the dominant crops of the region, those villages are singled out for which the residual value is greater than 10% of the TCA. As figure 30 illustrates, only 19% of the villages in the study region contained residual values greater than 10%. Since the remaining four crop types rarely make up more than 10% of the TCA in any one village, the locations of residual values that represent greater than 5% of the total number of hectares under cultivation have been pointed out (figures 31-34). Among these four, the largest number of residual villages (21%) is associated with the pulses crop type (figure 31). The smallest number of "significant" residuals (4%) is found on the map that represents the relationship between the predicted and observed number of hectares under the cultivation of cotton (figure 32). As figures 33 and 34 illustrate, the model was able to predict the amount of land devoted to both oilseeds and fruits and vegetables within a relatively low margin of error. For these two crop types, only 15% of the villages in the study area contained residual land-use quantities greater than 5% of their TCA.

Although the modeled landscape seems generally to reflect the observed agricultural land-use patterns of the region, various spatial residual patterns surface upon a more detailed examination. What follows examines the difference between predicted and observed land-use quantities for each individual crop type. In this more detailed analysis, percentage data, rather than the actual difference in number of hectares between predicted and observed values for each crop type, have been mapped and analyzed.

Residual Pattern Analysis: Cereals and Millets

The first apparent feature of the cereals and millets residual map is the small number of villages with residual values greater than +10% and less than -10% (figure 35). As discussed in an earlier section of this chapter concerning the calibration of the model land MDIS, these residual values are generated by taking the difference between corresponding cells of the predicted and observed land-use matrices. The rows of these matrices represent, therefore, the proportion of the TCA in a village devoted to a particular crop type. The villages with relatively large underpredictions (< -10%) are clustered mainly in small groups in the extreme southern region of the study area (area A, figure 36). After examining information gathered by interview questionnaires administered to farmers in the region, along with

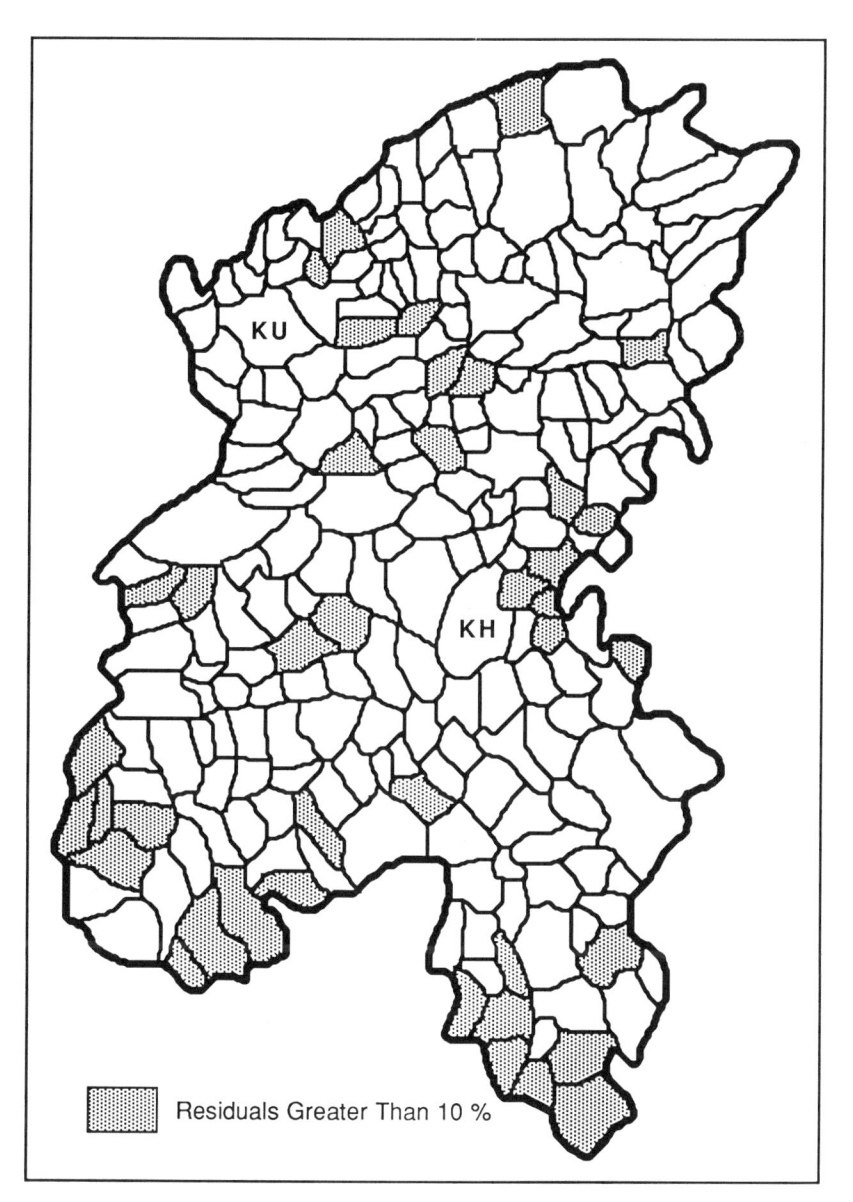

Fig. 30. Villages with Residuals Greater than or Equal to 10 Percent of Total Cropped Area: Cereals and Millets.

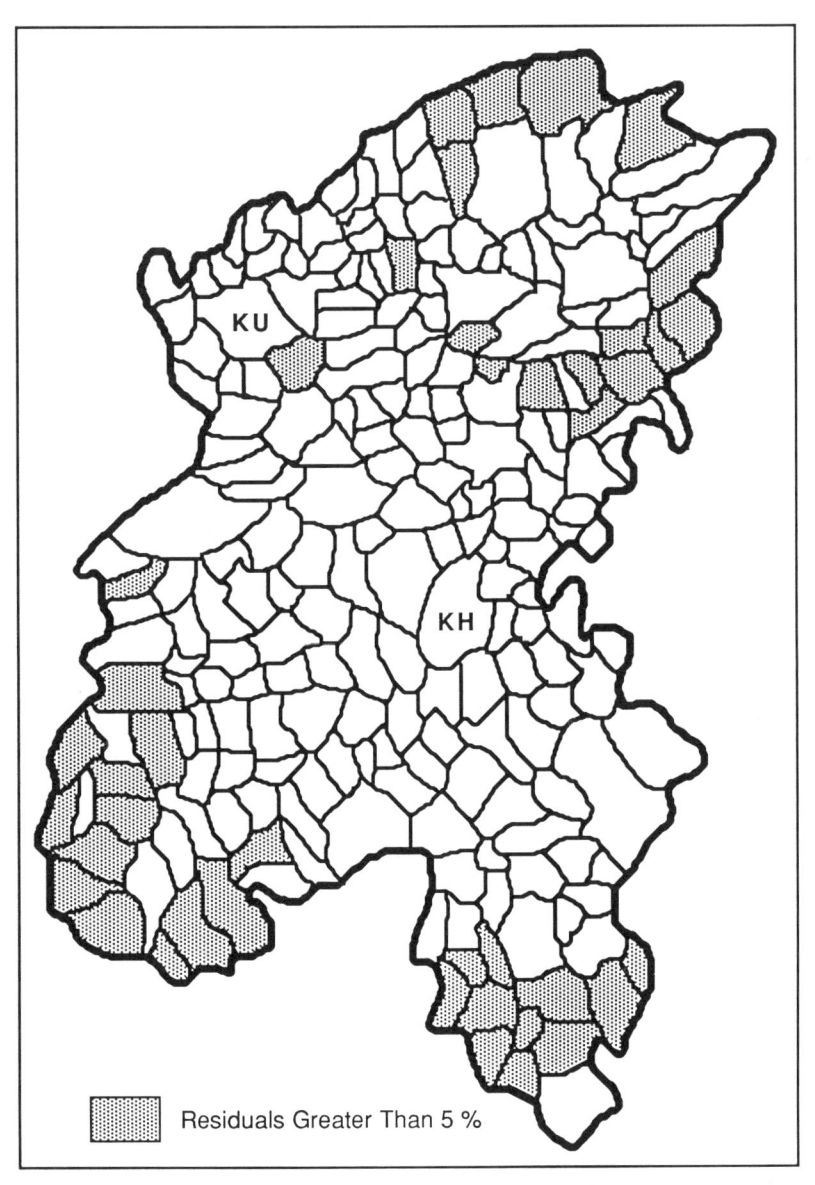

Fig. 31. Villages with Residuals Greater than or Less than 5 Percent of Total Cropped Area: Pulses.

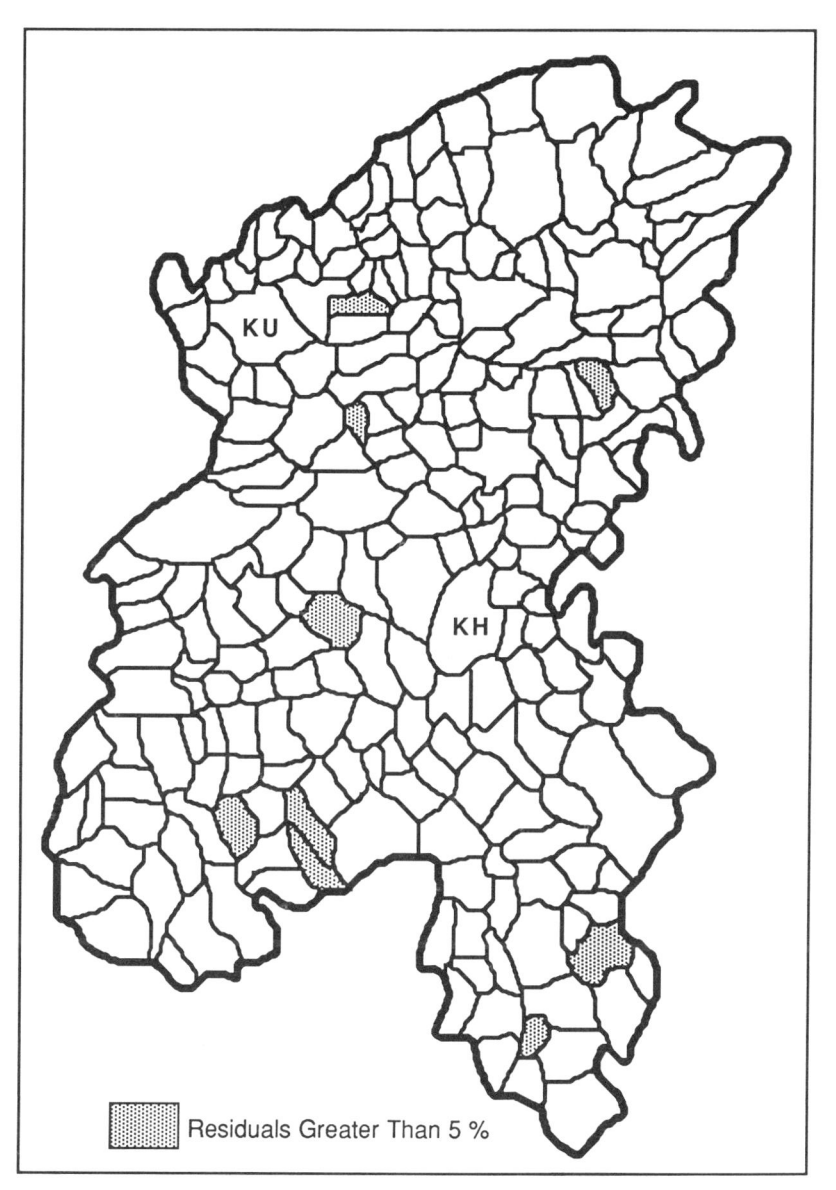

Fig. 32. Villages with Residuals Greater than or Less than 5 Percent of Total Cropped Area: Cotton.

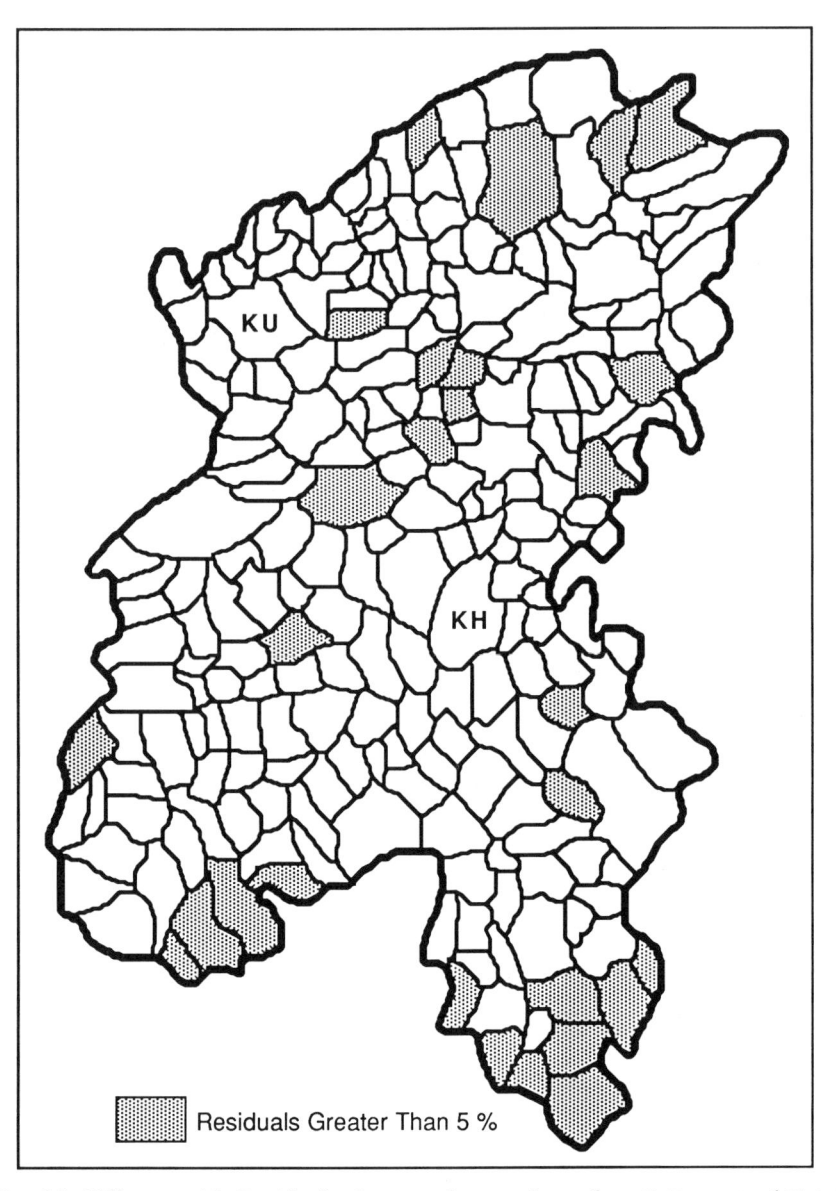

Fig. 33. Villages with Residuals Greater than or Less than 5 Percent of Total Cropped Area: Oilseeds.

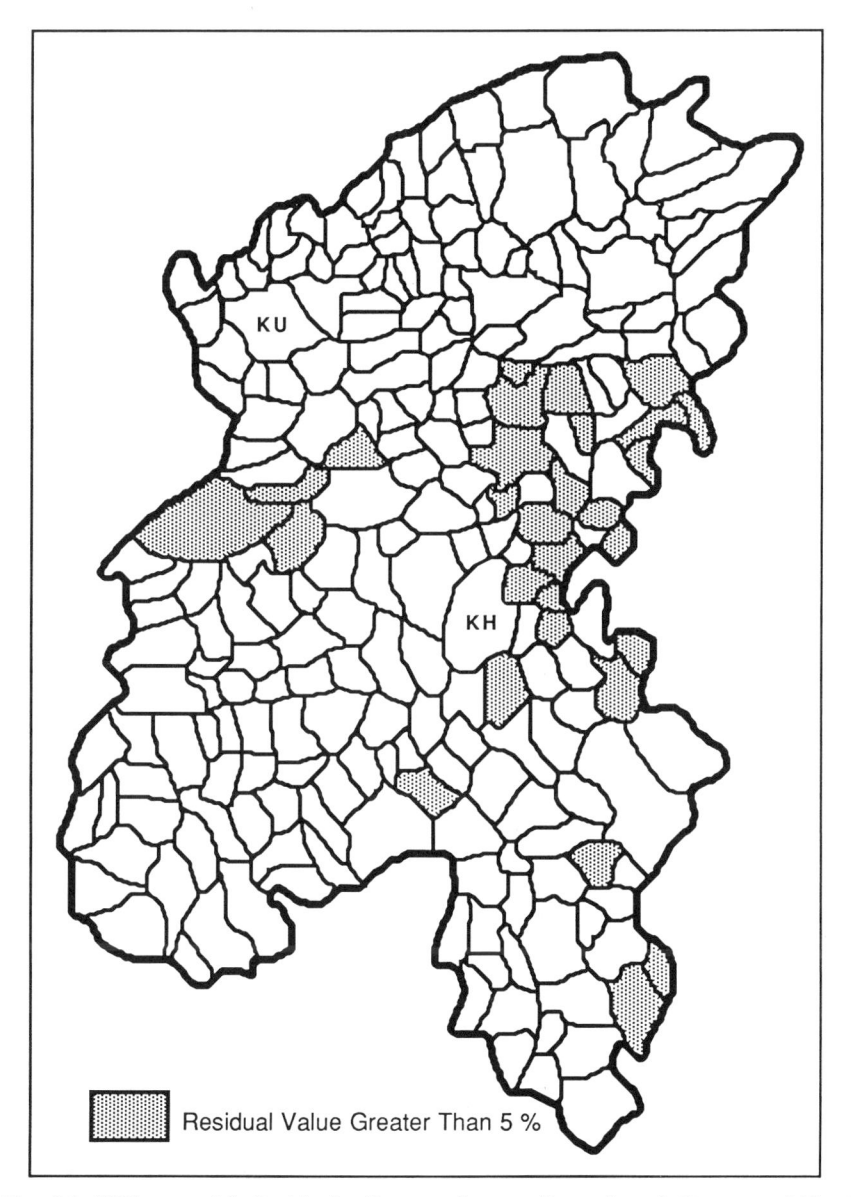

Fig. 34. *Villages with Residuals Greater than or Less than 5 Percent of Total Cropped Area: Fruits and Vegetables.*

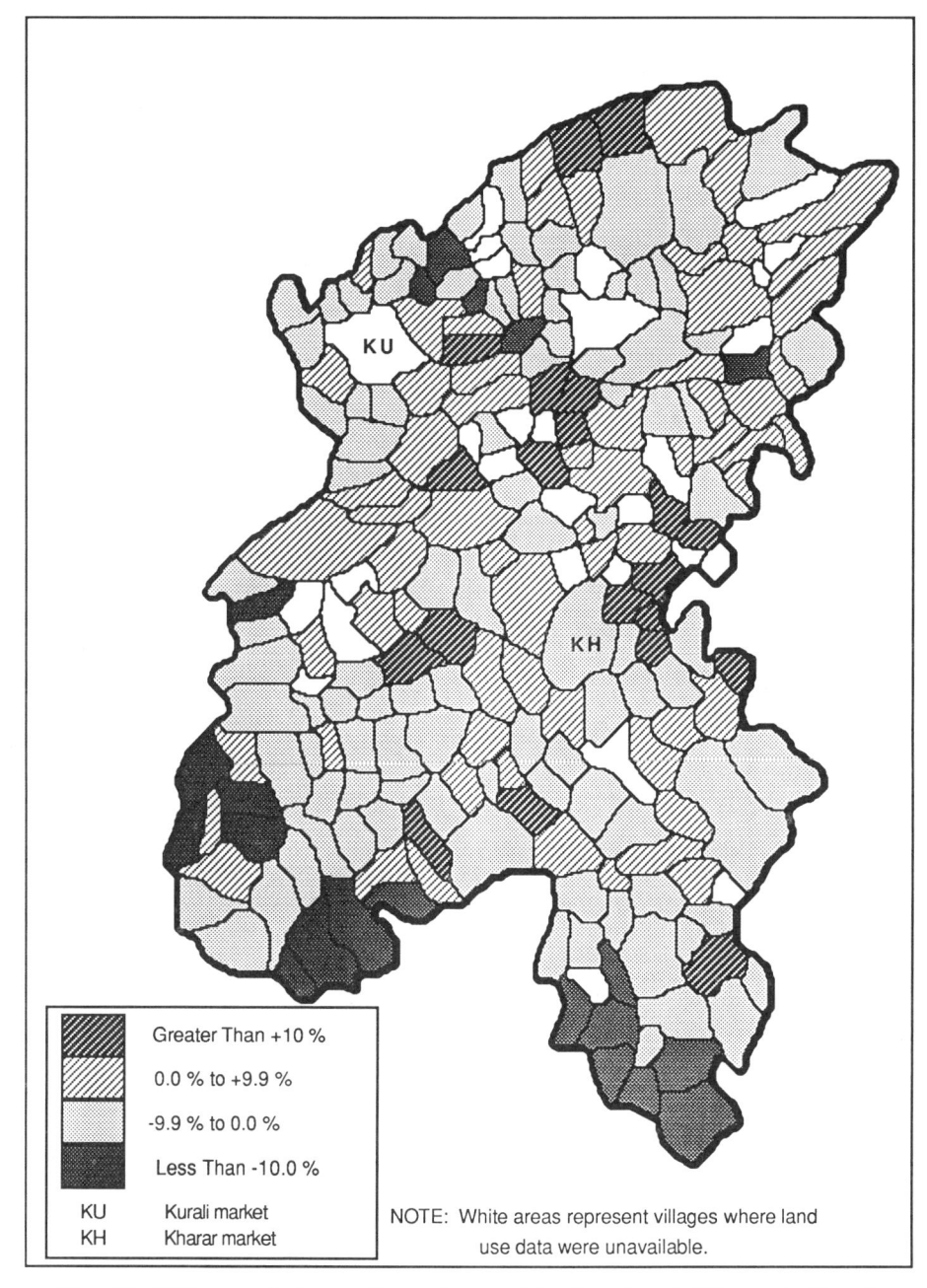

Fig. 35. *Difference between Percentages of Predicted and Observed: Cereals and Millets.*

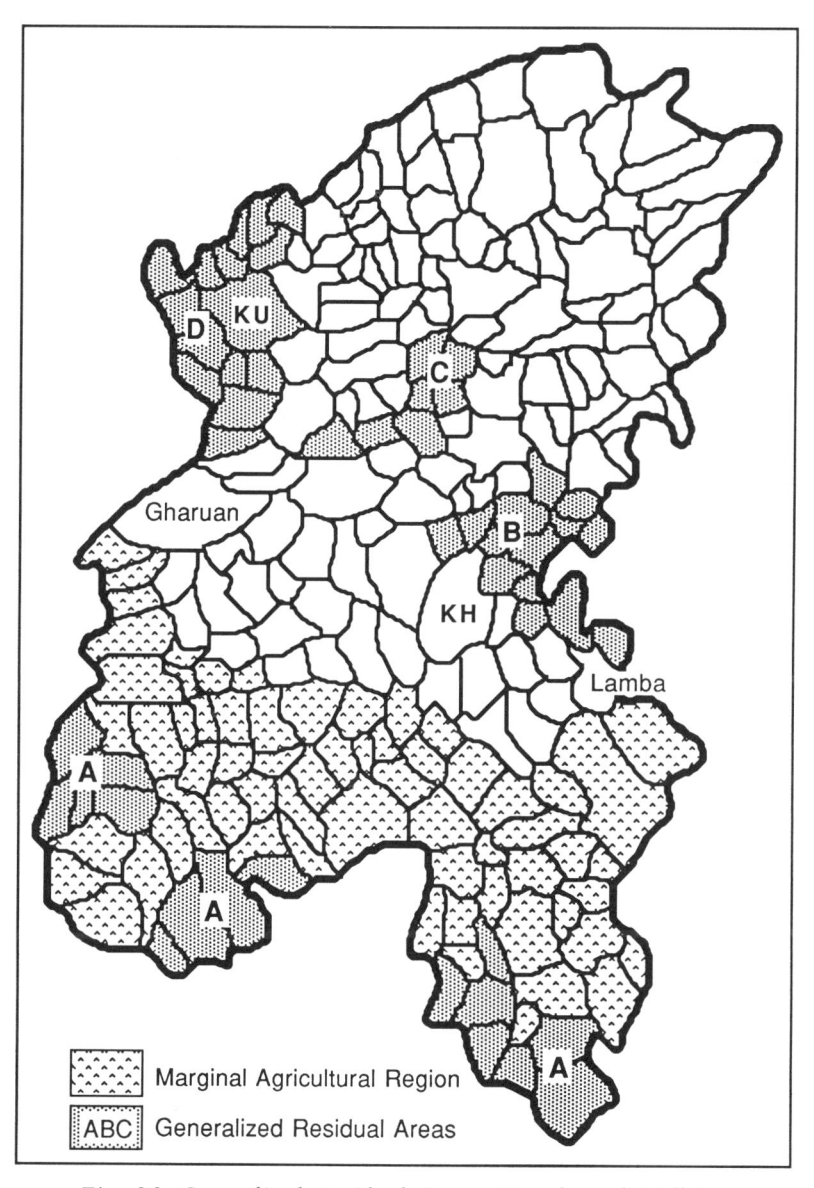

Fig. 36. Generalized Residual Areas: Cereals and Millets.

data concerning soils, depth of water table, and incidence of seasonal flooding, I concluded that these residuals were the byproduct of an unfavorable physical environment. In general, the area south of the villages Lamba in the east and Gharuan in the west is thought by local farmers to be among the poorest agricultural regions in the tehsil (figure 36). Prior to the partitioning of India in 1947, the southwest portion of the study area was dominated by Muslim farmers and artisans. This is another indication of unfavorable natural conditions, for in this region the Muslims traditionally occupied the most marginal agricultural lands. Among the environmental constraints that plague the region, lack of water is a major limiting factor. In some areas the water table lies over 200' beneath the surface. As a result, the majority of cultivated land throughout the region remains unirrigated.

Faced with such unfavorable environmental conditions, a peasant farmer is less concerned with market demand than with meeting his household sustenance requirements. Accordingly, his agricultural land-use patterns will be dominated by subsistence food crops and the least risky market crops. It is not surprising, therefore, that nearly 90% of the TCA in many villages in this southern region is devoted to the cultivation of cereals and millets. This contention is supported by the fact that the few scattered villages containing relatively high underpredictions outside this southern region are also located in marginal natural environments. These villages, along with other areas of underprediction in the north, are situated on the floodplains of the Siswan Nadi and Bhudh bi Nadi. These two intermittent rivers are responsible for eroding large tracts of land in this northern region (figure 20).

In analyzing the patterns of relatively high overprediction, one is compelled to examine simultaneously the areal distribution of significant underpredictions on the fruits and vegetables residual map (figure 37). In comparing the two maps, one can readily see that the extreme eastern portion of the fruits and vegetable map contains a cluster of relatively large negative residuals, or areas of significant underprediction. In contrast, this same general area on the cereals and millets map is dominated by numerous relatively large positive residuals, or areas of significant overprediction. In both cases, the somewhat poor fit between the predicted and observed values can be attributed to the impact of Chandigarh. As discussed in chapter 4, Chandigarh's main influence on the agricultural land-use patterns of Kharar tehsil is mainly confined to two areas: fruit and vegetable production and commercial dairying. Since cereals and millets command the largest proportion of TCA, it is not surprising to find that the extra land given over to fruit and vegetable cultivation would come from this crop type.

The withdrawal of land from cereal and millet production, however, is fueled not only by the large urban demand for fresh fruits and vegetables but also by the barriers to movement of wheat and paddy into the Union

THE STUDY AREA AND RESEARCH METHODOLOGY 111

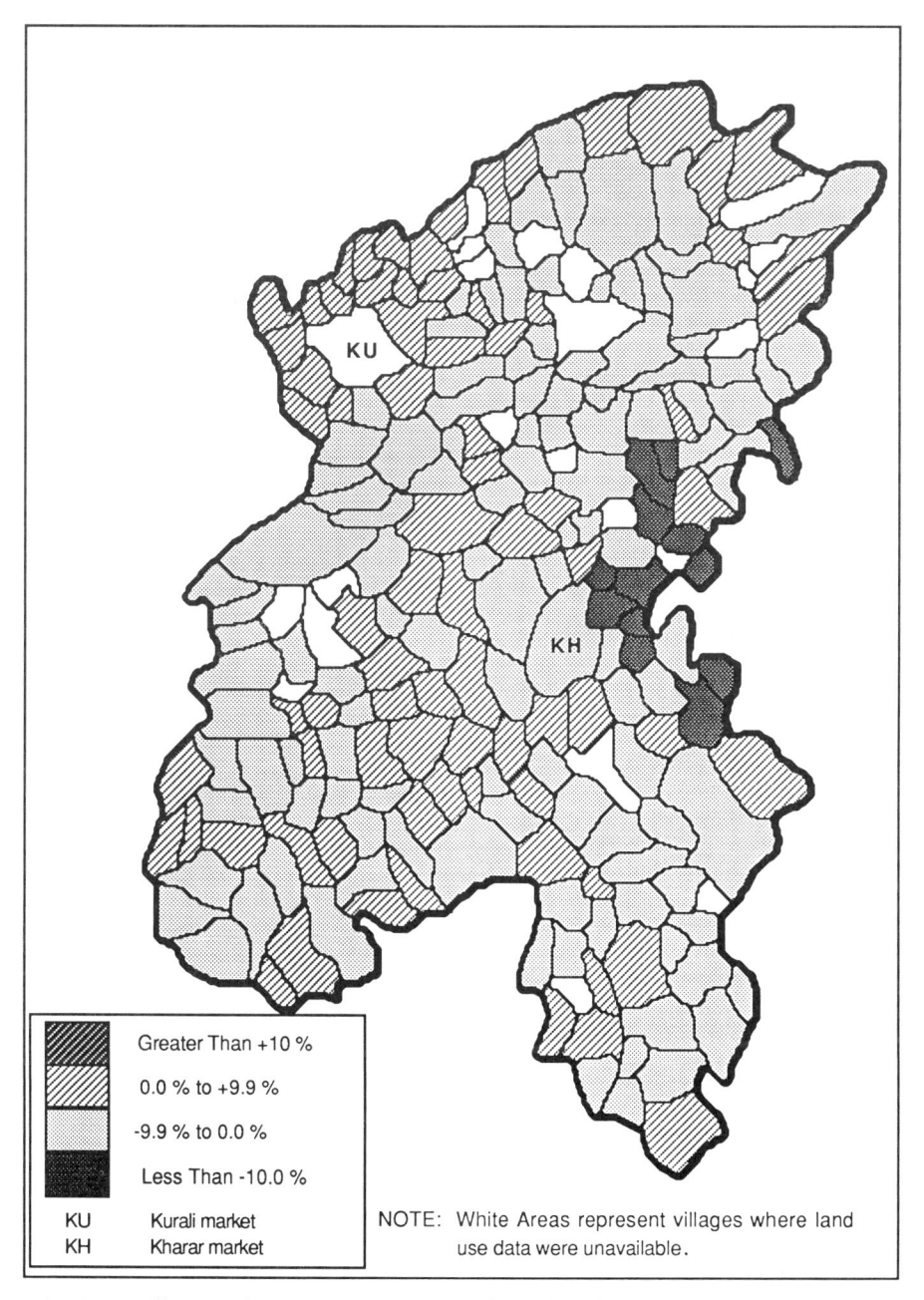

Fig. 37. Difference between Percentages of Predicted and Observed: Fruits and Vegetables.

112 UNDERSTANDING PEASANT AGRICULTURE

Territory. One could speculate that if the interstate trade of paddy were allowed, then the percentage of land devoted to the cereals and millets crop type in the region of Chandigarh would be significantly larger.

A second cluster of villages for which the model has overallocated a sizable percentage of land to cereal and millet is located on the border of the two market areas (area C, figure 38). This area of overprediction results both from the destination constraint incorporated into the model and from the influence, once again, of Chandigarh. As far as the model is concerned, the amount of land under fruit and vegetable cultivation in the market area of Kurali is related to the level of demand for these crops in Kurali, and not elsewhere. Therefore, owing to the steep distance decay parameter associated with fruits and vegetables ($-\beta^k = -0.80$), the model will allocate a larger percentage of the TCA to fruit and vegetable cultivation in those villages immediately surrounding Kurali. Given that the real market demand for fruits and vegetables is located in Chandigarh, however, it is not surprising to discover that the actual intensity of cultivation increases as one moves eastward, away from Kurali (figure 37). Consequently, this area of overprediction greater than 10%, along with other smaller positive residuals in the eastern region, is the result of land being diverted from cereal and millet production to fruit and vegetable cultivation (figures 35 and 37). In contrast, the general area of slight underprediction adjacent to Kurali (area D) is due to the model assigning fruits and vegetables to land actually occupied by three of the other four crop types (fruits and vegetables, pulses, and cotton).

The other scattered areas of significant overprediction can be attributed to localized environmental factors. This was discovered by noticing that, for each of these remaining villages of overprediction on the cereal and millet map, the corresponding village on the pulses map contained a slight underprediction (figures 35 and 39). Interviews with farmers in each of these villages revealed that the soil is particularly well suited for the cultivation of pulses such as lentils (*Lens esculenta* Moench.) and field peas (*Pisum arvense* L.); therefore farmers were devoting a relatively large proportion of land to their cultivation.

Residual Pattern Analysis: Fruits and Vegetables

One of Chandigarh's major impacts on the agricultural land-use patterns in Kharar tehsil concerns the cultivation of fruits and vegetables. This influence comes into sharper focus by examining, in more detail, the patterns of residuals in figures 34 and 37. As figure 37 illustrates, unlike the cereal and millet map, there is only one cluster of significantly large residuals. This one cluster, located in the extreme eastern portion of the study area, contains positive residuals greater than 10%. In other words, in these villages nearest to Chandigarh, the model has allocated a smaller percentage

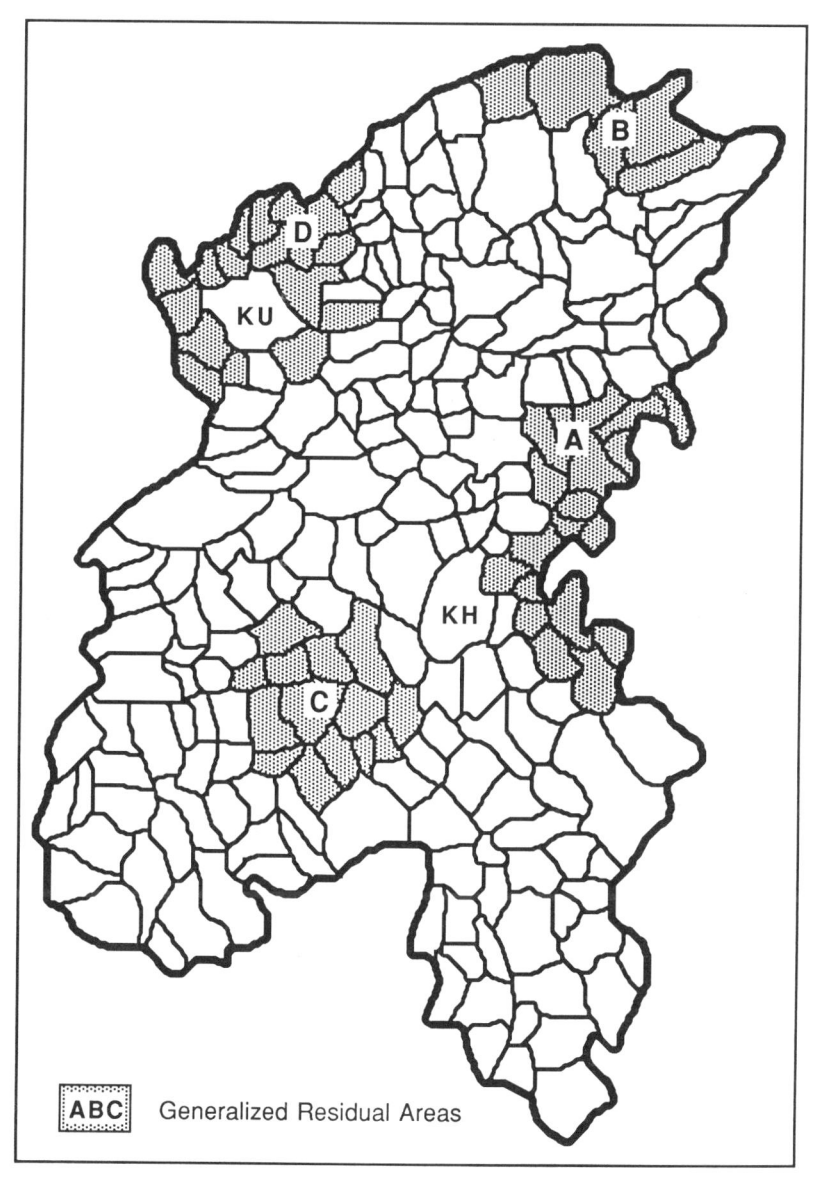

Fig. 38. Generalized Residual Areas: Fruits and Vegetables.

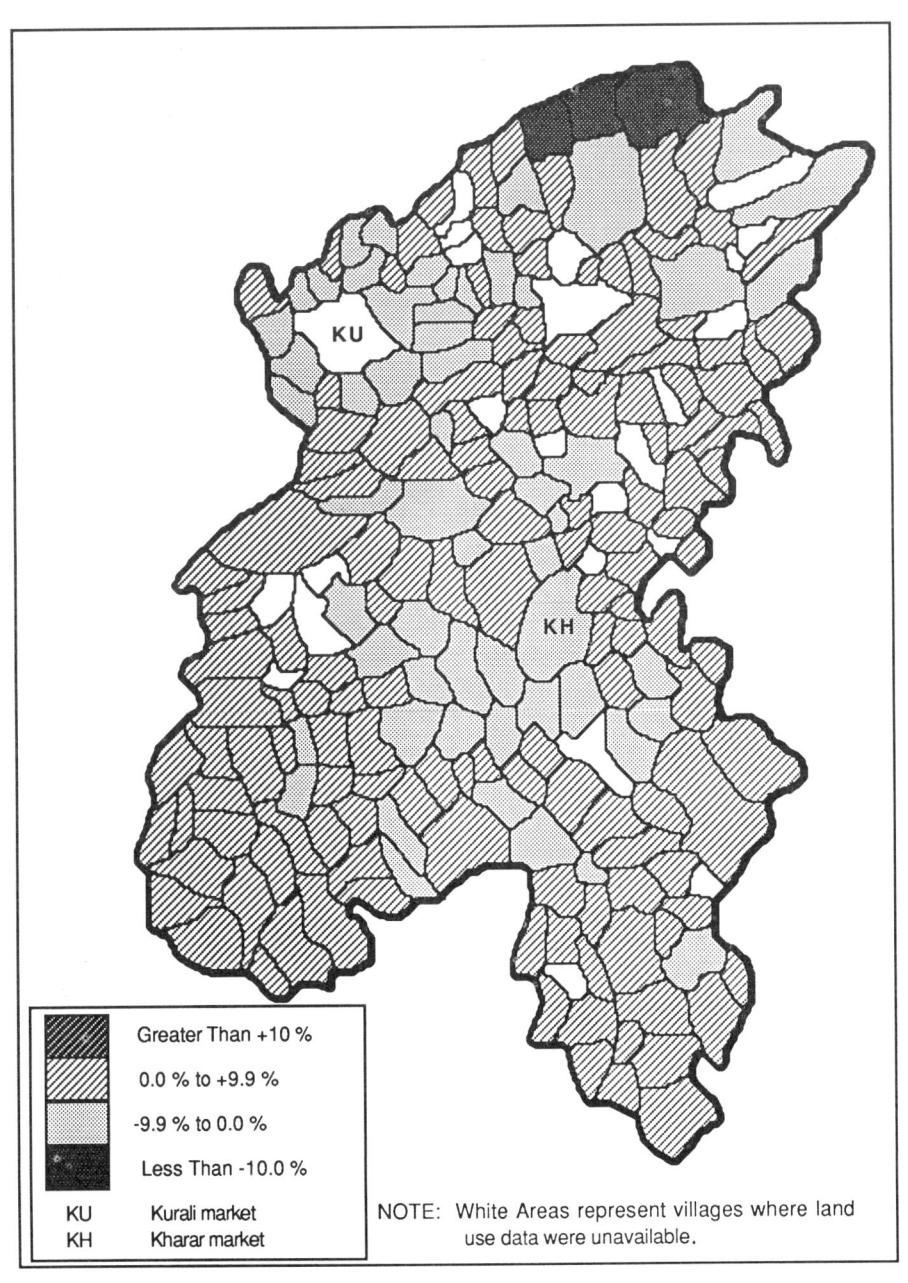

Fig. 39. Difference between Percentages of Predicted and Observed: Pulses.

of land to the cultivation of fruits and vegetables than their actual land-use patterns contain (area A, figure 38).

If one examines the spatial patterns of villages where the difference between the predicted and observed values reflects more than 5% of the TCA of a village, then the influence of Chandigarh on fruit and vegetable cultivation in the study region appears to be more extensive. As figure 34 demonstrates, the affected area extends further west. As one would suspect, this western extension of greater-than-predicted fruit and vegetable cultivation is located along two of the major feeder roadways into Chandigarh (figure 24). Further analysis of the patterns of residuals on the fruit and vegetable map reveals the existence of three areas of minor overprediction (areas B,C, and D, figure 38). Areas B and C can be attributed to localized environmental conditions that prevent the extensive cultivation of fruits and vegetables. The most limiting environmental constraint in both areas is the extreme depth of the water table and lack of adequate groundwater supplies. Given the general semiarid condition of the study region, it is impossible to undertake large-scale fruit and vegetable production without adequate, and economically feasible, supplies of irrigation water. As discussed in the preceding section, the remaining cluster of marginal overprediction, area D, results from the model's assumption that the production of fruits and vegetables in the study region is in response to the market demand of Kurali. On the basis of this assumption, and the steep distance decay parameter ($-\beta^k = -0.80$) assigned to this crop type, the model allocated a large percentage of the TCA of the villages immediately adjacent to Kurali to fruits and vegetables. Because the actual concentration of cultivation is located in the easternmost region of the market area, one would expect to find an area of overprediction surrounding Kurali.

One last feature of the fruit and vegetable map worth noting concerns the widespread marginal underprediction of fruits and vegetables throughout much of the study area. This extensive distribution of small negative residuals is related to the cultivation of potatoes in the test site. As mentioned earlier, for the most part the cultivation of potatoes is undertaken on a contract basis. A dealer will come to a village and contract for a certain number of hectares to be devoted to potatoes. A price per quintal is agreed upon at the time of sowing and the merchant is responsible for supplying all transportation and labor at the time of harvest. Even when a farmer plants potatoes upon his own initiative, he will more often than not end up selling his produce to a dealer in the village at the time of harvest. Once again he will not be directly responsible for transportation or labor costs. Under such marketing arrangements, distance from the market does not play an important factor in the land-use decision-making process of the farmer. In contrast to other vegetables, one therefore finds a more equal distribution of potatoes cultivation through the region, with site rather than situation characteristics being the greatest locational factor.

Residual Pattern Analysis: Pulses

Three distinctive features of the residual patterns (figure 39) associated with the pulses crop type have already been discussed in preceding sections. These three features include: (1) the area of slight underprediction surrounding Kurali (area D, figure 40) that is the result of a localized overallocation of land by the model to fruits and vegetables (area D, figure 38); (2) the several villages in the northernmost portion of the study area (area C, figure 40) that contain values of underprediction greater than 10% (figure 39) owing to localized soil conditions favoring the production of pulses; and (3) the area south of a line drawn between Lamba and Gharuan villages that is dominated by marginal overprediction, the result of the predominance of subsistence cereal crops in the region (figure 36).

Upon closer examination of the generalized patterns of residuals, however, one notices that the southern area of marginal overprediction extends northward along the extreme eastern and western portions of the study area (area A and B, figure 40). Both extensions are related to the cultivation of crops not included in the test case. In the east, the excluded crops that play a role in the formation of a generalized area of overprediction are the green fodder crops utilized by commercial dairy farmers. Three of the most common fodder crops of the region are: Egyptian clover, *jowar*, and *bajra*. As figure 26 confirms, the eastern area of overprediction corresponds to the generalized location of farming households supplying fresh milk to Chandigarh. Likewise, the western area of overprediction falls within the same general region of intensive sugarcane cultivation (figure 41). Sugarcane, like the green fodder crops, was not incorporated into the model for reasons discussed in chapter 4.

Residual Pattern Analysis: Oilseeds

The pattern of residuals on the oilseeds map is very similar to that associated with pulses. The southern third of the study area is marked by a predominance of slight overprediction (figure 42). Even more so than is the case with pulses, lands that would otherwise be turned over to oilseed cultivation have been given over to wheat and to paddy whenever adequate water supplies exist. The same general pattern of positive residuals extending along the eastern and western borders of the study area on the pulses map can also be found on the oilseeds map (areas A and B, figures 40 and 43). Here, once again, the formation of these positive residual patterns results from not incorporating fodder and sugarcane into the model.

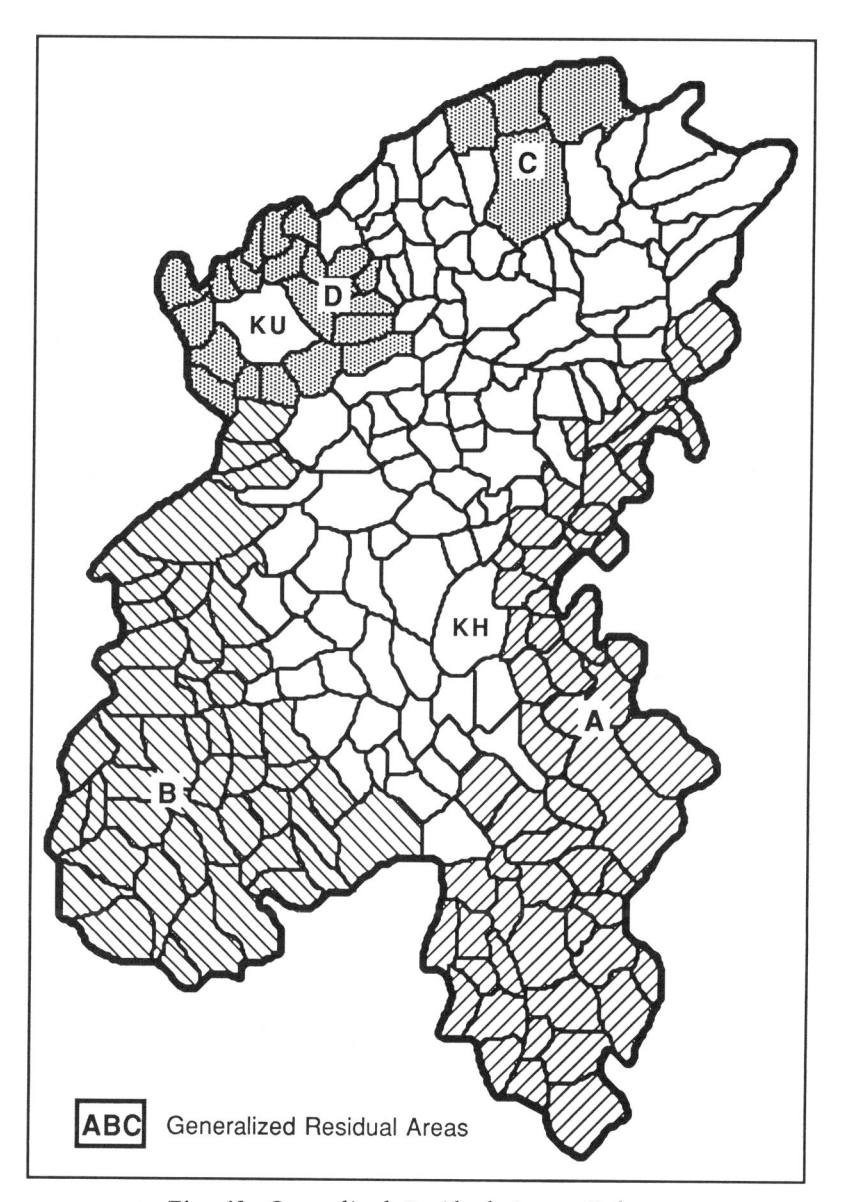

Fig. 40. Generalized Residual Areas: Pulses.

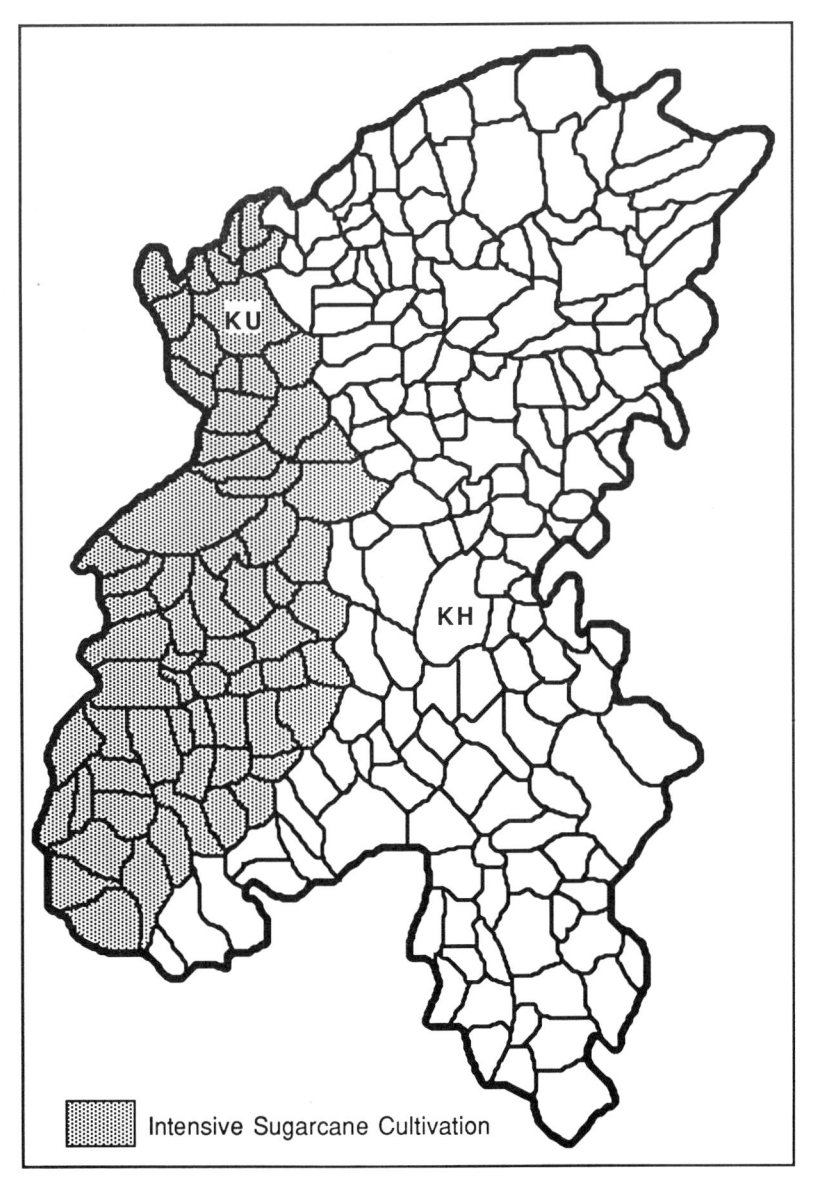

Fig. 41. Generalized Area of Intensive Sugarcane Cultivation, 1982.
SOURCE: Field survey, 1982.

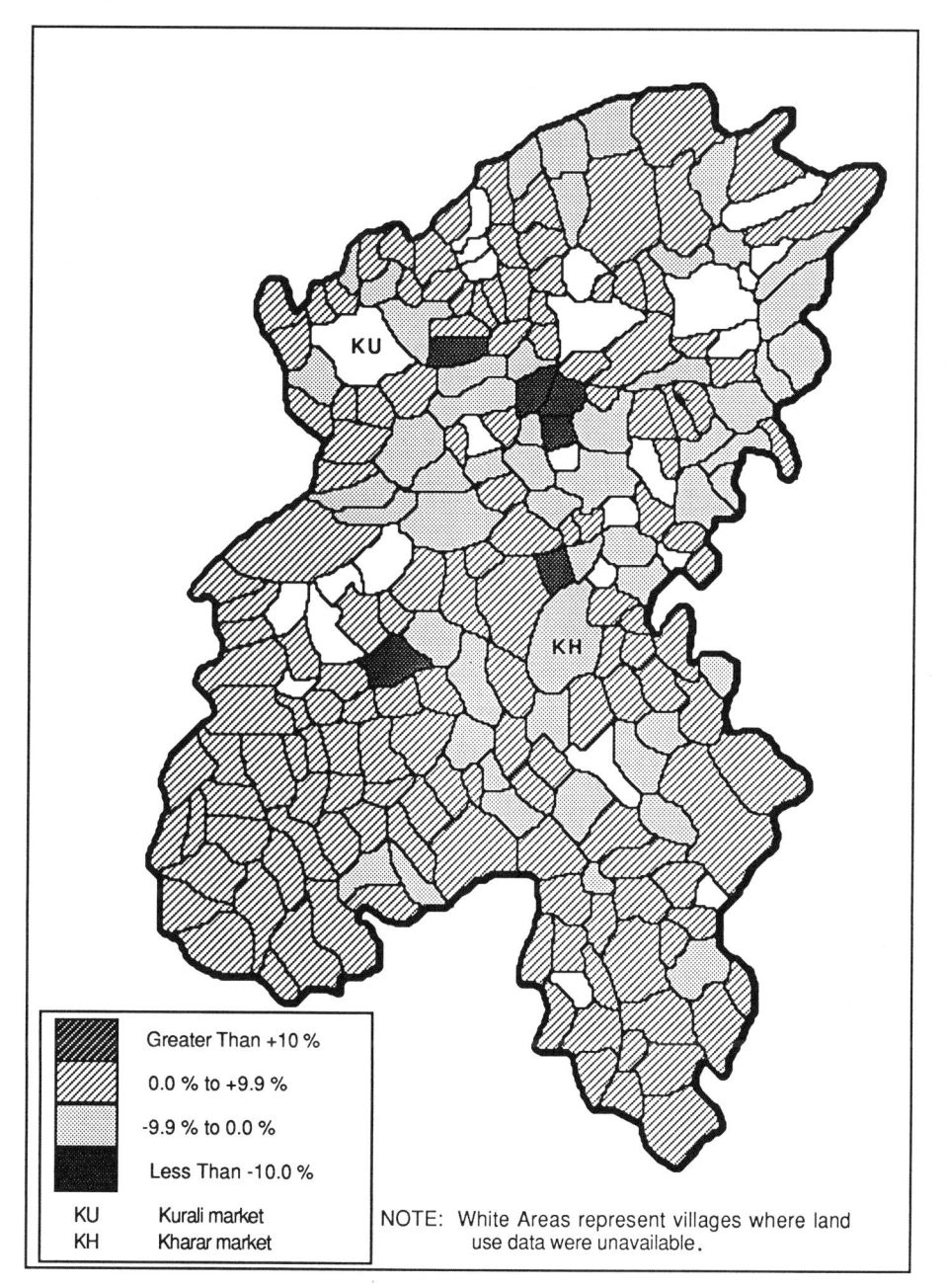

Fig. 42. *Difference between Percentages of Predicted and Observed: Oilseeds.*

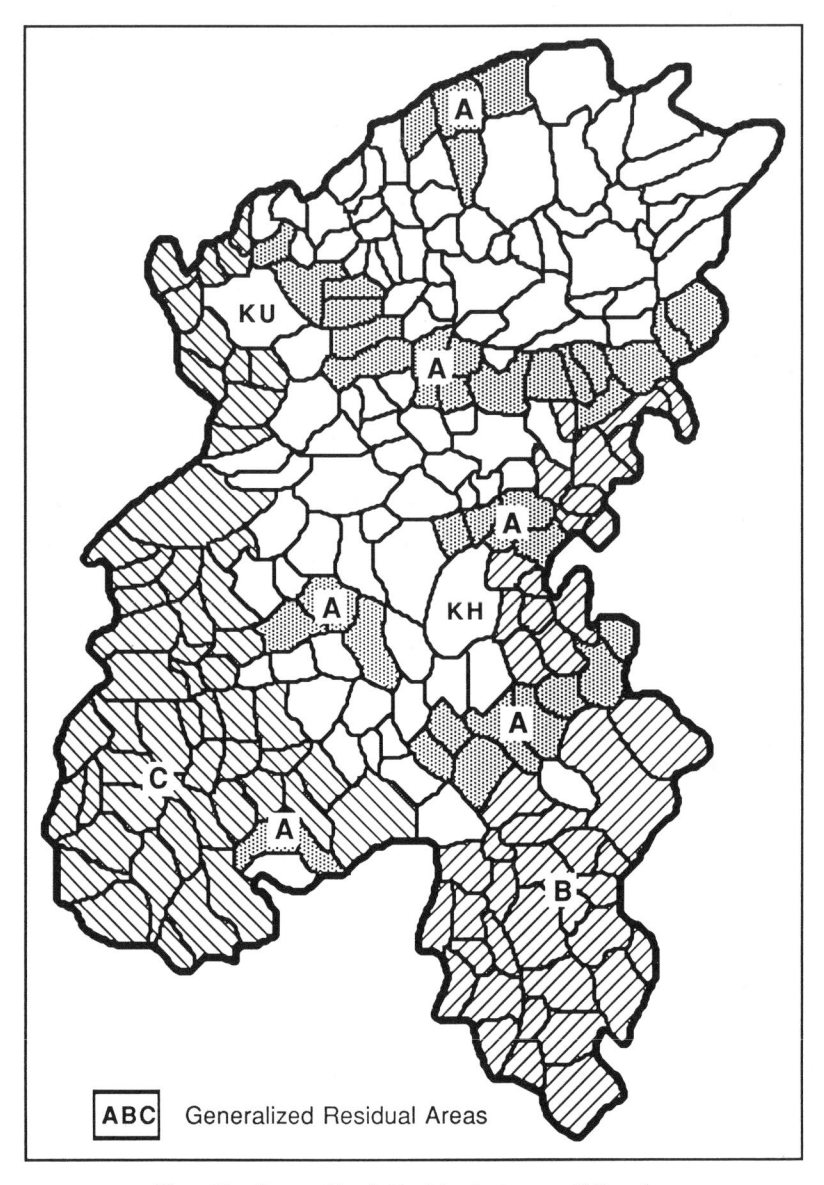

Fig. 43. Generalized Residual Areas: Oilseeds.

The major difference between the two maps lies within the areas of the intermittent rivers (figure 20). In these areas, where sandy soils dominate, the land devoted to pulses has consistently been overpredicted by the model (figures 20 and 39). This soil type is well suited for the cultivation not of pulses, but of groundnuts, the major oilseed of this region. Accordingly, in these villages susceptible to seasonal flooding, one finds the largest negative residuals associated with the oilseed crop type (figures 20 and 43).

Residual Pattern Analysis: Cotton

Although several general spatial patterns of residuals are evident on the cotton map (figure 44), one must be reminded of how small their values are (Appendix B). In fact, only 4% of the total number of residuals account for more than 5% of the TCA of their respective villages (figure 32). In this light, the three general areas of small overprediction that appear on the residual map are not overwhelmingly significant; nevertheless they do highlight two underlying contrasts that have not been incorporated into the model (areas A, B, and C, figure 45). Areas A and C can be attributed to environmental constraints, whereas area B is related to the influence once again of Chandigarh. The soils in area A contain a relatively high clay content, and this, coupled with the fact that the water table is not prohibitively deep, makes the area suitable for paddy cultivation. Although these physical features are not particularly restrictive to the cultivation of cotton, the choice goes to paddy because of its greater profitability. Whereas the environment is not necessarily a limiting condition in area A, this appears to be the case in area C. In this area, which is located along the Siswan Nadi (figure 20), the extremely sandy soils prohibit the widespread cultivation of cotton. Oilseeds are the major nonfood cash crops grown under these physical conditions (figure 42).

Unlike in areas A and C, the natural environment does not play a major role leading to the existence of numerous minor positive residuals in area B (figure 45). On the contrary, here the more profitable cash crops of fruits and vegetables have diverted production away from cotton.

The existence of a large number of small negative residuals is due to the fairly steep distance-deterrence parameter ($-\beta^k = -0.30$) assigned to cotton. One must keep in mind, however, that the size of these residuals is extremely small.

Summary

The procedure that was followed to operationalize and calibrate the maximum-likelihood model utilized in this test case involves, first, the transformation of the standard fully constrained equation of a maximum-likelihood model (equation 9) into a more appropriate form for agricultural

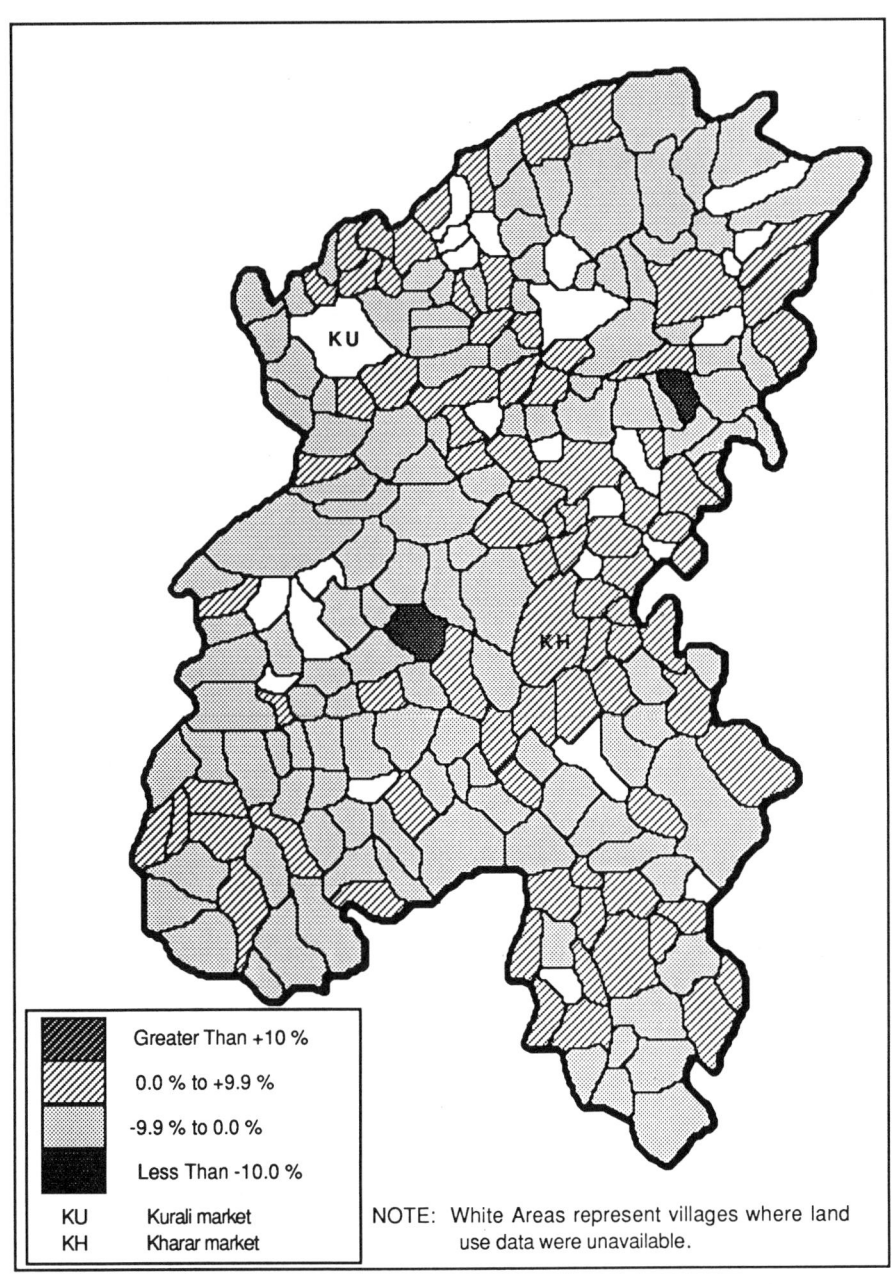

Fig. 44. Difference between Percentages of Predicted and Observed: Cotton.

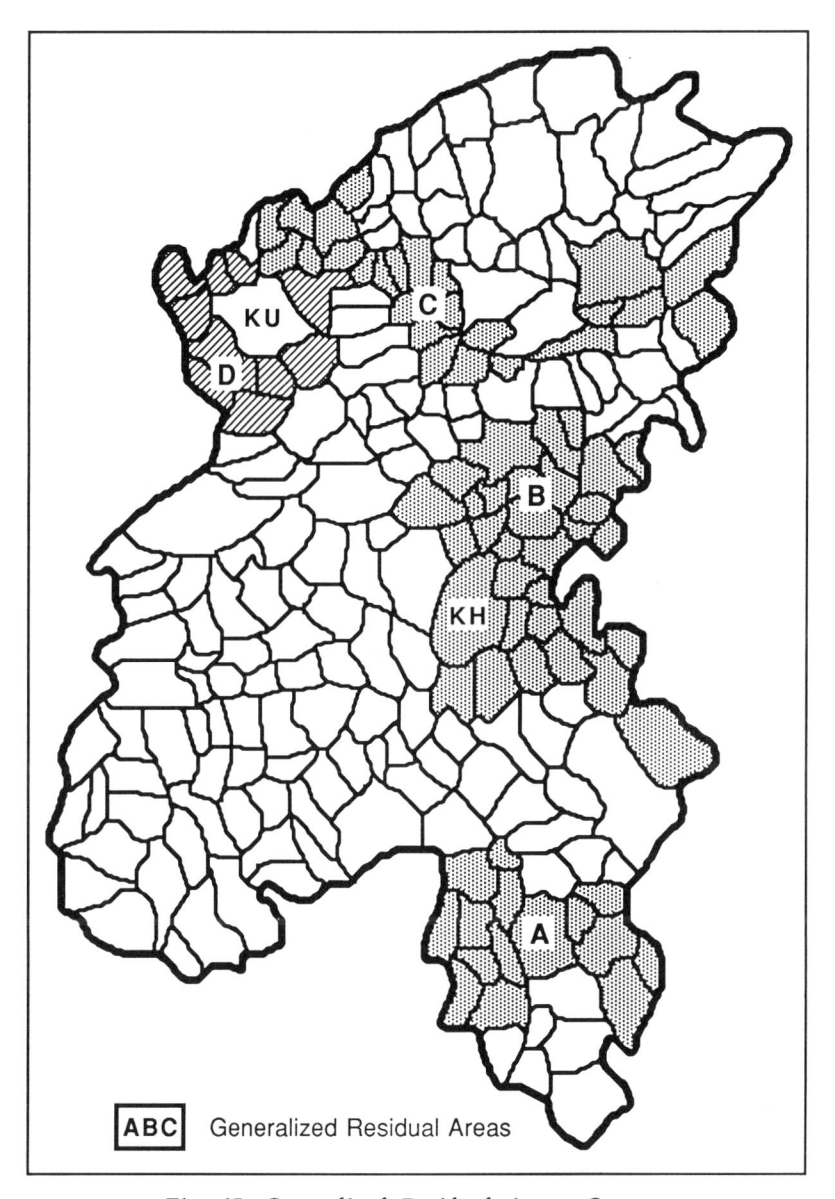

Fig. 45. Generalized Residual Areas: Cotton.

land-use modeling. One such equation with its own specific D_j^k and $-\beta^k$ values is required for each crop type associated with the test case. Second, the cost matrix, c_{ij}, remains constant between crop types, therefore representing a distance matrix. The market demand component of the equation, D_j^k, is derived by setting it equal to the total number of hectares devoted to each crop type. In selecting the initial set of distance-deterrence parameters, $-\beta^k$, perishability, transportation costs, and degree of market orientation were all taken into account.

Calibration of the model involves deciding which goodness-of-fit statistic to use in estimating the most appropriate distance-deterrence parameters, $-\beta^k$, for each crop type. Based on recent findings by Ayeni, the minimum information discrimination statistic (MDIS) appears to be the best statistic for parameter estimation.[15] As the results of the parameter estimation of the test case indicate, there are also problems associated with the use of MDIS. The problems encountered in the calibration of the test-case model are related to MDIS being too overly sensitive to the existence of either numerous small residuals or a few large residuals.

The benefits of analyzing the residual patterns of each crop type are twofold. First, as Baxter has pointed out, it may be possible to explain clusters of over- or underpredicted residuals "in terms of particular characteristics of a system's structure that may, in turn, increase understanding of that system."[16] Second, once a feature of the underlying system structure has been found to be related to the pattern of residuals, it may be utilized to recalibrate and improve the model. In the test case, three different aspects of the agricultural land-use system of the study area appear to be related to spatial distribution of the residuals. One causal factor underlying the patterns of over- and underprediction for all crop types is that quality of the natural environment varies significantly throughout the study area. An important initial assumption of the model is that both markets are located on a homogeneous agricultural plain. In that case, no village enjoys a site advantage over any other village in the study region. Analysis of the residuals has led us to discover, however, that soil, water table depth, and other environmental features vary widely throughout the study area. One could incorporate environmental variability into the model by assigning penalty values to the cost matrix for those villages located in marginal agricultural regions (e.g., adjacent to an intermittent river or in an area where the water table is extremely deep).

A second important influence on the agricultural land-use system of the study area is related to the impact of Chandigarh on fruit and vegetable

---

[15] Ayeni, "Algorithm 11."

[16] M. Baxter, "Estimation and Inference in Spatial Interaction Models," *Progress in Human Geography* (1983): 55.

cultivation and dairy farming. These two features could be incorporated into the model by: (1) including Chandigarh as a third market in the equation associated with fruits and vegetables, along with the appropriate changes in the cost matrix; and (2) incorporating fodder as a sixth crop type and once again including Chandigarh as the third and dominant market.

A third significant factor in the residual patterns associated with several crop types is the sizable percentage of the agricultural land devoted to the cultivation of sugarcane in the western region of the study area. Once again, modifications to the model would consist of incorporating sugarcane as an additional crop type and Morinda as a third market.

From the above discussion one can see how easy it is to incorporate modifications into a maximum-likelihood model without making the model overly complex. One word of caution, however, is warranted with regard to improved results based on the recalibration of the model. Significant improvement in the model's performance is not an appropriate test of importance for those factors discovered in the residual analysis. As Baxter has stated: "What is required is that many data sets be analyzed (or reanalyzed) in the manner suggested in order to identify the most important influences on aggregate trip distribution. The pervasiveness of such influences could then be tested on new data sets."[17] Accordingly, before the true merits of this test case can accurately be judged, the maximum-likelihood model developed in this monograph needs to be applied to other areas of peasant agricultural land use.

---

[17] Ibid., p. 55.

Chapter 6

TOWARD AN INTEGRATED APPROACH TO MODELING PEASANT AGRICULTURAL LAND USE

As far back as the eighteenth century, geographers and other social scientists have been concerned with modeling the areal distribution of agricultural production. This interest in agricultural land-use modeling remains, to this day, an active area of research among scholars in both geography and economics. Throughout its history, agricultural location theory has been dominated by two seemingly incompatible approaches: an older and more widely followed normative economic approach originally introduced, at least in a modeling sense, by von Thünen; and a more recent but rarely adopted probabilistic/behavioral approach.

There are various reasons for the apparently incongruent nature of the two approaches. One is that their initial assumptions seem to be in direct conflict. "Economic models treat decision-making as a parameter, whereas the behavioral explanations owe their existence to the variability of this factor."[1] Economic models of agricultural location assume that farmers are highly responsive to the demands of the market and, operating in a sphere of perfect information, make land-use decisions based solely upon the principles of profit maximization. As a result, agricultural land-use patterns are determined purely by economic factors, such as transportation costs and market prices. In contrast, behavioral models are founded upon the premise that there is often a significant differential response among farmers to actual or potential opportunities in the economic sphere. The degree to which farmers respond to economic stimuli, therefore, is largely determined by their sociopersonal characteristics, rather than economic forces. Proponents of the behavioral approach also believe that among peasant farmers, risk aversion, rather than profit maximization, is the norm.

---

[1] P.W.E. Hart, "Problems and Potentialities of the Behavioural Approach to Agricultural Location," pp. 102-103.

In addition to the actual construction of analytical models, many geographers have been concerned with the empirical testing of such models in various economic settings throughout the world. Although a large portion of this testing has taken place within predominantly peasant agricultural societies, no attempt has been made to build a location model specifically tailored to the characteristics of these less developed economies. As a result, land-use models from either tradition have had limited success in modeling the agricultural land-use patterns of peasant farmers. It was this apparent need for a more appropriate peasant agricultural land-use model that prompted this study. From its inception, the primary goal of this research effort has been to introduce a new approach to agricultural land-use modeling, one specifically designed to fit the characteristics of a peasant agricultural system.

I have argued in this monograph that peasant agricultural production landscapes are systems characterized by lack of information and dominated by uncertainty. Farmers in developing economies often possess minimal, if any, reliable information concerning market conditions and forces, and they know little about the production behavior of competitors, other than their fellow villagers. Under such conditions of minimum information, farmers practice mixed cropping to minimize risk. Systems governed by uncertainty are also characterized by a variety of individual behaviors. It is also true, however, that transportation costs play an important role in determining land-use patterns in peasant agricultural systems.

It is evident from the preceding discussion that both behavioral and economic forces greatly influence the patterns of agricultural land use found within less developed economies. Therefore, the construction of an appropriate peasant agricultural land-use model appears to require the selective integration of the economic and behavioral paradigms. An integrated approach to modeling peasant agricultural land use is one which incorporates a variety of risk-aversion behaviors, including mixed cropping, while at the same time recognizing the importance of, for example, transportation costs in the decision-making process of peasant farmers. On the basis of the favorable results of the test case presented in this monograph, a location model founded upon maximum-likelihood principles seems to offer a viable integrated approach to modeling peasant agricultural land use.

Possible Modifications and Further Testing of the Model

Despite the promising results of this initial test case, much work remains to be done. As stated earlier, this study is exploratory in nature, and further testing is required in a variety of settings before a valid judgment can be made concerning its usefulness as an integrated approach to agricultural land-use modeling. Before further testing of the model takes place,

however, I believe the performance of the model could be improved by incorporating one or more of the following recommendations:
1. A disaggregated land-use data base.
2. Examination of other families of spatial-deterrence functions.
3. Inclusion of an additional modal-split constraint to differentiate between the available means of transportation.
4. A more satisfactory method of calibrating the model.
5. Utilization of information gained through the analysis of residuals to reformulate the general maximum-likelihood equation.

In regard to the first suggestion, it should be useful to regroup the data, possibly according to the two main agricultural seasons of the region. Two main benefits may be realized by doing so. First, by regrouping the data according to agricultural season, crop types will be more homogeneous in regard to cost of production, degree of market orientation, and cost of transportation. In other words, as the groupings now stand, crops may be assigned to a general distance-deterrence parameter which is not well suited to their particular interaction space. Paddy, for example, has a significantly greater degree of market orientation and transportation cost than the other crops in the cereal and millet crop group. After the crop groupings have been refined, a more appropriate distance-deterrence function may be assigned. This in turn may result in a better fit between the predicted and observed land-use values. Second, reorganizing the land-use data by *kharif* and *rabi* cropping periods may bring out seasonal differences in the agricultural landscape of the region.

In reference to the second recommended modification, the *beta* functions utilized in this study were derived from Wilson's work concerning urban and regional modelling.[2] Other families of spatial-deterrence parameters, such as Weibull, Gamma, or Tanner functions, may be more appropriate to agricultural land-use applications of a maximum-likelihood model. Performance of the model also may be increased by assigning a different family of spatial-deterrence functions to each of the five crop groups (i.e., cereal and millet may be better represented by Gamma functions, whereas Tanner functions are more appropriate for fruits and vegetables).

As for the third modification, more accurate results might be achieved by including an additional modal-split constraint into each of the k maximum-likelihood equations utilized in a particular land-use model. These additional modal-split constraints will account for the various means of transportation being utilized by farmers of varying economic levels. The cost curve for a wealthy farmer who uses a tractor to transport his goods to

---

[2] Wilson, *Entropy in Urban and Regional Modelling.*

130 UNDERSTANDING PEASANT AGRICULTURE

market is significantly different from that of a poor farmer who must rely on his overworked bullocks. Incorporating such constraint would require the estimation of the percentage of farmers using each means of transportation. It should be noted that this percentage might vary between crop types, thereby requiring a unique modal-split constraint for each maximum-likelihood equation utilized in the model.

In regard to the fourth suggested modification, a finer calibration of the model could be achieved by employing an alternative best-fit statistic. As discussed in chapter 5, the statistic utilized in the calibration of the test-case model, the minimum information discrimination statistic (MDIS), appears to be overly sensitive to either a few large residual values or numerous insignificant ones. A problem associated with the use of MDIS is that the actual distribution of 2Ψ is not known, although it is thought to approximate chi-square distribution with $(m - 1)(n - 1)$ degrees of freedom.

As far as the fifth suggestion is concerned, a more accurate replication of the observed land-use patterns may be obtained by reformulating the general maximum-likelihood equation. From analysis of the residual patterns for each of the five crop groups, several possible modifications to the basic equation came to light. The important role the physical environment plays in the land-use decision-making process of peasant farmers was evident from the residual patterns associated with all five crop types. In order to incorporate this site characteristic, an environmental constraint could be programmed into the model by assigning a penalty cost to those villages situated within unfavorable environmental zones. These penalty costs would be incorporated into the distance metric (c_{ij} matrix) of the model.

In order to improve the fit between the modeled and observed values associated with the two crop types, fruits and vegetables, and cereal and millet, the city of Chandigarh could be added as a third market in the runs associated with these two crop types. The distance matrix mentioned above would also have to be modified to include the distance between Chandigarh *mandi* and all 207 villages in the study area.

To achieve a better fit between the predicted and observed values associated with the three remaining crop groups—pulses, oilseeds, and cotton—two of the crops excluded from the test case should be incorporated into the model. Doing so would involve formulating two additional maximum-likelihood equations, each with its own specific spatial-deterrence parameter. The inclusion of fodder as a crop type would inevitably improve the fit on the eastern side of the study area, whereas the addition of sugarcane would undoubtedly reduce the number and size of the residuals on the western portion of the test site.

It should be noted that incorporating one or all of these five modifications will increase the data requirements and equational complexity of the model. Neither of these two outcomes may be desirable given that two of the main advantages of utilizing a maximum-likelihood approach to model agricultural land use are its unsophisticated nature and minimal data requirements.

Potential Planning Applications of the Model

The notable similarity between the "most likely" and observed agricultural landscape in the study region indicates the model's potential usefulness as a planning tool in less developed economies. Two of the more useful planning applications are : (1) the model's ability to predict what changes are most likely to occur in land-use patterns as a result of induced change; and (2) the manner in which the model can be used to identify barriers to agricultural development.

In regard to the first planning application, one could determine the most likely effects of changing the transportation or marketing system of a region. This could be accomplished by simply altering the distance-cost matrix of the model or, as discussed in the previous section, adding an additional agricultural market to the general maximum-likelihood formula. Given that the maximum-likelihood formulation lends itself to the inclusion of additional information concerning the characteristics of the system, the benefits and negative impacts of various forms of induced change can be readily analyzed.

The second planning application—identification of barriers to agricultural development—can be accomplished by an in-depth analysis of the spatial patterns of the residuals between the predicted and observed agricultural landscapes of the study area. Within the test site several environmental, political, and economic obstacles to development (e.g, scarcity of water, soil quality, trade restrictions, and high cost of agricultural inputs) were identified as a result of such an analysis. After the barriers have been identified, more appropriate development strategies can be formulated to foster economic growth.

I would like to conclude by issuing a call for further empirical testing of this integrated approach to modeling peasant agricultural land use. Based on the promising results of this initial test case, additional testing will not only aid in judging the usefulness of such an approach as a planning tool, but also promises to shed further light on the factors which affect a peasant farmer's agricultural decision-making process.

Appendix A

MARKETING AND LAND-USE QUESTIONNAIRE

I. Sample Information
   1. Interview no.
   2. Date
   3. Time taken
   4. Interviewers
II. Personal Information
   1. Village
   2. Age
   3. Education
   4. Caste
   5. Religion
   6. Family
      a. Relation to interviewee
      b. Age
      c. Education
      d. Occupation
      e. Employer
      f. Location of employer
III. Land-Use and Marketing Information
   1. Land
      a. Owned
      b. Rented (cash/kind)
      c. *Bataai*
   2. Amount irrigated
   3. Type of irrigation
   4. Tractor ownership
      a. Date
      b. Cost
      c. Location

        d. Origin of funds
    5. Milch livestock, buffaloes, and dairy cows
        a. Number
        b. Domestic/foreign/crossbred
        c. Cost
        d. Location
        e. Origin of funds
    6. Commercial dairying
        a. Date
        b. Quantity sold/day
        c. Location
        d. Means of transportation
    7. Perceived market demand for milk
    8. Fodder crops
    9. Oilseeds
        a. Type
        b. Use
    10. Pulses
    11. Soil test
        a. Date
        b. Location
        c. Collected by
    12. Factors that determine the farmer's cropping pattern (i.e., what determines which crops are grown and how much land is devoted to each crop)
    13. Agricultural produce dealer (*Arhtiya*)
        a. Name
        b. Location
        c. Type of produce
    14. Reasons for selling to the above mentioned dealer(s)
    15. Produce purchased by the dealers in the village itself
        a. Type of produce
        b. *Mandi* selling price
        c. Village selling price
    16. Estimated shipping cost perceived by the farmer
        a. Type of produce
        b. Cost
    17. Farmer's "measurement" of distance
    18. Additional notes and observations
IV. Farmer's opinion on which of the following programs/policies the government should concentrate their time and resources on in order to best help the farmers
    1. Increased subsidy of fertilizers (cheaper fertilizers)

2. Set support price at time of sowing
   3. Set support price at time of harvest
   4. Promote free trade
   5. Strengthen trade barriers
   6. Replace *arhtiyas* with government dealers
   7. Additional irrigation facilities
   8. Increase supply of herbicides and insecticides
   9. Lower electricity rates and increased availability
  10. Soil and water testing
  11. Lower rates and greater supply of HYV seeds
  12. Education program for the farmers
  13. Lower rates and greater supply of diesel fuel
  14. Construction and repair of feeder roads
  15. Higher support prices

V. Crops Grown and Their Market Destinations (*Kharif*).

Crop	Amt. land	Qty prod	% sold	Irrig./ unirrig.	Market	Trans. medium	Pay % cash	Selling price	Mkt demand lim./unlim.
Rice									
Jowar									
Bajra									
Maize									
Maize/ pulse									
Pulses									
Sugarcane									
Cotton									
Oilseeds									
Fodder									
Fruits									
Vegetables									
Other									

136 UNDERSTANDING PEASANT AGRICULTURE

VI. Crops Grown and Their Market Destinations (*Rabi*).

Crop	Amt. land	Qty prod	% sold	Irrig./ unirrig.	Market	Trans. medium	Pay % cash	Selling price	Mkt demand lim./unlim.
Wheat									
Barley									
Gram									
Wheat-gram									
Barley-gram									
Barley-pulse									
Pulses									
Oilseeds									
Fodder									
Fruits									
Vegetables									
Other									

Appendix B

DIFFERENCE MATRICES OF PREDICTED AND OBSERVED LAND USE

Cereals and Millets

Village I.D. (Hadbast no.)	Percentage of Total Cropped Area		Residual (Predicted minus observed)
	Predicted	Observed	
1	81.72	85.64	-3.92
2	81.72	88.06	-6.34
7	85.85	95.14	-9.29
21	87.55	82.89	4.66
25	88.17	66.21	21.95
26	87.61	79.01	8.60
27	86.61	87.64	-1.03
28	84.38	70.21	14.17
29	84.38	69.31	15.07
30	86.60	34.68	51.92
31	84.38	42.04	42.34
32	86.61	87.70	-1.09
33	86.61	89.18	-2.58
34	86.56	78.37	8.18
35	84.51	86.46	-1.94
36	86.74	83.06	3.68
37	87.79	90.82	-3.03
38	87.09	85.63	1.46
39	85.85	83.51	2.34
40	86.74	94.60	-7.86
41	88.34	84.37	3.97
42	85.85	89.16	-3.31
43	85.69	90.90	-5.22
44	85.85	86.77	-0.92
45	86.74	84.77	1.97

138 UNDERSTANDING PEASANT AGRICULTURE

Village I.D. (Hadbast no.)	Percentage of Total Cropped Area		Residual (Predicted minus observed)
	Predicted	Observed	
46	87.78	92.30	-4.52
47	87.44	75.22	12.22
48	86.80	91.17	-4.37
49	87.78	87.12	0.67
50	84.58	86.28	-1.70
51	87.44	90.83	-3.39
52	85.85	88.77	-2.92
53	86.00	92.79	-6.79
54	85.13	86.87	-1.74
55	86.80	90.09	-3.29
56	86.80	89.85	-3.05
57	83.87	69.10	14.77
58	83.43	77.89	5.54
59	80.44	92.24	-11.80
60	81.72	77.98	3.73
61	77.03	87.29	-10.26
62	80.26	94.79	-14.53
63	80.43	87.20	-6.77
63	75.87	91.02	-15.15
69	87.07	83.09	3.97
70	87.70	70.84	16.85
71	86.61	82.87	3.74
72	87.65	65.35	22.30
73	87.32	81.25	6.08
74	86.47	88.84	-2.37
75	84.37	85.62	-1.24
76	84.14	79.72	4.42
77	86.04	89.88	-3.84
78	84.37	81.92	2.45
79	87.32	81.81	5.51
80	86.47	87.25	-0.78
81	87.32	77.86	9.46
82	87.87	74.05	13.82
84	87.46	77.96	9.50
85	86.04	78.37	7.67
86	84.01	81.57	2.44
87	84.05	87.80	-3.75
88	84.87	79.28	5.58
89	85.85	72.05	13.80
90	87.41	71.42	15.99
92	87.80	75.00	12.80
93	86.74	80.44	6.29
94	87.61	88.44	-0.83
95	86.74	77.40	9.33

APPENDIX B 139

Village I.D. (Hadbast no.)	Percentage of Total Cropped Area		Residual (Predicted minus observed)
	Predicted	Observed	
96	86.31	78.04	8.27
97	87.36	75.86	11.51
98	87.78	84.71	3.08
99	87.36	78.87	8.50
100	87.37	89.88	-2.52
102	87.44	84.27	3.18
103	85.28	70.99	14.30
104	84.28	86.86	-2.58
105	84.28	88.88	-4.60
106	85.14	74.15	10.98
107	84.50	78.90	5.60
108	86.49	83.16	3.33
109	85.05	77.85	7.20
110	84.00	78.16	5.84
111	83.29	84.00	-0.71
112	85.82	88.96	-3.14
113	84.40	92.20	-7.80
114	84.50	88.20	-3.70
115	83.81	83.63	0.18
116	82.88	89.16	-6.28
117	83.47	91.19	-7.72
119	83.30	88.78	-5.48
120	82.03	86.56	-4.53
122	81.53	89.88	-8.36
123	83.30	81.63	1.67
125	83.30	87.75	-4.45
126	82.88	87.69	-4.80
127	81.53	95.29	-13.76
128	81.53	77.85	3.68
129	83.09	86.30	-3.20
130	82.88	96.95	-14.06
133	83.93	83.60	0.33
134	83.33	83.69	-0.36
135	83.89	85.96	-2.07
136	82.78	80.22	2.56
137	83.89	94.31	-10.42
138	82.03	88.31	-6.27
139	81.27	84.12	-2.85
140	82.19	87.82	-5.63
141	79.48	76.47	3.02
142	77.30	78.76	-1.46
144	80.26	87.80	-7.54
145	81.22	86.95	-5.73
146	79.17	76.47	2.70

Village I.D.	Percentage of Total Cropped Area		Residual
(*Hadbast* no.)	Predicted	Observed	(Predicted minus observed)
147	75.06	80.87	-5.81
149	82.29	82.88	-0.59
150	83.43	93.18	-9.75
151	83.43	86.59	-3.16
152	84.34	79.48	4.86
153	85.47	86.66	-1.19
154	82.72	77.96	4.76
155	81.72	87.50	-5.78
156	81.23	92.05	-10.82
157	82.50	72.97	9.53
158	82.37	79.54	2.83
159	80.59	82.95	-2.36
164	84.22	83.92	0.30
170	86.00	80.64	5.36
173	86.77	87.84	-1.07
174	87.44	58.62	28.83
179	87.65	80.82	6.83
182	79.79	65.85	13.95
183	80.40	72.78	7.62
184	73.86	76.00	-2.14
185	80.27	82.17	-1.91
186	84.38	91.37	-6.99
187	86.60	83.79	2.81
188	84.38	78.01	6.37
189	87.61	86.70	0.92
190	87.91	84.15	3.76
191	86.56	91.08	-4.52
192	87.61	89.36	-1.74
193	87.79	88.29	-0.51
195	87.61	80.91	6.70
212	82.34	80.53	1.82
213	82.34	92.21	-9.87
214	82.37	87.27	-4.90
215	80.43	83.75	-3.31
216	80.49	91.53	-11.05
217	78.18	90.54	-12.36
218	75.75	81.18	-5.44
219	80.49	88.86	-8.38
282	79.26	90.52	-11.27
284	81.72	94.14	-12.42
285	78.33	92.34	-14.01
286	79.26	92.18	-12.92
287	81.43	85.00	-3.56
288	83.43	93.03	-9.60

APPENDIX B 141

Village I.D. (Hadbast no.)	Percentage of Total Cropped Area		Residual (Predicted minus observed)
	Predicted	Observed	
289	83.43	68.69	14.74
292	83.43	87.58	-4.15
293	86.19	92.53	-6.35
294	85.69	93.77	-8.08
295	84.75	97.52	-12.77
296	80.44	97.00	-16.56
299	81.72	95.69	-13.98
301	84.58	93.93	-9.35
306	80.40	96.59	-16.20
307	80.49	94.94	-14.45
308	82.42	93.10	-10.68
309	78.20	94.37	-16.17
315	82.23	91.39	-9.16
317	79.75	84.48	-4.72
318	75.55	68.00	7.55
319	79.31	77.77	1.54
320	73.03	58.13	14.90
321	70.48	58.51	11.98
322	75.87	76.01	-0.14
323	72.35	73.64	-1.29
324	71.82	62.93	8.89
327	72.34	72.09	0.26
328	67.47	69.91	-2.44
329	71.82	66.66	5.16
330	80.85	75.06	5.79
332	79.17	70.96	8.21
334	75.05	67.53	7.52
337	75.05	72.41	2.65
364	87.69	90.14	-2.44
365	87.60	97.28	-9.67
366	87.70	91.01	-3.31
367	87.22	96.26	-9.05
368	86.85	93.33	-6.48
370	85.47	87.00	-1.53
371	85.53	83.89	1.63
373	84.03	93.10	-9.06
374	85.53	88.17	-2.64
375	85.44	84.86	0.58
376	86.59	88.83	-2.24
377	86.67	82.19	4.48
378	84.87	93.49	-8.62
379	87.07	85.03	2.04
380	86.49	84.47	2.02
381	87.80	80.20	7.60

Village I.D. (Hadbast no.)	Percentage of Total Cropped Area		Residual (Predicted minus observed)
	Predicted	Observed	
385	87.91	90.44	-2.52
386	87.91	94.52	-6.60
387	84.16	88.46	-4.30
388	82.50	92.80	-10.30
389	84.01	88.48	-4.47
390	84.11	90.52	-6.41

Fruits and Vegetables

Village I.D. (Hadbast no.)	Percentage of Total Cropped Area		Residual (Predicted minus observed)
	Predicted	Observed	
1	0.10	9.88	-9.78
2	0.10	6.71	-6.61
21	2.56	15.78	-13.22
25	1.61	24.32	-22.71
26	2.48	14.81	-12.33
27	4.26	8.42	-4.16
28	7.20	23.40	-16.20
29	7.20	27.84	-20.64
30	4.25	64.16	-59.91
31	7.20	55.68	-48.48
32	4.26	5.34	-1.08
33	4.26	5.94	-1.68
34	4.75	1.80	2.95
35	0.16	4.02	-3.85
36	0.54	2.11	-1.57
37	1.48	1.93	-0.45
38	0.52	3.31	-2.79
39	0.38	9.89	-9.50
40	0.54	2.07	-1.53
42	0.38	4.58	-4.19
43	0.31	1.13	-0.83
44	0.38	5.44	-5.06
45	0.54	0.41	0.13
46	1.48	1.44	0.04
47	0.95	9.17	-8.22
50	0.22	1.24	-1.03
52	0.38	1.02	-0.63
53	0.56	0.90	-0.34
54	0.52	0.62	-0.10
56	0.68	0.72	-0.04
57	0.29	0.81	-0.52
60	0.10	1.25	-1.15
61	0.05	0.66	-0.62
63	0.04	1.34	-1.30
71	4.26	2.44	1.82
72	2.68	6.69	-4.01
73	2.85	6.25	-3.40
74	4.39	2.39	2.00
75	7.18	6.53	0.65
76	7.41	10.48	-3.08
77	4.86	1.94	2.92

Village I.D. (Hadbast no.)	Percentage of Total Cropped Area		Residual (Predicted minus observed)
	Predicted	Observed	
78	7.18	6.02	1.16
79	2.85	6.06	-3.21
80	4.39	10.78	-6.39
81	2.85	10.13	-7.28
82	1.52	20.54	-19.02
84	0.85	18.64	-17.79
85	0.91	10.81	-9.89
86	0.15	2.63	-2.48
87	0.15	5.48	-5.34
88	0.32	5.71	-5.39
89	0.38	1.47	-1.08
90	0.82	1.14	-0.32
92	1.43	2.77	-1.34
93	3.54	1.11	2.43
94	2.48	2.51	-0.03
95	3.54	2.01	1.53
96	2.76	7.92	-5.16
97	1.18	7.47	-6.28
98	1.48	0.63	0.85
99	1.18	2.81	-1.63
100	1.18	1.12	0.07
102	0.95	3.37	-2.42
103	0.92	1.52	-0.60
104	0.53	1.01	-0.48
105	0.53	2.77	-2.25
107	1.81	3.12	-1.31
108	1.60	5.94	-4.34
109	2.95	4.69	-1.75
110	5.05	4.57	0.47
111	5.37	6.00	-0.62
112	1.62	2.59	-0.98
119	3.54	0.93	2.61
120	6.04	2.98	3.06
123	3.54	2.04	1.50
128	6.34	3.57	2.77
133	1.93	3.27	-1.34
134	1.10	1.08	0.02
135	1.04	1.75	-0.71
136	0.59	1.64	-1.06
139	0.33	3.17	-2.84
140	0.63	0.87	-0.24
141	0.41	2.94	-2.53
144	0.17	2.43	-2.26
145	0.17	2.17	-2.00

APPENDIX B   145

Village I.D. (Hadbast no.)	Percentage of Total Cropped Area		Residual (Predicted minus observed)
	Predicted	Observed	
146	0.04	1.47	-1.43
147	0.01	1.09	-1.07
149	0.16	2.25	-2.08
150	0.18	2.27	-2.09
151	0.18	6.18	-6.00
152	0.17	0.85	-0.68
154	0.10	2.54	-2.44
155	0.10	0.89	-0.79
156	0.07	0.66	-0.59
157	0.08	9.54	-5.86
158	0.08	3.78	-3.70
159	0.05	4.54	-4.50
164	0.16	10.71	-10.55
170	0.56	9.67	-9.12
174	0.95	39.65	-38.70
179	2.68	11.64	-8.96
182	12.71	18.29	-5.58
183	11.89	20.00	-8.11
184	19.26	19.95	-0.70
185	12.07	15.84	-3.77
186	7.20	1.72	5.48
187	4.25	3.91	0.34
188	7.20	12.06	-4.87
189	2.48	0.53	1.95
190	0.92	1.98	-1.05
191	4.75	1.91	2.84
192	2.48	5.31	-2.84
193	1.48	2.12	-0.64
195	2.48	3.81	-1.33
212	0.08	2.65	-2.57
213	0.08	0.29	-0.21
215	0.04	2.50	-2.45
217	0.02	2.90	-2.88
218	0.01	1.98	-1.97
219	0.05	0.58	-0.54
284	0.10	1.21	-1.11
285	0.05	1.31	-1.26
286	0.09	2.05	-1.96
287	0.05	3.33	-3.28
288	0.18	1.49	-1.31
289	0.18	1.73	-1.56
292	0.18	4.82	-4.65
293	0.30	4.47	-4.18
294	0.31	0.20	0.10

Village I.D. (Hadbast no.)	Percentage of Total Cropped Area		Residual (Predicted minus observed)
	Predicted	Observed	
301	0.22	0.60	-0.38
308	0.09	0.69	-0.60
319	0.42	3.47	-3.04
320	0.06	1.16	-1.10
322	0.05	4.26	-4.21
323	0.01	1.35	-1.34
330	0.05	1.35	-1.30
337	0.02	1.72	-1.70
364	2.72	0.70	2.02
366	0.90	2.24	-1.34
367	0.53	1.49	-0.96
373	0.15	0.57	-0.42
374	0.27	2.15	-1.87
375	0.26	5.40	-5.14
376	0.47	1.45	-0.98
377	0.48	7.54	-7.05
378	0.32	2.43	-2.12
379	1.70	3.74	-2.03
380	1.60	2.16	-0.57
381	1.43	8.85	-7.42
385	0.92	0.73	0.19
387	0.15	1.53	-1.38
388	0.09	2.87	-2.79
389	0.15	0.71	-0.57
390	0.15	0.35	-0.19

Pulses

Village I.D. (*Hadbast* no.)	Percentage of Total Cropped Area		Residual (Predicted minus observed)
	Predicted	Observed	
1	9.39	2.11	7.28
2	9.39	2.98	6.41
7	6.58	3.88	2.70
21	3.90	1.31	2.59
25	4.39	1.35	3.04
26	3.96	3.70	0.26
27	3.40	2.24	1.15
28	2.85	1.27	1.58
29	2.85	0.56	2.28
30	3.37	0.57	2.80
31	2.85	1.13	1.72
32	3.40	3.74	-0.34
33	3.40	2.16	1.24
34	3.19	4.50	-1.31
35	7.89	3.21	4.68
36	5.92	2.64	3.28
37	4.55	3.38	1.17
38	5.94	5.52	0.42
39	6.58	2.19	4.39
40	5.92	1.24	4.68
41	4.83	6.25	-1.42
42	6.58	2.50	4.09
43	6.80	3.40	3.40
44	6.58	5.44	1.14
45	5.92	7.40	-1.48
46	4.55	2.88	1.67
47	5.14	5.50	-0.36
48	5.73	1.47	4.26
49	4.55	4.54	0.01
50	7.54	3.99	3.55
51	5.26	4.16	1.10
52	6.58	6.12	0.47
53	6.30	2.70	3.60
54	6.83	7.50	-0.66
55	5.73	0.99	4.74
56	5.73	3.62	2.11
57	7.82	13.82	-6.00
58	8.25	5.26	2.99
59	10.13	7.36	2.77
60	9.39	3.14	6.25
61	12.19	5.35	6.84

Village I.D. (Hadbast no.)	Percentage of Total Cropped Area		Residual (Predicted minus observed)
	Predicted	Observed	
62	10.04	2.08	7.97
63	10.41	6.73	3.68
63	12.82	6.41	6.41
69	4.72	9.39	-4.66
70	4.44	7.38	-2.94
71	3.40	6.72	-3.33
72	3.91	5.90	-1.99
73	3.80	3.75	0.06
74	3.32	1.99	1.33
75	2.83	1.96	0.87
76	2.78	4.19	-1.41
77	3.22	3.11	0.11
78	2.83	2.41	0.42
79	3.80	8.08	-4.27
80	3.32	0.98	2.34
81	3.80	5.86	-2.06
82	4.60	1.62	2.99
84	5.36	1.69	3.67
85	5.94	1.08	4.87
86	8.11	1.31	6.80
87	8.06	2.43	5.62
88	7.22	2.85	4.37
89	6.58	3.67	2.91
90	5.34	2.85	2.49
92	4.62	11.11	-6.49
93	3.65	12.84	-9.20
94	3.96	3.01	0.95
95	3.65	8.72	-5.07
96	4.42	4.87	-0.46
97	4.96	4.59	0.37
98	4.55	4.45	0.09
99	4.96	7.04	-2.08
100	4.96	4.49	0.47
102	5.14	1.12	4.02
103	6.37	4.58	1.80
104	7.32	3.03	4.29
105	7.32	3.70	3.62
106	5.84	7.86	-2.02
107	6.12	6.25	-0.13
108	5.14	1.98	3.17
109	5.03	5.36	-0.34
110	4.27	11.97	-7.70
111	4.47	5.33	-0.86
112	5.52	1.94	3.57

APPENDIX B 149

Village I.D. (Hadbast no.)	Percentage of Total Cropped Area		Residual (Predicted minus observed)
	Predicted	Observed	
113	5.26	2.59	2.67
114	6.12	6.18	-0.06
115	5.44	5.45	-0.01
116	5.66	5.83	-0.16
117	6.49	3.14	3.35
119	5.57	5.60	-0.03
120	4.72	7.46	-2.73
122	4.80	5.61	-0.82
125	5.57	9.18	-3.61
126	5.66	9.23	-3.56
128	4.80	5.71	-0.91
129	6.60	9.58	-2.99
130	5.66	1.82	3.84
133	6.33	9.83	-3.50
134	7.30	10.87	-3.56
135	7.06	7.01	0.04
136	8.09	14.83	-6.74
137	7.06	2.27	4.79
138	8.83	9.09	-0.25
139	9.23	7.93	1.30
140	8.37	5.21	3.16
141	10.03	13.23	-3.20
142	11.85	10.61	1.23
144	10.04	3.65	6.39
145	9.52	4.34	5.18
146	11.07	7.35	3.72
147	13.52	7.65	5.88
149	8.92	6.30	2.62
150	8.25	2.27	5.98
151	8.25	1.03	7.22
152	7.78	7.69	0.09
153	7.05	8.33	-1.28
154	8.86	1.69	7.17
155	9.39	3.57	5.82
156	9.77	1.98	7.79
157	9.05	2.70	6.35
158	9.17	3.03	6.15
159	10.27	4.54	5.73
164	8.04	1.78	6.26
173	5.47	0.39	5.08
179	3.91	2.05	1.86
182	2.27	2.43	-0.17
183	2.33	0.32	2.01
184	1.85	1.91	-0.06

Village I.D. (Hadbast no.)	Percentage of Total Cropped Area		Residual (Predicted minus observed)
	Predicted	Observed	
186	2.85	4.02	-1.17
187	3.37	8.38	-5.00
188	2.85	4.74	-1.89
189	3.96	5.31	-1.35
190	5.09	2.97	2.12
191	3.19	4.45	-1.26
192	3.96	1.06	2.90
193	4.55	1.06	3.49
195	3.96	6.87	-2.90
212	9.24	8.85	0.40
213	9.24	3.89	5.36
214	9.17	8.48	0.69
215	10.41	5.00	5.41
216	10.46	5.38	5.08
217	11.84	3.63	8.21
218	13.32	5.94	7.39
219	10.46	4.49	5.97
282	10.79	6.84	3.96
284	9.39	1.81	7.57
285	11.46	2.18	9.27
286	10.79	1.64	9.15
287	9.98	3.33	6.65
288	8.25	1.74	6.51
289	8.25	13.04	-4.79
292	8.25	2.75	5.50
293	6.73	2.98	3.75
294	6.80	4.56	2.24
295	7.97	0.82	7.15
296	10.13	1.90	8.23
299	9.39	2.68	6.71
301	7.54	3.03	4.51
306	10.49	2.72	7.77
307	10.46	4.28	6.18
308	9.22	2.75	6.46
309	11.85	2.68	9.17
315	7.69	6.45	1.24
317	9.93	8.62	1.32
318	12.71	9.33	3.38
319	10.08	4.86	5.22
320	14.27	24.41	-10.14
321	16.07	26.59	-10.52
322	12.82	14.83	-2.02
323	15.15	14.86	0.29
324	15.34	26.72	-11.38

APPENDIX B   151

Village I.D. (Hadbast no.)	Percentage of Total Cropped Area		Residual (Predicted minus observed)
	Predicted	Observed	
327	15.15	11.62	3.52
328	17.98	23.00	-5.02
329	15.34	11.11	4.24
330	10.07	11.92	-1.85
332	11.07	16.12	-5.06
334	13.53	12.98	0.55
337	13.53	17.24	-3.71
364	3.86	4.22	-0.36
365	5.28	0.54	4.74
366	5.22	2.24	2.97
368	6.08	2.66	3.42
370	7.11	7.00	0.11
371	7.08	8.47	-1.39
373	8.12	2.29	5.83
374	7.08	5.37	1.71
375	7.10	6.48	0.62
376	6.19	3.39	2.80
377	6.06	4.88	1.18
378	7.22	2.43	4.79
379	4.72	3.40	1.33
380	5.14	5.05	0.09
381	4.62	1.56	3.06
385	5.09	5.14	-0.06
386	5.09	2.74	2.35
387	7.95	3.07	4.88
388	9.05	2.15	6.90
389	8.11	6.47	1.64
390	8.09	3.86	4.24

Oilseeds

Village I.D. (Hadbast no.)	Percentage of Total Cropped Area		Residual (Predicted minus observed)
	Predicted	Observed	
1	7.12	0.70	6.42
2	7.12	1.11	6.01
25	3.15	5.40	-2.25
26	2.95	1.23	1.72
27	2.51	1.12	1.39
28	2.11	2.12	-0.02
34	2.29	10.81	-8.51
35	5.71	4.15	1.56
36	4.45	10.05	-5.60
38	4.28	2.76	1.53
39	4.97	1.64	3.32
40	4.45	0.41	4.04
41	3.42	9.37	-5.95
42	4.97	2.91	2.06
43	5.11	2.27	2.84
44	4.97	0.77	4.19
45	4.45	3.70	0.75
46	3.40	0.96	2.44
47	3.86	6.42	-2.56
48	4.32	2.94	1.39
49	3.40	0.75	2.64
50	5.69	2.99	2.70
51	3.93	3.33	0.60
52	4.97	1.02	3.95
53	4.78	0.90	3.88
54	5.21	1.25	3.96
55	4.32	0.99	3.34
56	4.32	2.17	2.15
57	5.96	5.69	0.27
58	6.26	9.47	-3.21
59	7.72	0.38	7.34
60	7.12	12.57	-5.45
61	9.33	3.34	5.99
62	7.73	0.78	6.95
63	7.74	3.36	4.38
63	9.87	0.64	9.23
69	3.58	2.81	0.77
70	3.33	14.02	-10.69
71	2.51	5.50	-2.99
72	2.84	5.90	-3.06
73	2.85	1.25	1.61

APPENDIX B 153

Village I.D. (Hadbast no.)	Percentage of Total Cropped Area		Residual (Predicted minus observed)
	Predicted	Observed	
74	2.48	1.19	1.29
75	2.10	0.65	1.45
76	2.08	0.69	1.38
77	2.42	1.94	0.48
78	2.10	7.22	-5.12
79	2.85	2.02	0.84
81	2.85	3.46	-0.61
82	3.36	1.62	1.74
85	4.53	7.02	-2.49
86	6.00	11.84	-5.84
88	5.48	10.00	-4.52
89	4.97	21.32	-16.35
90	3.97	21.71	-17.74
92	3.43	9.44	-6.01
93	2.75	2.79	-0.04
94	2.95	2.51	0.44
95	2.75	8.50	-5.74
96	3.36	4.26	-0.90
97	3.74	7.47	-3.72
98	3.40	7.64	-4.24
99	3.74	2.81	0.93
100	3.74	2.24	1.50
102	3.86	7.86	-4.00
103	4.88	20.61	-15.73
104	5.60	6.06	-0.45
105	5.60	2.77	2.83
106	4.50	14.60	-10.10
107	4.73	3.12	1.61
108	3.92	6.93	-3.01
109	3.87	8.72	-4.85
110	3.29	2.81	0.47
111	3.45	2.00	1.46
112	4.23	1.94	2.28
113	4.06	1.29	2.77
115	4.23	5.45	-1.22
116	4.44	1.66	2.78
117	5.06	1.25	3.81
119	4.35	0.93	3.42
122	3.76	4.49	-0.73
123	4.35	10.20	-5.85
125	4.35	1.02	3.33
126	4.44	1.53	2.90
127	3.76	1.17	2.59
128	3.76	8.57	-4.81

Village I.D. (Hadbast no.)	Percentage of Total Cropped Area		Residual (Predicted minus observed)
	Predicted	Observed	
134	5.67	2.17	3.50
135	5.46	1.75	3.71
136	6.26	1.09	5.16
137	5.46	1.13	4.32
139	7.14	2.38	4.76
140	6.50	2.60	3.90
141	7.90	4.41	3.49
142	9.16	7.08	2.09
144	7.73	3.65	4.08
145	7.29	4.34	2.95
146	8.35	10.29	-1.94
147	10.26	7.10	3.16
149	6.80	6.30	0.49
150	6.26	1.13	5.12
151	6.26	4.12	2.14
152	5.84	10.25	-4.41
154	6.66	4.23	2.42
155	7.12	5.35	1.77
156	7.38	2.64	4.73
157	6.76	15.13	-8.37
158	6.82	11.36	-4.54
159	7.68	7.95	-0.27
170	4.78	9.67	-4.90
173	4.15	10.98	-6.83
179	2.84	3.42	-0.58
182	1.65	12.19	-10.54
183	1.73	1.31	0.42
184	1.36	1.48	-0.12
185	1.72	0.99	0.73
187	2.51	2.79	-0.28
188	2.11	0.86	1.25
189	2.95	3.72	-0.77
190	3.65	6.93	-3.27
193	3.40	5.31	-1.92
195	2.95	4.58	-1.63
212	6.81	4.42	2.39
213	6.81	1.79	5.02
214	6.82	3.33	3.49
215	7.74	3.33	4.41
216	7.67	2.30	5.36
218	9.86	9.40	0.46
219	7.67	4.68	2.99
282	8.27	1.05	7.22
284	7.12	1.01	6.11

Village I.D. (Hadbast no.)	Percentage of Total Cropped Area		Residual (Predicted minus observed)
	Predicted	Observed	
285	8.73	2.40	6.33
286	8.27	0.82	7.45
288	6.26	0.99	5.27
289	6.26	7.82	-1.56
292	6.26	4.13	2.12
294	5.11	1.45	3.66
295	5.58	1.65	3.93
299	7.12	1.07	6.05
301	5.69	0.60	5.09
307	7.67	0.38	7.28
308	6.76	2.75	4.00
309	8.73	1.22	7.51
317	7.78	5.17	2.62
318	9.96	18.66	-8.70
319	7.97	11.11	-3.14
320	11.18	16.27	-5.09
321	12.38	14.89	-2.51
322	9.87	3.45	6.41
323	11.49	6.75	4.74
324	11.75	8.19	3.57
327	11.50	13.95	-2.45
328	13.71	2.65	11.06
329	11.75	20.00	-8.25
330	7.56	10.29	-2.73
332	8.35	12.90	-4.55
334	10.26	18.18	-7.92
337	10.26	5.17	5.09
364	2.80	0.70	2.10
366	3.78	1.12	2.66
368	4.42	1.33	3.09
370	5.24	5.00	0.24
371	5.19	3.39	1.81
374	5.19	1.07	4.12
376	4.58	3.88	0.70
377	4.53	2.44	2.09
378	5.48	1.62	3.85
379	3.58	4.76	-1.18
380	3.92	4.69	-0.77
381	3.43	4.68	-1.25
387	5.94	3.84	2.10
388	6.77	1.43	5.33
389	6.00	2.15	3.85
390	5.94	2.80	3.13

Cotton

Village I.D. (*Hadbast* no.)	Percentage of Total Cropped Area		Residual (Predicted minus observed)
	Predicted	Observed	
1	1.65	1.64	0.01
2	1.65	1.11	0.54
7	2.19	9.71	1.22
25	2.66	2.70	-0.04
26	2.97	1.23	1.74
27	3.20	0.56	2.64
28	3.44	2.97	0.47
29	3.44	2.27	1.18
30	3.25	0.57	2.68
31	3.44	1.13	2.31
32	3.20	3.20	-0.00
33	3.20	2.70	0.50
34	3.19	4.50	-1.31
35	1.70	2.14	-0.44
36	2.32	2.11	0.21
37	2.77	3.86	-1.09
38	2.15	2.76	-0.61
39	2.19	2.74	-0.55
40	2.32	1.66	0.67
42	2.19	0.83	1.36
43	2.08	2.27	-0.19
44	2.19	1.55	0.64
45	2.32	3.70	-1.38
46	2.77	2.40	0.37
47	2.59	3.67	-1.08
48	2.45	4.41	-1.96
49	2.77	7.57	-4.81
50	1.95	5.48	-3.53
51	2.49	1.66	0.83
52	2.19	3.06	-0.87
53	2.35	2.70	-0.35
54	2.28	3.75	-1.46
55	2.45	7.92	-5.47
56	2.45	3.62	-1.17
57	2.03	10.56	-8.53
58	1.86	7.36	-5.50
60	1.65	5.03	-3.37
61	1.38	3.34	-1.96
62	1.77	2.34	-0.57
63	1.36	1.34	0.01
63	1.37	1.92	-0.55

APPENDIX B 157

Village I.D. (Hadbast no.)	Percentage of Total Cropped Area		Residual (Predicted minus observed)
	Predicted	Observed	
69	2.90	4.69	-1.79
70	2.87	7.74	-4.88
71	3.20	2.44	0.76
72	2.90	16.14	-13.24
73	3.16	7.50	-4.34
74	3.33	5.57	-2.25
75	3.50	5.22	-1.73
76	3.58	4.89	-1.31
77	3.44	3.11	0.33
78	3.50	2.41	1.09
79	3.16	2.02	1.14
80	3.33	0.98	2.35
81	3.16	2.66	0.49
82	2.63	2.16	0.47
84	2.37	1.69	0.68
85	2.55	2.70	-0.15
86	1.70	2.63	-0.92
87	1.73	4.26	-2.53
88	2.10	2.14	-0.04
89	2.19	1.47	0.72
90	2.43	2.85	-0.42
92	2.70	1.66	1.04
93	3.30	2.79	0.51
94	2.97	3.51	-0.54
95	3.30	3.35	-0.05
96	3.12	4.87	-1.75
97	2.72	4.59	-1.87
98	2.77	2.54	0.22
99	2.72	8.45	-5.72
100	2.72	2.24	0.48
102	2.59	3.37	-0.78
103	2.52	2.29	0.23
104	2.25	3.03	-0.77
105	2.25	1.85	0.40
106	2.80	3.37	-0.57
107	2.82	8.59	-5.77
108	2.83	1.98	0.86
109	3.09	3.35	-0.26
110	3.37	2.46	0.91
111	3.40	2.66	0.73
112	2.80	4.54	-1.74
113	3.11	3.89	-0.78
114	2.82	5.61	2.79
115	3.16	5.45	-2.29

158 UNDERSTANDING PEASANT AGRICULTURE

Village I.D. (Hadbast no.)	Percentage of Total Cropped Area		Residual (Predicted minus observed)
	Predicted	Observed	
116	3.28	3.33	-0.05
117	2.91	4.40	-1.48
119	3.21	3.73	-0.52
120	3.50	2.98	0.52
123	3.22	6.12	-2.90
125	3.21	2.04	1.18
126	3.28	1.53	1.74
127	3.56	3.52	0.03
128	3.56	4.28	-0.72
129	2.97	4.11	-1.13
130	3.28	1.22	2.06
133	2.86	3.27	-0.41
134	2.57	2.17	0.40
135	2.54	3.50	-0.97
136	2.26	2.19	0.07
137	2.54	2.27	0.27
138	2.00	2.59	-0.59
139	2.01	2.38	-0.36
140	2.30	3.47	-1.18
141	2.15	2.94	-0.78
142	1.57	3.54	-1.97
144	1.77	2.43	-0.66
145	1.78	2.17	-0.39
146	1.35	4.41	-3.05
147	1.12	3.27	-2.15
149	1.81	2.25	-0.44
150	1.86	1.13	0.73
151	1.86	2.06	-0.19
152	1.85	1.70	0.14
153	1.95	5.00	-3.05
154	1.64	13.55	-11.91
155	1.65	2.67	-1.02
156	1.54	2.64	-1.11
157	1.58	3.24	-1.66
158	1.53	2.27	-0.73
164	1.69	3.57	-1.88
173	2.62	0.78	1.84
174	2.59	1.72	.87
179	2.90	2.05	0.85
182	3.56	1.22	2.35
183	3.63	5.57	-1.94
184	3.65	0.63	3.02
185	3.59	0.99	2.60
186	3.44	2.87	0.58

APPENDIX B 159

Village I.D. (Hadbast no.)	Percentage of Total Cropped Area		Residual (Predicted minus observed)
	Predicted	Observed	
187	3.25	1.11	2.14
188	3.44	4.31	-0.86
189	2.97	3.72	-0.74
190	2.40	3.96	-1.55
191	3.19	2.54	0.65
192	2.98	4.25	-1.28
193	2.77	3.19	-0.42
195	2.98	3.81	-0.84
212	1.50	3.54	-2.04
213	1.50	1.79	-0.29
214	1.54	0.90	0.63
215	1.36	5.41	-4.06
216	1.32	0.76	0.56
217	1.17	2.90	-1.73
218	1.03	1.48	-0.45
219	1.32	1.36	-0.04
282	1.57	1.57	-0.01
284	1.65	1.81	-0.16
285	1.41	1.75	-0.34
286	1.57	3.29	-1.72
287	1.35	8.33	-6.98
288	1.86	2.73	-0.87
289	1.86	8.69	-6.83
292	1.86	0.69	1.18
296	1.60	1.09	0.51
299	1.65	0.53	1.12
301	1.95	1.81	0.14
306	1.32	0.68	0.65
307	1.32	0.38	0.94
308	1.50	0.69	0.81
309	1.17	1.71	-0.54
315	2.72	2.15	0.58
317	2.11	1.72	0.39
318	1.64	4.00	-2.35
319	2.19	2.77	-0.58
322	1.37	1.42	-0.05
323	0.98	3.37	-2.39
324	1.05	2.15	-1.10
327	0.98	2.32	-1.34
328	0.82	4.42	-3.60
329	1.05	2.22	-1.16
330	1.45	1.35	0.10
334	1.13	1.29	-0.17
337	1.12	3.44	-2.32

Village I.D. (Hadbast no.)	Percentage of Total Cropped Area		Residual (Predicted minus observed)
	Predicted	Observed	
364	2.91	4.22	-1.31
365	2.37	2.17	0.20
366	2.38	3.37	-0.98
367	2.16	2.23	-0.08
368	2.13	2.66	-0.53
370	1.90	1.00	0.90
371	1.90	4.23	-2.34
373	1.69	4.02	-2.33
374	1.90	3.22	-1.33
375	1.92	3.24	-1.32
376	2.15	2.42	-0.28
377	2.24	2.93	-0.69
379	2.90	3.06	-0.16
380	2.83	3.61	-0.77
381	2.70	4.68	-1.98
385	2.40	3.67	-1.27
386	2.40	2.74	-0.33
387	1.78	3.07	-1.29
388	1.58	0.71	0.86
389	1.71	2.15	-0.45
390	1.69	2.45	-0.77

BIBLIOGRAPHY

Abalu, G.O.I. "A Note on Crop Mixtures under Indigenous Conditions in Northern Nigeria." *Journal of Development Studies* 12 (1976): 212-220.

Alonzo. W. *Location and Land Use: Toward a General Theory of Land Rent.* Boston: Harvard University Press, 1964.

Astroth, J.H., Jr. "Cropping and Land Use Patterns in a Newly Developing Urban Fringe: A Case Study of the Chandigarh Region, India." Paper presented at the annual meeting of the Missouri Academy of Sciences, Kirksville, Mo., April 1980.

_____. "Influence of a Growth Center on Indian Rural Life." M.A. Thesis, University of Missouri, 1980.

Astroth, J.H., Jr., and Meyer, J.T. "A New Approach to Modelling the Interregional Trade Flows of Foodgrains in a Developing Economy: The Case of Wheat and Pulse Flows between Trade Blocks in India, 1975." Paper presented at the 78th annual meeting of the Association of American Geographers, San Antonio, Tex., 28 April 1982.

Ayeni, B. "The Testing of Hypotheses on Interaction Data Matrices." *Geographical Analysis* 14 (1982): 79-84.

_____. "Algorithm 11: Information Statistics for Comparing Predicted and Observed Trip Matrices." *Environmental and Planning* A 15 (1983): 1259-1266.

Baker, O.E. "The Increasing Importance of the Physical Condition in Determining the Utilization of Land for Agricultural and Forest Production in the United States." *Annals of the Association of American Geographers* 11 (1921): 17-46.

Batty, M., and Mackie, S. "The Calibration of Gravity, Entropy and Related Models of Spatial Interaction." *Environment and Planning* 4 (1972): 205-233.

Baxter, R.S. "Entropy Maximizing Models of Spatial Interaction." *Computer Applications* 1 (1973): pp. 57-83.

Benedict, E.T., ed. *Theodor Brinkman's Economics of the Farm Business.* Berkeley: University of California Press, 1935.

Blaikie, P.M. "Spatial Organization of Some North Indian Villages I." *Transactions of the Institute of British Geographers* 52 (1971): 1-40.

_____. "Spatial Organization of Agriculture in Some North Indian Villages: Part II." *Transactions of the Institute of British Geographers* 53 (1971): 15-30.

Buchanan, K., and Hurwitz, N. "Land Use in Natal." *Economic Geography* 27 (1951): 230-242.

Burton, I. *Types of Agricultural Occupance of Flood Plains in the United States.* University of Chicago Department of Geography Research Papers no. 75. Chicago: Department of Geography, University of Chicago, 1962.

Casetti, E. "Spatial Equilibrium Distribution of Agricultural Production and Land Values." *Economic Geography* 48 (1972): 193-198.

Caucian, F. *Change and Uncertainty in a Peasant Economy.* Stanford: Stanford University Press, 1972.

Cesario, F.J. "A Primer on Entropy Modelling." *Journal of the American Institute of Planners* 41 (1975): 40-48.

Chakravarti, A.K. "Green Revolution in India." *Annals of the Association of American Geographers* 63 (1973): 319-330.

_____. "The Impact of the High-Yielding Varieties Program on Foodgrain Production in India." *Canadian Geographer* 20 (1976): 199-223.

Champion, A.G. "Antecedents of von Thünen." *Area* 11 (1979): 258.

Chenery, H.B. "Interregional and International Input-Output Analysis." In *Structural Interdependence of the Economy,* edited by T. Barnes. New York: Wiley, 1954.

Chisholm, M. *Rural Settlement and Land Use: An Essay in Location.* 3d ed. London: Hutchinson University Library, 1979.

_____. "Von Thünen Anticipated." *Area* 11 (1979): 37-40.

Coppock, J.T. "The Geography of Agriculture." *Journal of Agricultural Economics* 19 (1968): 153-175.

Darby, H.C. "Settlement in Northern Rhodesia." *Geographical Review* 21 (1931): 559-573.

Day, R.H., and Tinney, E.H. "A Dynamic von Thünen Model." *Geographical Analysis* 1 (1969): 137-151.

Dean, G.W. "Firm Theory Incorporating Growth and Risk: Integration into Farm Management Research." *International Journal of Agrarian Affairs,* Supplement 1974-1975 (1975): 110-120.

de Garis De Lisle, D. "Effects of Distance on Cropping Patterns Internal to the Farm." *Annals of the Association of American Geographers* 72 (1982): 88-98.

Dillon, J.L., and Heady, E.O. *Theories of Choice in Relation to Farmer Decisions.* Iowa Agricultural and Home Economics Experiment Station Research Bulletin no. 485. Ames, Ia.: 1960.

Doabia, T.S. *The Punjab Agricultural Produce Markets Act,* 1961. Chandigarh: The New Chandigarh Printing Press, 1980.

Dunn, E.S. *The Location of Agricultural Production.* Gainesville: University of Florida Press, 1954.

Durand, L. "The Major Milksheds of the Northeastern Quarter of the United States." *Economic Geography* 40 (1964): 9-33.

Edwards, W., and Tversky, A., eds. *Decision-Making.* Hammondsworth: Penguin, 1967.

Egbert, A.C., and Heady, E.O. *Regional Adjustments in Grain Production: A Linear Programming Analysis.* U.S. Department of Agriculture, Technical Bulletin no. 1241. Washington: U.S. Government Printing Office, 1961.

Elmes, Gregory A. "Modeling Spatial Interaction of Utility Coal in Pennsylvania." *Annals of the Association of American Geographers* 75 (June 1985): 212-226.

Evans, S.P. "A Relationship between the Gravity Model for Trip Distribution and the Transportation Problem of Linear Programming." *Transportation Research* 7 (1973): 39-61.

Farmer, B.H. "The Green Revolution in South Asian Ricefields: Environment and Production." *Journal of Development Studies* 15 (1979): 304-319.

Found, W.C. *A Theoretical Approach to Rural Land-Use Patterns.* London: Edward Arnold, 1971.

Foust, J.B., and de Souza, A.R. *The Economic Landscape: A Theoretical Introduction.* Columbus: Charles E. Merrill Pub. Co., 1978.

Fox, K.A. "A Spatial Equilibrium Model of Livestock-Feed Economy of the United States." *Econometrica* 21 (1953): 547-566.

Fox, K.A., and Taeuber, R.C. "Spatial Equilibrium Models of the Livestock-Feed Economy." *American Economic Review* 45 (1955): 584-608.

Fung, K. "Suburban Agricultural Land-Use." In *China: Urbanization and National Development*, edited by C.K. Leung and N. Ginsburg, pp. 156-184. University of Chicago Department of Geography Research Paper no. 196. Chicago: Department of Geography, University of Chicago, 1980.

Garrison, W.L., and Marble, D.F. "The Spatial Structure of Agricultural Activities." *Annals of the Association of American Geographers* 47 (1957): 137-144.

Geertz, C. "The Bazaar Economy: Information and Search in Peasant Marketing." *American Economic Review* 68 (1978): 28-32.

Gould, P. "Man against His Environment: A Game Theoretic Framework." *Annals of the Association of American Geographers* 53 (1963): 290-297.

──────. "Pedagogic Review." *Annals of the Association of American Geographers* 62 (1972): 689-700.

Gourou, P. "The Quality of Land Use of Tropical Cultivators." In *Man's Role in Changing the Face of the Earth*, edited by W.L. Thomas, Jr., pp. 336-350. Chicago: University of Chicago Press, 1956.

Gregor, H.F. *Geography of Agriculture: Themes in Research*. Englewood Cliffs: Prentice-Hall, 1970.

Griffin, E. "Testing von ThünenTheory in Uruguay." *Geographical Review* 63 (1973): 500-516.

Grotewold, A. "Von Thünen in Retrospect." *Economic Geography* 35 (1959): 346-355.

Harriss, B. "The Role of Punjab Wheat Markets as Growth Centres." *Geographical Journal* 140 (1974): 52-71.

Hart, P.W.E. "Problems and Potentialities of the Behavioural Approach to Agricultural Location." *Geografiska Annaler* 62B (1980): 99-107.

Harvey, D. "Theoretical Concepts and the Analysis of Agricultural Land-Use Patterns in Geography." *Annals of the Association of American Geographers* 56 (1966): 361-374.

Harwood, R.R., and Price, E.C. "Multiple Cropping in Tropical Asia." In *Multiple Cropping*, edited by R.I. Papendick, P.A. Sanchez, and G.B. Triplett, pp. 11-40. ASA Special Publication no. 27. Madison: American Society of Agronomy, Crop Science Society of America, Soil Science Society of America, 1976.

Heady, E.O., and Egbert, A.C. "Regional Programming of Efficient Agricultural Production Patterns." *Econometrica* 32 (1964): 374-386.

Heady, E.O., and Hall, H.H. "Linear and Non-Linear Spatial Models in Agricultural Competition, Land-Use and Production Potential." *American Journal of Agricultural Economics* 50 (1968): 1539-1548.

Henderson, J.M. "The Utilization of Agricultural Land: A Theoretical and Empirical Inquiry." *Review of Economics and Statistics* 41 (1959): 242-260.

Henshall, J.D. "Models of Agricultural Activity." In *Socio-Economic Models in Geography*, edited by R.J. Chorley and P. Haggett, pp. 423-458. London: Methuen and Co., 1968.

Herath, G.H.M. "Crop Mixtures under Peasant Conditions: A Decision Theoretic Interpretation." *Journal of Development Studies* 16 (1980): 322-331.

Hoel, P.G. *Introduction to Mathematical Statistics*. New York: John Wiley, 1971.

Hoover, E.M. *Location Theory and the Shoe and Leather Industries*. Cambridge, Mass.: Harvard University Press, 1937.

Horvath, R.J. "Von Thünen's Isolated State and the Area around Addis Ababa, Ethiopia." *Annals of the Association of American Geographers* 59 (1969): 308-323.

Howes, R. "A Test of a Linear Programming Model for Agriculture." *Papers of the Regional Science Association* 19 (1967): 123-140.

Hunter, J.M. "The Social Roots of Dispersed Settlement in Northern Ghana." *Annals of the Association of American Geographers* 57 (1967): 340-352.

Ilbery, B.W. "Point Score Analysis: A Methodological Framework for Analyzing the Decision-Making Process in Agriculture." *Tijdschrift voor Economische en Sociale Geographie* 68 (1977): 66-71.

_____. "Agricultural Decision-Making: A Behavioral Perspective." *Progress in Human Geography* 2 (1978): 448-466.

Isard, W. *Location and Space Economy*. Cambridge, Mass.: Massachusetts Institute of Technology Press, 1956.

_____. *Methods of Regional Analysis*. New York: John Wiley, 1960.

Jackson, R. "Some Observations on the Thünen Method of Analysis with Reference to South-East Ethiopia." *East African Geographical Review* 8 (1970): 39-46.

Jodha, N.S. "Intercropping in Traditional Farming Systems." *Journal of Development Studies* 16 (1980): 426-442.

Johnson, A.W. *Sharecroppers of the Sertao*. Stanford: Stanford University Press, 1971.

Jonasson, O. "Agricultural Regions of Europe." *Economic Geography* 1 (1925): 277-314; and 2 (1926): 19-48.

Jones, A.P.; McGuire; W.J. and Witte, A.D. "A Reexamination of Some Aspects of von Thünen's Model of Spatial Location." *Journal of Regional Science* 18 (1978): 1-16.

Jones, D.W. "The Price Theory of Thünen's Theory of Rent: Assumptions and Implications of a Familiar Model." *Canadian Geographer* 4 (1979): 322-336.

Jones, R.C. "Testing Macro-Thünen Models by Linear Programming." *Professional Geographer* 28 (1976): 353-361.

Junakar, P.N. "Do Indian Farmers Maximize Profits?" *Journal of Development Studies* 16 (1980): 48-59.

Katzman, M.T. "The von Thünen Paradigm, the Industrial-Urban Hypothesis, and the Spatial Structure of Agriculture." *American Journal of Agricultural Economics* 56 (1974): 683-696.

Kellerman, A. "The Pertinence of the Macro-Thünen Analysis." *Economic Geography* 53 (1977): 255-264.

Kelly, K. "Agricultural Change in Hooghly, 1850-1910." *Annals of the Association of American Geographers* 71 (1981): 237-252.

Knox, P.L. *Social Well-Being: A Spatial Perspective*. London: Oxford Clarendon Press, 1975.

Kullback, S. *Information Theory and Statistics*. New York: John Wiley, 1958.

Lösch, A. *The Economics of Location*. Translated from 2d rev. ed by W.H. Woglom and W.F. Stolper. New Haven: Yale University Press, 1954.

Low, A.R. "Decision-Making under Uncertainty: A Linear Programming Model of Peasant Farmer Behaviour." *Journal of Agricultural Economics* 25 (1974): 311-321.

Lowe, J.C., and Moryadas, S. *The Geography of Movement*. Boston: Houghton Mifflin Co., 1975.

McClelland, D.C. "The Achievement Motive in Economic Growth." In *Development and Society: The Dynamics of Economic Change*, edited by D.E. Novack and R. Lekachman. New York: St. Martin's Press, 1964.

Maclennan, D. "Steuart, Smith and von Thünen." *Area* 11 (1979): 312-313.

Macmillan, W.D. "Some Comments on the Stevens Linear and Quadratic Programming Versions of von Thünen's Theory of Agricultural Land Usage." *Environment and Planning* A 11 (1979): 943-962.

Maltz, A., and Weissbrod, R. "Entropy Procedures: A Research Note." *Professional Geographer* 28 (1976): 385-386.

Marsh, G.P. *Man and Nature: Or, Physical Geography as Modified by Human Action.* Edited by D. Lowenthal. Cambridge, Mass.: Belknap Press of Harvard University, 1965.

Medvedkov, Y. "Entropy: An Assessment of Potentialities in Geography." *Economic Geography* 46 (1970): 306-316.

Meyer, J.T., and Elmes, G.A. "Investigation of Maximum Entropy Methods for Agricultural Land Use Theory." Paper presented at the 78th annual meeting of the Association of American Geographers, San Antonio, Tex., 28 April 1982.

Mitchell, W.A. "Turkish Villages in Interior Anatolio and von Thünen's Isolated State." *Middle East Journal* 25 (1971): 355-369.

Moerman, M. *Agricultural Change and Peasant Choice in a Thai Village.* Berkeley: University of California Press, 1968.

Moran, W. "Spatial Patterns of Agriculture on the Urban Periphery: The Auckland Case." *Tijdschrift voor Economische en Sociale Geografie* 70 (1979): 164-176.

Morgan, W.B. "The Doctrine of the Rings," *Geography* 58 (1978): 301-312.

Moses, L. "A General Equilibrium Model of Production, Interregional Trade, and Location of Industry." *Review of Economics and Statistics* 42 (1960): 373-397.

Muller, P.O. "Trend Surfaces of American Agricultural Patterns: A Macro-Thünian Analysis." *Economic Geography* 49 (1973): 228-242.

Myren, D.T. "The Role of Information in Farm Decisions under Conditions of High Risk and Uncertainty." In *First Interamerican Research Symposium on the Role of Communications in Agricultural Development*, edited by D.T. Myren, pp. 94-100. Mexico City: Imp. Venecia, 1964.

Nair, K. *The Lonely Furrow: Farming in the United States, Japan, and India.* Ann Arbor: University of Michigan Press, 1969.

———. *In Defense of the Irrational Peasant: Indian Agriculture since the Green Revolution.* Chicago: University of Chicago Press, 1979.

Nitz, H. "Studies in the Field Patterns of Northern India and Germany." *Geographer* 13 (1966): 61-74.

Norman, D.W. "Rationalizing Mixed Cropping under Indigenous Conditions: The Example of Northern Nigeria." *Journal of Development Studies* 11 (1974): 3-21.

Openshaw, S. "An Empirical Study of Some Spatial Interaction Models." *Environment and Planning* 8 (1976): 23-42.

Papendick, R.I.; Sanchez, P.A.; and Triplett, G.B., eds. *Multiple Cropping.* ASA Special Publication no. 27. Madison: American Society of Agronomy, Crop Science Society of America, Soil Science Society of America, 1976.

Peet, J.R. "The Spatial Expansion of Commercial Agriculture in the Nineteenth Century: A von Thünen Interpretation." *Economic Geography* 45 (1969): 283-301.

Peterson, G.H., and Heady, E.O. *Application of Input-Output Analysis to a Single Model Emphasizing Agriculture.* Iowa Agricultural and Home Economics Experiment Station Research Bulletin no. 427. Ames, Ia.: 1956.

Pitfield, D.E. "Algorithm 6: The X Test for Predicted Trip Matrices." *Environment and Planning,* A 10 (1978): 1201-1206.

Prothero, R.M. "Land Use at Soba, Zaria Province, Northern Nigeria." *Economic Geography* 33 (1957): 72-86.

Rhind, David, and Hudson, Ray. *Land Use.* New York: Methuen and Co., 1980.

Ricardo, D. *Principles of Political Economy and Taxation.* London: J.M. Dent and Sons, 1817.

Richardson, R.C. "Distance Regularities in Guyanese Rice Cultivation." *Journal of Developing Areas* 8 (1974): 235-256.

Sauer, C.O. "The Agency of Man on Earth." In *Man's Role in Changing the Face of the Earth,* edited by W.L. Thomas. Chicago: University of Chicago, 1956.

Scott, J.C. *The Moral Economy of the Peasant: Rebellion and Subsistence in Southeast Asia.* New Haven: Yale University Press, 1976.

Senior, M.L. "From Gravity Modelling to Entropy Maximizing: A Pedagogic Guide." *Progress in Human Geography* 3 (1979): 179-210.

Shantz, H.L. "Agricultural Regions of Africa." *Economic Geography* 16-19 (1940-43).

Simon, H.A. *Models of Man: Social and Rational.* New York: Wiley and Sons, 1957.

Sinclair, R. "Von Thünen and Urban Sprawl." *Annals of the Association of American Geographers* 57 (1967): 72-87.

Singh, V.R. "Agricultural Typology of India." *Geographia Polonica* 40 (1979): 113-131.

Smith, A. *An Inquiry into the Nature and Causes of the Wealth of Nations.* Edited by E. Cannan. 6th ed. 2 vols. London, 1950. Originally published in 1789.

Snickars, F., and Weibull, J.W. "A Minimum Information Principle: Theory and Practice." *Regional Science and Urban Economics* 7 (1977): 137-168.

Stamp, D.L. *Man and the Land*. London: Collins, 1964.

Steuart, J. *An Inquiry into the Principles of Political Economy*. London, 1767.

Stevens, B.H. "Location Theory and Programming Models: The von Thünen Case." *Papers and Proceedings of the Regional Science Association* 21 (1968): 29-34.

Stevens, R., and Lee, Y. "A Spatial Analysis of Agricultural Intensity in a Basotho Village of Southern Africa." *Professional Geographer* 31 (1979): 177-183.

Tarrant, J.R. *Agricultural Geography*. New York: John Wiley and Sons, 1974.

Taylor, G. "The Agricultural Regions of Australia." *Economic Geography* 6 (1930).

Thomas, R.S., and Corbin, P.B. *The Geography of Economic Activity*. 3d ed. New York: McGraw-Hill, 1974.

Thomas, R.W. and Huggett, R.J. *Modelling in Geography: A Mathematical Approach*. Totowa, N.J.: Barnes and Noble Books, 1980.

Thomas, W.L. *Man's Role in Changing the Face of the Earth*. 2 vols. Chicago: University of Chicago Press, 1956.

Thornthwaite, C.W. "Modification of Rural Microclimates." In *Man's Role in Changing the Face of the Earth*, pp. 567-584. Edited by W.L. Thomas, Jr. Chicago: University of Chicago Press, 1956.

Thünen, J.H. von. *Von Thünen's Isolated State*. Translated by Carla M. Wortenberg. Edited by Peter Hall. Oxford: Pergammon Press, 1966. Originally published as *Der Isolierte Staat in Beziehung auf Landwirtschaft und Nationalökonomie*. Rostock, 1826.

Troughton, M.J. "Application of the Revised Scheme of Typology of World Agriculture to Canada." *Geographia Polonica* 40 (1979): 95-111.

Visser, S. "Technological Change and the Spatial Structure of Agriculture." *Economic Geography* 56 (1980): 311-319.

von Neumann, J., and Morgenstern, O. *Theory of Games and Economic Behavior*. Princeton: Princeton University Press, 1944.

Weaver, J.C. "Crop Combination Regions in the Middle West." *Geographical Review* 44 (1954): 104-130.

_____. "A Design for Research in the Geography of Agriculture." *Professional Geographer* 10 (1958): 2-8.

Webber, M.J. "Pedagogy Again: What is Entropy?" *Annals of the Association of American Geographers* 67 (1977): 254-266.

Whyte, R.O. *The Spatial Geography of Rural Economies.* London: Oxford University Press, 1982.

Williams, K. *Linear Programming: The Simplex Algorithm.* London: Longmans, 1969.

Wilson, A.G. *Inter-regional Commodity Flows: Entropy Maximizing Approaches.* Centre for Environmental Studies Working Paper 19. London: 1968.

_____. *Entropy in Urban and Regional Modelling.* London: Prior, 1970.

_____. *Urban and Geographical Models in Geography and Planning.* London: John Wiley and Sons, 1974.

_____. "A Statistical Theory of Spatial Distribution Models." *Transportation Research* 1 (1967): 253-266.

Wilson, A.G., and Senior, M.L. "Some Relationships between Entropy Maximizing Models, Linear Programming Models, and Their Duals." *Journal of Regional Science* 14 (1974): 207-215.

Wilson, A.G. et al. "Calibration and Testing of the SELNEC Transport Model." *Regional Studies* 3 (1969): 337-350.

Wilson, E.B., and Hilferty, M.M. "The Distribution of Chi-Square." *Proceedings of the National Academy of Science* 17 (1931): 684-688.

Wolpert, J. "The Decision Process in Spatial Context." *Annals of the Association of American Geographers* 54 (1964): 537-558.

Yamane, T. *Statistics: An Introductory Analysis.* New York: Harper and Row, 1973.

INDEX

agricultural land use in the study area 89
agricultural location theory 7
agroeconomic climate 69
Alonzo 14
arthiya 75
Astroth 21
Ayeni 99

baaraanii zamiin 68
Baxter 43
behavioral approach 27, 29
Benedict 14
Blaikie 21
Buchanan 16

calibration of the model 99
cereals and millets 87
Cesario 36
Champion 7
Chandigarh 51, 77
Chenery 24
Chisholm 7
chi-square 99
cost matrix 97
crops 72, 86

dairy farming 79
data sources 88
Dean 28
decision theory 27
De Garis De Lisle 18
distance-deterrence parameters 98
Dunn 14
Durand 17

economic approach 8
Edwards 30

ENT-3 model 95
environmental constraints 57
erosion 63

Fatehgarh Sahib 51
fiber crops 87
fodder crops 87
Food Corporation of India 73
Found 14
Fox 24
fruits and vegetables 79, 87
Fung 20

game theory 29
geologic structure 59
Gottmann 17
Green Revolution 68
Grotewold and Sublett 18
gur 72

Hart 30
Harvey 27
Haryana 51
Heady and Egbert 25
Held 16
Henderson 24
Henshall 30
Horvath 20
household crops 87
Howes 26
Hurwitz 16

Ilbery 27, 31
illustrative concepts 42
input-output models 24
intercropping 70
interregional equilibrium models 23

INDEX

Isard 24

Jackson 21
Jonasson 16
Jones 17
Judge 24

Katzman 21
Kellerman 19
Kelly 20
Khandi Watershed and Area Development Project 64
Kharar 51, 72
Kharar tehsil 51
kharif crops 57
Kurali 51, 70

lal kitab 89
landholdings 67
land-use and cropping data 88
Laplace criterion 27
Leontieff 24
limiting assumptions 26
linear programming 25
Lösch 14

mandi 51
mandi development scheme 73
market areas 72, 96
market crops 86
market interaction factors 98
MARKFED 73
mathematical programming models 38
maximum likelihood and agricultural land use 40, 93
maximum-likelihood modeling 35
minimum discrimination information statistic (MDIS) 100
Mitchell 20
mixed cultivation 70
modal split and crop types 41
Moran 19
Morinda 72
Moses 24
Muller 17
multiple crops–multiple markets case 11, 45
multiple crops–single market case 10, 43

Nair 21
Norman 28

oilseeds 87
operationalization of the model 96

peasant agricultural land use 127
Peet 17
Pitfield 99
Prothero 20
pulses 87
Punjab 51
PUNSUP 73

rabi crop 57
Rajpura 51
research methodology 51
residual pattern analysis
Ricardo 7
Richardson 21
risk-aversion techniques 70
road network 89
Roscher 16
Rupnagar 51

"safety first" attitude 70
SAS Nagar (Mohali) 75
"satisficer" model 28
Shivalik Hills 51
shukr 72
Simon 28
Smith 7
spatial equilibrium models 24
Stevens and Lee 22
study area 51
sugarcane 87

Taeuber 24
tehsildar 88
total market demand 96
trade restrictions 82
transportation costs 89
transportation problem 38
Tversky 30

umland 51

Valkenburg 16
Valkenburg and Held 17
von Neumann and Morgenstern 27
von Thünen model 8, 11, 15, 16, 22

Wald's "standards for judgment" 27

Wallace 24
Weber 14
Wilson 35, 41
Wilson and Senior 39

THE UNIVERSITY OF CHICAGO
GEOGRAPHY RESEARCH PAPERS
(Lithographed, 6 x 9 inches)

Titles in Print

48. BOXER, BARUCH. *Israeli Shipping and Foreign Trade.* 1957. x + 162 p.
56. MURPHY, FRANCIS C. *Regulating Flood-Plain Development.* 1958. x + 204 p.
62. GINSBURG, NORTON, ed. *Essays on Geography and Economic Development.* 1960. xx + 173 p.
71. GILBERT, EDMUND W. *The University Town in England and West Germany.* 1961. viii + 74 p.
72. BOXER, BARUCH. *Ocean Shipping in the Evolution of Hong Kong.* 1961. x + 95 p.
91. HILL, A. DAVID. *The Changing Landscape of a Mexican Municipio, Villa Las Rosas, Chiapas.* 1964. xiii + 121 p.
97. BOWDEN, LEONARD W. *Diffusion of the Decision to Irrigate: Simulation of the Spread of a New Resource Management Practice in the Colorado Northern High Plains.* 1965. xxvii + 146 p.
98. KATES, ROBERT W. *Industrial Flood Losses: Damage Estimation in the Lehigh Valley.* 1965. xi + 76 p.
101. RAY, D. MICHAEL. *Market Potential and Economic Shadow: A Quantitative Analysis of Industrial Location in Southern Ontario.* 1965. xvii + 164 p.
102. AHMAD, QAZI. *Indian Cities: Characteristics and Correlates.* 1965. viii + 184 p.
103. BARNUM, H. GARDINER. *Market Centers and Hinterlands in Baden-Württemberg.* 1966. xviii + 172 p.
105. SEWELL, W. R. DERRICK, ed. *Human Dimensions of Weather Modification.* 1966. xii + 423 p.
107. SOLZMAN, DAVID M. *Waterway Industrial Sites: A Chicago Case Study.* 1967. x + 138 p.
108. KASPERSON, ROGER E. *The Dodecanese: Diversity and Unity in Island Politics.* 1967. xiv + 184 p.
109. LOWENTHAL, DAVID, ed. *Environmental Perception and Behavior.* 1967. vi + 88 p.
112. BOURNE, LARRY S. *Private Redevelopment of the Central City: Spatial Processes of Structural Change in the City of Toronto.* 1967. xii + 199 p.
113. BRUSH, JOHN E., and HOWARD L. GAUTHIER, JR. *Service Centers and Consumer Trips: Studies on the Philadelphia Metropolitan Fringe.* 1968. x + 182 p.
115. BURTON, IAN, ROBERT W. KATES, and RODMAN E. SNEAD. *The Human Ecology of Coastal Flood Hazard in Megalopolis.* 1968. xiv + 196 p.
117. WONG, SHUE TUCK. *Perception of Choice and Factors Affecting Industrial Water Supply Decisions in Northeastern Illinois.* 1968. x + 93 p.
118. JOHNSON, DOUGLAS L. *The Nature of Nomadism: A Comparative Study of Pastoral Migrations in Southwestern Asia and Northern Africa.* 1969. viii + 200 p.
119. DIENES, LESLIE. *Locational Factors and Locational Developments in the Soviet Chemical Industry.* 1969. x + 262 p.
120. MIHELIC, DUESAN. *The Political Element in the Port Geography of Trieste.* 1969. ix + 104 p.

121. BAUMANN, DUANE D. *The Recreational Use of Domestic Water Supply Reservoirs: Perception and Choice.* 1969. ix + 125 p.
122. LIND, AULIS O. *Coastal Landforms of Cat Island, Bahamas: A Study of Holocene Accretionary Topography and Sea-Level Change.* 1969. ix + 156 p.
123. WHITNEY, JOSEPH B. R. *China: Area, Administration and Nation Building.* 1970. xiii + 198 p.
124. EARICKSON, ROBERT. *The Spatial Behavior of Hospital Patients: A Behavioral Approach to Spatial Interaction in Metropolitan Chicago.* 1970. xi + 138 p.
125. DAY, JOHN C. *Managing the Lower Rio Grande: An Experience in International River Development.* 1970. xii + 274 p.
126. MacIVER, IAN. *Urban Water Supply Alternatives: Perception and Choice in the Grand Basin, Ontario.* 1970. ix + 178 p.
127. GOHEEN, PETER G. *Victorian Toronto, 1850 to 1900: Pattern and Process of Growth.* 1970. xiii + 278 p.
128. GOOD, CHARLES M.*Rural Markets and Trade in East Africa.* 1970. xvi + 252 p.
129. MEYER, DAVID R. *Spatial Variation of Black Urban Households.* 1970. xiv + 127 p.
130. GLADFELTER, BRUCE G. *Meseta and Campina Landforms in Central Spain: A Geomorphology of the Alto Henares Basin.* 1971. xii + 204 p.
131. NEILS, ELAINE M. *Reservation to City: Indian Migration and Federal Relocation.* 1971. x + 198 p.
132. MOLINE, NORMAN T. *Mobility and the Small Town, 1900-1930.* 1971. ix + 169 p.
133. SCHWIND, PAUL J. *Migration and Regional Development in the United States, 1950-1960.* 1971. x + 170 p.
134. PYLE, GERALD F. *Heart Disease, Cancer and Stroke in Chicago: A Geographical Analysis with Facilities, Plans for 1980.* 1971. ix + 292 p.
135. JOHNSON, JAMES F. *Renovated Waste Water: An Alternative Source of Municipal Water Supply in the United States.* 1971. ix + 155 p.
136. BUTZER, KARL W. *Recent History of an Ethiopian Delta: The Omo River and the Level of Lake Rudolf.* 1971. xvi + 184 p.
139. McMANIS, DOUGLAS R. *European Impressions of the New England Coast, 1497-1620.* 1972. viii + 147 p.
140. COHEN, YEHOSHUA S. *Diffusion of an Innovation in an Urban System: The Spread of Planned Regional Shopping Centers in the United States, 1949-1968.* 1972. ix + 136 p.
141. MITCHELL, NORA. *The Indian Hill-Station: Kodaikanal.* 1972. xii + 199 p.
142. PLATT, RUTHERFORD H. *The Open Space Decision Process: Spatial Allocation of Costs and Benefits.* 1972. xi + 189 p.
143. GOLANT, STEPHEN M. *The Residential Location and Spatial Behavior of the Elderly: A Canadian Example.* 1972. xv + 226 p.
144. PANNELL, CLIFTON W. *T'ai-Chung, T'ai-wan: Structure and Function.* 1973. xii + 200 p.
145. LANKFORD, PHILIP M. *Regional Incomes in the United States, 1929-1967: Level, Distribution, Stability, and Growth.* 1972. x + 137 p.
146. FREEMAN, DONALD B. *International Trade, Migration, and Capital Flows: A Quantitative Analysis of Spatial Economic Interaction.* 1973. xiv + 201 p.
147. MYERS, SARAH K. *Language Shift among Migrants to Lima, Peru.* 1973. xiii + 203 p.
148. JOHNSON, DOUGLAS L. *Jabal al-Akhdar, Cyrenaica: An Historical Geography of Settlement and Livelihood.* 1973. xii + 240 p.

149. YEUNG, YUE-MAN. *National Development Policy and Urban Transformation in Singapore: A Study of Public Housing and the Marketing System.* 1973. x + 204 p.
150. HALL, FRED L. *Location Criteria for High Schools: Student Transportation and Racial Integration.* 1973. xii + 156 p.
151. ROSENBERG, TERRY J. *Residence, Employment, and Mobility of Puerto Ricans in New York City.* 1974. xi + 230 p.
152. MIKESELL, MARVIN W., ed. *Geographers Abroad: Essays on the Problems and Prospects of Research in Foreign Areas.* 1973. ix + 296 p.
153. OSBORN, JAMES. *Area, Development Policy, and the Middle City in Malaysia.* 1974. x+ 291 p.
154. WACHT, WALTER F. *The Domestic Air Transportation Network of the United States.* 1974. ix + 98 p.
155. BERRY, BRIAN J. L. et al. *Land Use, Urban Form and Environmental Quality.* 1974. xxiii + 440 p.
156. MITCHELL, JAMES K. *Community Response to Coastal Erosion: Individual and Collective Adjustments to Hazard on the Atlantic Shore.* 1974. xii + 209 p.
157. COOK, GILLIAN P. *Spatial Dynamics of Business Growth in the Witwatersrand.* 1975. x + 144 p.
160. MEYER, JUDITH W. *Diffusion of an American Montessori Education.* 1975. xi + 97 p.
161. SCHMID, JAMES A. *Urban Vegetation: A Review and Chicago Case Study.* 1975. xii + 266 p.
162. LAMB, RICHARD F. *Metropolitan Impacts on Rural America.* 1975. xii + 196 p.
163. FEDOR, THOMAS STANLEY. *Patterns of Urban Growth in the Russian Empire during the Nineteenth Century.* 1975. xxv + 245 p.
164. HARRIS, CHAUNCY D. *Guide to Geographical Bibliographies and Reference Works in Russian or on the Soviet Union.* 1975. xviii + 478 p.
165. JONES, DONALD W. *Migration and Urban Unemployment in Dualistic Economic Development.* 1975. x + 174 p.
166. BEDNARZ, ROBERT S. *The Effect of Air Pollution on Property Value in Chicago.* 1975. viii + 111 p.
167. HANNEMANN, MANFRED. *The Diffusion of the Reformation in Southwestern Germany, 1518-1534.* 1975. ix + 235 p.
168. SUBLETT, MICHAEL D. *Farmers on the Road: Interfarm Migration and the Farming of Noncontiguous Lands in Three Midwestern Townships. 1939-1969.* 1975. xiii + 214 p.
169. STETZER, DONALD FOSTER. *Special Districts in Cook County: Toward a Geography of Local Government.* 1975. xi + 177 p.
171. SPODEK, HOWARD. *Urban-Rural Integration in Regional Development: A Case Study of Saurashtra, India—1800-1960.* 1976. xi + 144 p.
172. COHEN, YEHOSHUA S., and BRIAN J. L. BERRY. *Spatial Components of Manufacturing Change.* 1975. vi + 262 p.
173. HAYES, CHARLES R. *The Dispersed City: The Case of Piedmont, North Carolina.* 1976. ix + 157 p.
174. CARGO, DOUGLAS B. *Solid Wastes: Factors Influencing Generation Rates.* 1977. viii + 100 p.
175. GILLARD, QUENTIN. *Incomes and Accessibility: Metropolitan Labor Force Participation, Commuting, and Income Differentials in the United States, 1960-1970.* 1977. ix + 106 p.

176. MORGAN, DAVID J. *Patterns of Population Distribution: A Residential Preference Model and Its Dynamic.* 1978. xiii + 200 p.
177. STOKES, HOUSTON H., DONALD W. JONES, AND HUGH M. NEUBURGER. *Unemployment and Adjustment in the Labor Market: A Comparison between the Regional and National Responses.* 1975. ix + 125 p.
180. CARR, CLAUDIA J. *Pastoralism in Crisis. The Dasanetch and Their Ethiopian Lands.* 1977. xx + 319 p.
181. GOODWIN, GARY C. *Cherokees in Transition: A Study of Changing Culture and Environment Prior to 1775.* 1977. ix + 207 p.
182. KNIGHT, DAVID B. *A Capital for Canada: Conflict and Compromise in the Nineteenth Century.* 1977. xvii + 341 p.
183. HAIGH, MARTIN J. *The Evolution of Slopes on Artificial Landforms, Blaenavon, U.K.* 1978. xiv + 293 p.
184. FINK, L. DEE. *Listening to the Learner: An Exploratory Study of Personal Meaning in College Geography Courses.* 1977. ix + 186 p.
185. HELGREN, DAVID M. *Rivers of Diamonds: An Alluvial History of the Lower Vaal Basin, South Africa.* 1979. xix + 389 p.
186. BUTZER, KARL W., ed. *Dimensions of Human Geography: Essays on Some Familiar and Neglected Themes.* 1978. vii + 190 p.
187. MITSUHASHI, SETSUKO. *Japanese Commodity Flows.* 1978. x + 172 p.
188. CARIS, SUSAN L. *Community Attitudes toward Pollution.* 1978. xii + 211 p.
189. REES, PHILIP M.*Residential Patterns in American Cities: 1960.*1979. xvi +405 p.
190. KANNE, EDWARD A. *Fresh Food for Nicosia.* 1979. x + 106 p.
192. KIRCHNER, JOHN A. *Sugar and Seasonal Labor Migration: The Case of Tucumán, Argentina.* 1980. xii + 174 p.
193. HARRIS, CHAUNCY D., AND JEROME D. FELLMANN. *International List of Geographical Serials, Third Edition, 1980.* 1980. vi + 457 p.
194. HARRIS, CHAUNCY D. *Annotated World List of Selected Current Geographical Serials, Fourth Edition. 1980.* 1980. iv + 165 p.
195. LEUNG, CHI-KEUNG. *China: Railway Patterns and National Goals.* 1980. xv + 243 p.
196. LEUNG, CHI-KEUNG, AND NORTON S. GINSBURG, eds. *China: Urbanizations and National Development.* 1980. ix + 283 p.
197. DAICHES, SOL. *People in Distress: A Geographical Perspective on Psychological Wellbeing.* 1981. xiv + 199 p.
198. JOHNSON, JOSEPH T. *Location and Trade Theory: Industrial Location, Comparative Advantage, and the Geographic Pattern of Production in the United States.* 1981. xi + 107 p.
199-200. STEVENSON, ARTHUR J. *The New York-Newark Air Freight System.* 1982. xvi + 440 p.
201. LICATE, JACK A. *Creation of a Mexican Landscape: Territorial Organization and Settlement in the Eastern Puebla Basin, 1520-1605.* 1981. x + 143 p.
202. RUDZITIS, GUNDARS. *Residential Location Determinants of the Older Population.* 1982. x + 117 p.
203. LIANG, ERNEST P. *China: Railways and Agricultural Development, 1875-1935.* 1982. xi + 186 p.

204. DAHMANN, DONALD C. *Locals and Cosmopolitans: Patterns of Spatial Mobility during the Transition from Youth to Early Adulthood.* 1982. xiii + 146 p.
205. FOOTE, KENNETH E. *Color in Public Spaces: Toward a Communication-Bases Theory of the Urban Built Environment.* 1983. xiv + 153 p.
206. HARRIS, CHAUNCY D. *Bibliography of Geography. Part II: Regional. Volume 1. The United States of America.* 1984. viii + 178 p.
207-208. WHEATLEY, PAUL. *Nagara and Commandery: Origins of the Southeast Asian Urban Traditions.* 1983. xv + 472 p.
209. SAARINEN, THOMAS F., DAVID SEAMON, AND JAMES L. SELL, eds. *Environmental Perception and Behavior: An Inventory and Prospect.* 1984. x + 263 p.
210. WESCOAT, JAMES L., JR. *Integrated Water Development: Water Use and Conservation Practice in Western Colorado.* 1984. xi + 239 p.
211. DEMKO, GEORGE J., AND ROLAND J. FUCHS, eds. *Geographical Studies on the Soviet Union: Essays in Honor of Chauncy D. Harris.* 1984. vii + 294 p.
212. HOLMES, ROLAND C. *Irrigation in Southern Peru: The Chili Basin.* 1986. ix + 199 p.
213. EDMONDS, RICHARD LOUIS. *Northern Frontiers of Qing China and Tokugawa Japan: A Comparative Study of Frontier Policy.* 1985. xi + 209 p.
214. FREEMAN, DONALD B., AND GLEN B. NORCLIFFE. *Rural Enterprise in Kenya: Development and Spatial Organization of the Nonfarm Sector.* 1985. xiv + 180 p.
215. COHEN, YEHOSHUA S., AND AMNON SHINAR. *Neighborhoods and Friendship Networks:AStudy of Three Residential Neighborhoods in Jerusalem.*1985. ix+137 p.
216. OBERMEYER, NANCY J. *Bureaucrats, Clients, and Geography: The Bailly Nuclear Power Plant Battle in Northern Indiana.* 1989. x + 135 p.
217-218. CONZEN, MICHAEL P., ed. *World Patterns of Modern Urban Change: Essays in Honor of Chauncy D. Harris.* 1986. x + 479 p.
219. KOMOGUCHI, YOSHIMI. *Agricultural Systems in the Tamil Nadu: A Case Study of Peruvalanallur Village.* 1986. xvi + 175 p.
220. GINSBURG, NORTON, JAMES OSBORN, AND GRANT BLANK. *Geographic Perspectives on the Wealth of Nations.* 1986. ix + 1331 p.
221. BAYLSON, JOSHUA C. *Territorial Allocation by Imperial Rivalry: The Human Legacy in the Near East.* 1987. xi + 138 p.
222. DORN, MARILYN APRIL. *The Administrative Partitioning of Costa Rica.* 1989. xi + 126 p.
223. ASTROTH, JOSEPH H., JR. *Understanding Peasant Agriculture: An Integrated Land-Use Model for the Punjab.* 1990. xiii + 173 p.
224. PLATT, RUTHERFORD H., SHEILA G. PELCZARSKI, AND BARBARA K. BURBANK, eds. *Cities on the Beach: Management Issues of Developed Coastal Barriers.* 1987. vii + 324 p.
225. LATZ, GIL. *Agricultural Development in Japan: The Land Improvement District in Concept and Practice.* 1989. viii + 135 p.
226. GRITZNER, JEFFREY A. *The West African Sahel: Human Agency and Environmental Change.* 1988. xii + 170 p.
227. MURPHY, ALEXANDER B. *The Regional Dynamics of Language Differentiation in Belgium: A Study in Cultural-Political Geography.* 1988. xiii + 249 p.